W9-BTO-219

VOL. 32
VIZ Media Edition

Story and Art by
RUMIKO TAKAHASHI

English Adaptation by Gerard Jones

Translation/Mari Morimoto
Touch-up Art & Lettering/Bill Schuch
Cover and Interior Graphic Design/Yuki Ameda
Editor/Ian Robertson

Editor in Chief, Books/Alvin Lu
Editor in Chief, Magazines/Marc Weidenbaum
VP of Publishing Licensing/Rika Inouye
VP of Sales/Gonzalo Ferreyra
Sr. VP of Marketing/Liza Coppola
Publisher/Hyoe Narita

Printed in the U.S.A.

Published by VIZ Media, LLC
P.O. Box 77010
San Francisco, CA 94107

VIZ Media Edition
10 9 8 7 6 5 4 3 2 1
First printing, January 2008

www.viz.com

store.viz.com

INUYASHA

VOL. 32

VIZ Media Edition

STORY AND ART BY
RUMIKO TAKAHASHI

CONTENTS

THE STORY THUS FAR

Long ago, in the "Warring States" era of Japan's Muromachi period (*Sengoku-jidai*, approximately 1467-1568 CE), a legendary dog-like half-demon called "Inuyasha" attempted to steal the Shikon Jewel—or "Jewel of Four Souls"—from a village, but was stopped by the enchanted arrow of the village priestess, Kikyo. Inuyasha fell into a deep sleep, pinned to a tree by Kikyo's arrow, while the mortally wounded Kikyo took the Shikon Jewel with her into the fires of her funeral pyre. Years passed.

Fast-forward to the present day. Kagome, a Japanese high school girl, is pulled into a well one day by a mysterious centipede monster and finds herself transported into the past—only to come face to face with the trapped Inuyasha. She frees him, and Inuyasha easily defeats the centipede monster.

The residents of the village, now 50 years older, readily accept Kagome as the reincarnation of their deceased priestess Kikyo, a claim supported by the fact that the Shikon Jewel emerges from a cut on Kagome's body. Unfortunately, the jewel's rediscovery means that the village is soon under attack by a variety of demons in search of this treasure. Then, the jewel is accidentally shattered into many shards, each of which may have the fearsome power of the entire jewel.

Although Inuyasha says he hates Kagome because of her resemblance to Kikyo, the woman who "killed" him, he is forced to team up with her when Kaede, the village leader, binds him to Kagome with a powerful spell. Now the two grudging companions must fight to reclaim and reassemble the shattered shards of the Shikon Jewel before they fall into the wrong hands...

THIS VOLUME A fierce battle rages in the borderland that lies between the world of the living and the afterlife. A mysterious force is attacking Inuyasha, preventing him from obtaining the last Shikon shard—and this force claims to be acting on behalf of the will of the shard! Inuyasha also faces the dreaded Naraku, who will stop at nothing to obtain the shard. When all hope seems lost, Inuyasha receives help from a surprising source!

CHARACTERS

INUYASHA
Half-demon hybrid, son of a human mother and demon father. His necklace is enchanted, allowing Kagome to control him with a word.

KAGOME
Modern-day Japanese schoolgirl who can travel back and forth between the past and present through an enchanted well.

NARAKU
Enigmatic demon-mastermind behind the miseries of nearly everyone in the story.

MIROKU
Lecherous Buddhist priest cursed with a mystical "hellhole" in his hand that's slowly killing him.

KOGA
Leader of the Wolf Clan, Koga is himself a Wolf Demon and, because of several Shikon shards in his legs, possesses super speed. Enamored of Kagome, he quarrels with Inuyasha frequently.

SANGO
"Demon Exterminator" or slayer from the village where the Shikon Jewel was first born.

SCROLL 1
THE CHOICE

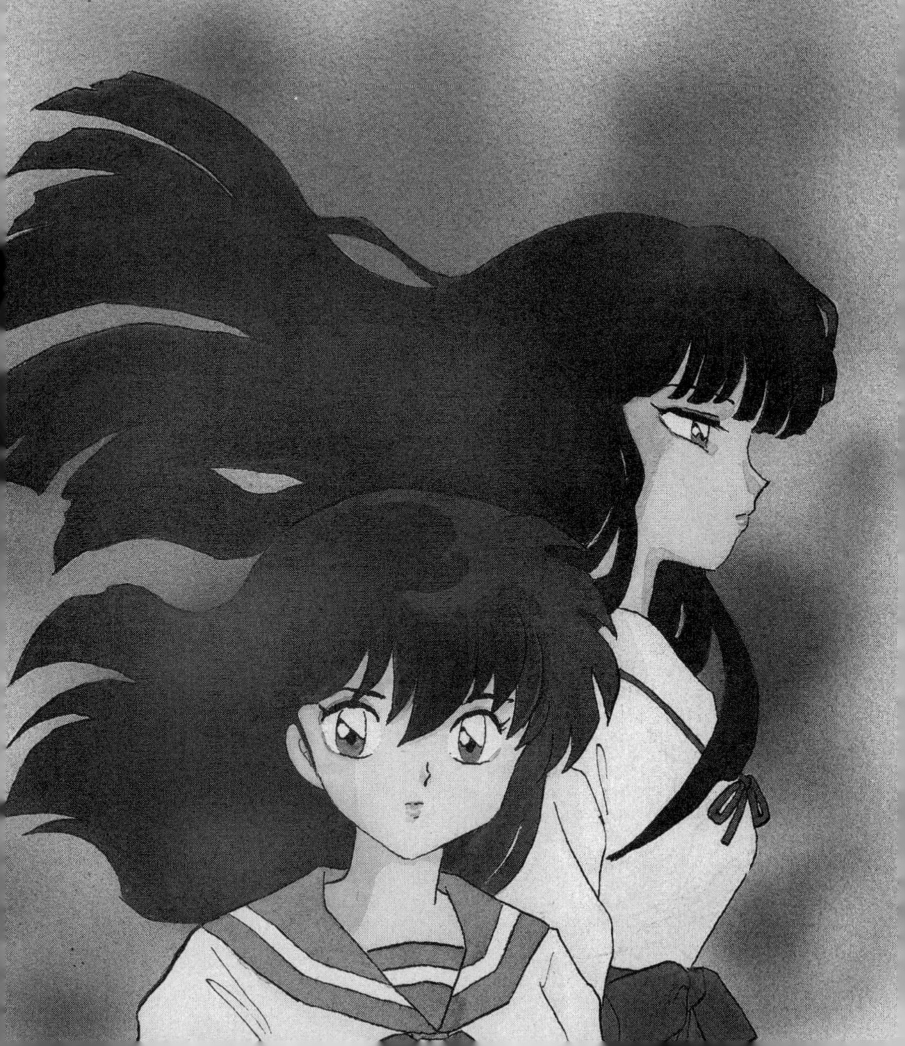

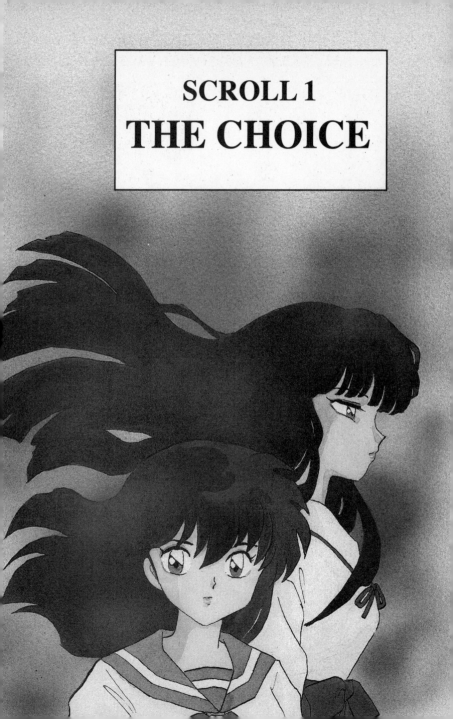

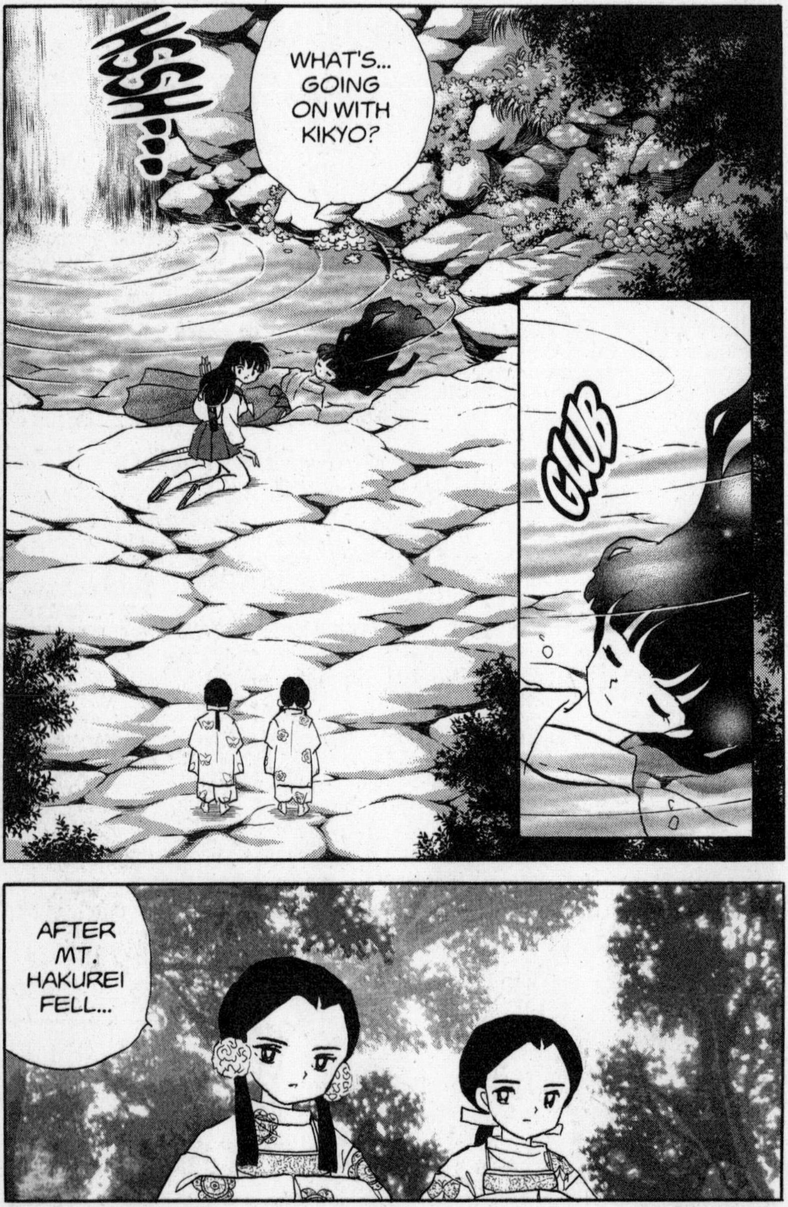
HSSH...
WHAT'S... GOING ON WITH KIKYO?
GLUB
AFTER MT. HAKUREI FELL...

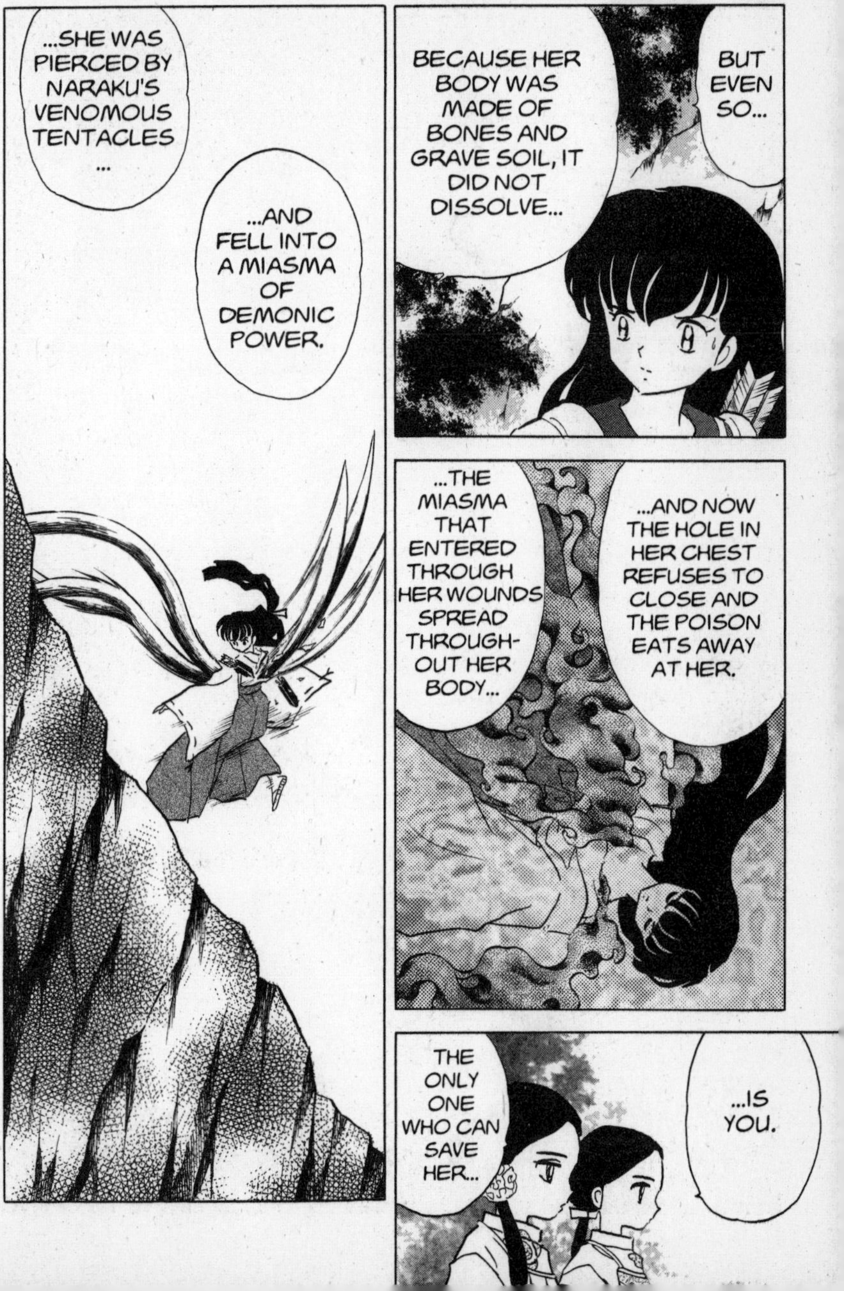
...SHE WAS PIERCED BY NARAKU'S VENOMOUS TENTACLES ...
...AND FELL INTO A MIASMA OF DEMONIC POWER.
BECAUSE HER BODY WAS MADE OF BONES AND GRAVE SOIL, IT DID NOT DISSOLVE...
BUT EVEN SO...
...THE MIASMA THAT ENTERED THROUGH HER WOUNDS SPREAD THROUGH-OUT HER BODY...
...AND NOW THE HOLE IN HER CHEST REFUSES TO CLOSE AND THE POISON EATS AWAY AT HER.
THE ONLY ONE WHO CAN SAVE HER...
...IS YOU.

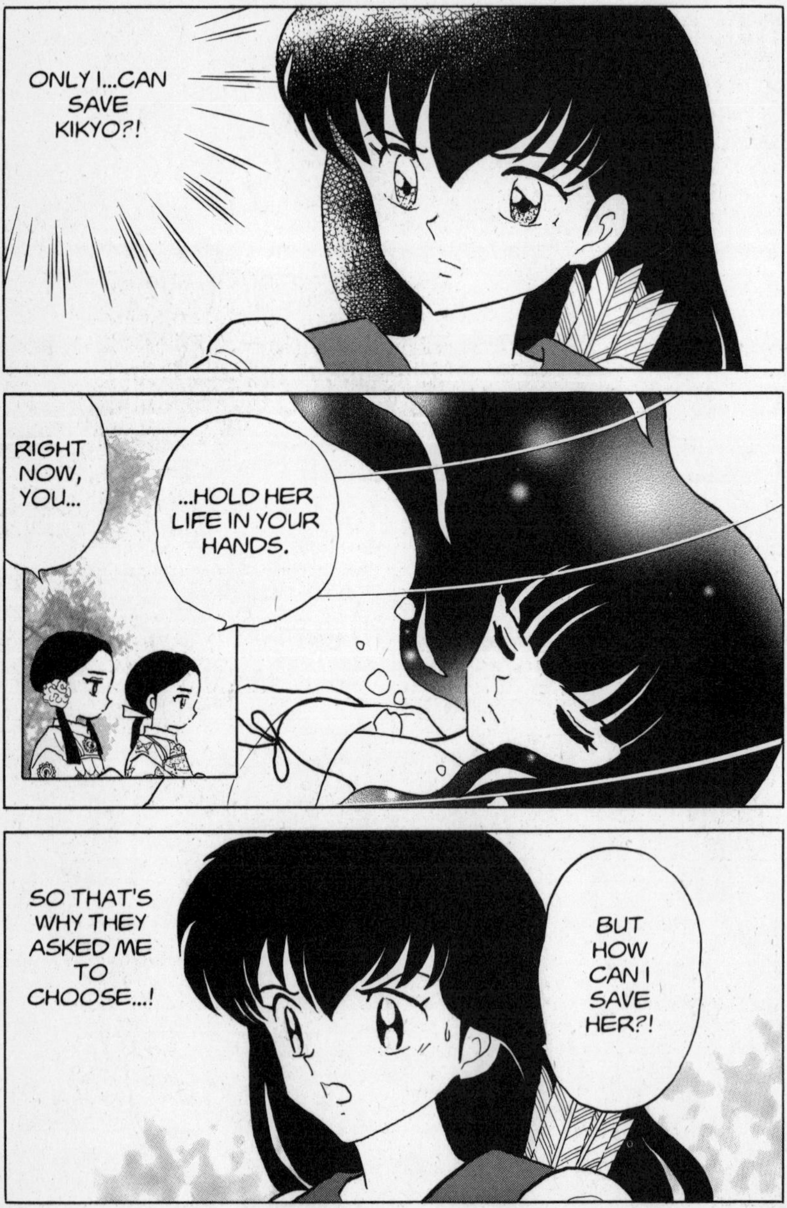
ONLY I...CAN SAVE KIKYO?!
RIGHT NOW, YOU...
...HOLD HER LIFE IN YOUR HANDS.
SO THAT'S WHY THEY ASKED ME TO CHOOSE...!
BUT HOW CAN I SAVE HER?!

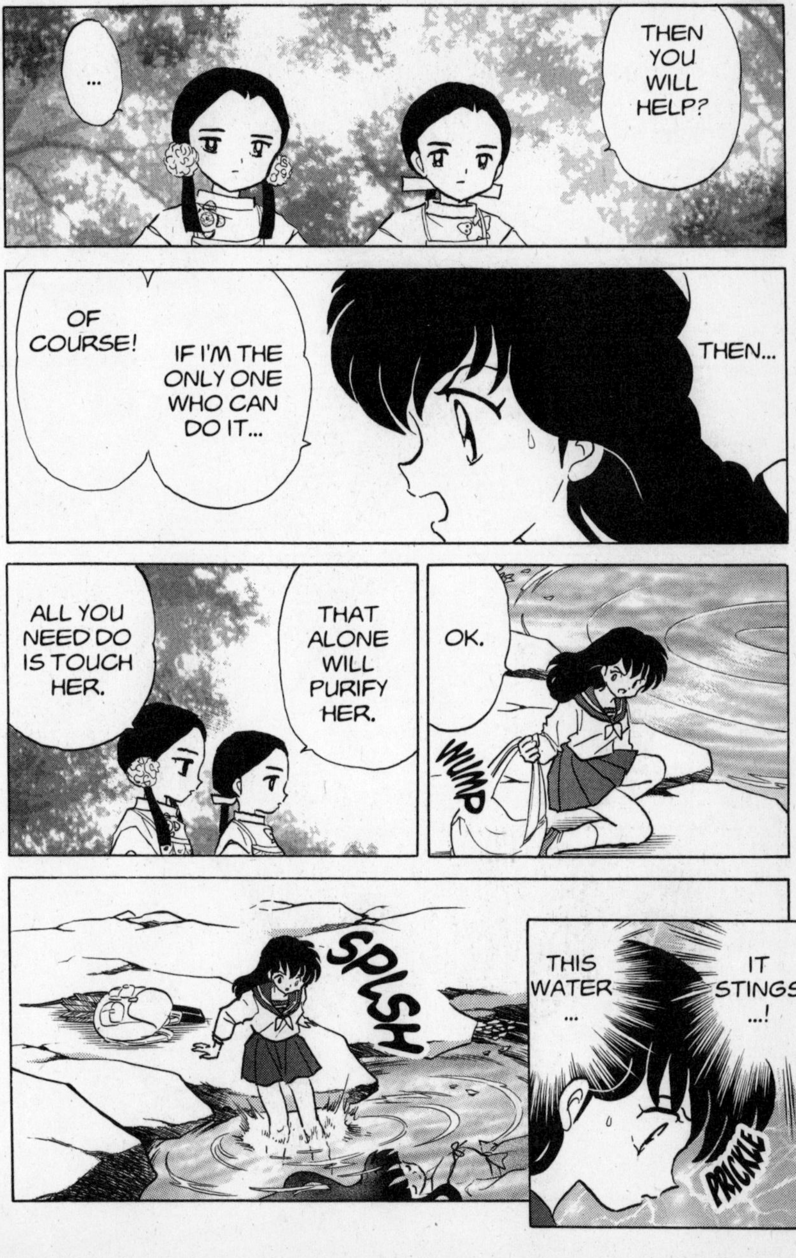
...
THEN YOU WILL HELP?
OF COURSE!
IF I'M THE ONLY ONE WHO CAN DO IT...
THEN...
ALL YOU NEED DO IS TOUCH HER.
THAT ALONE WILL PURIFY HER.
OK.
WUMP
SPLSH
THIS WATER ...
IT STINGS ...!
PRICKLE

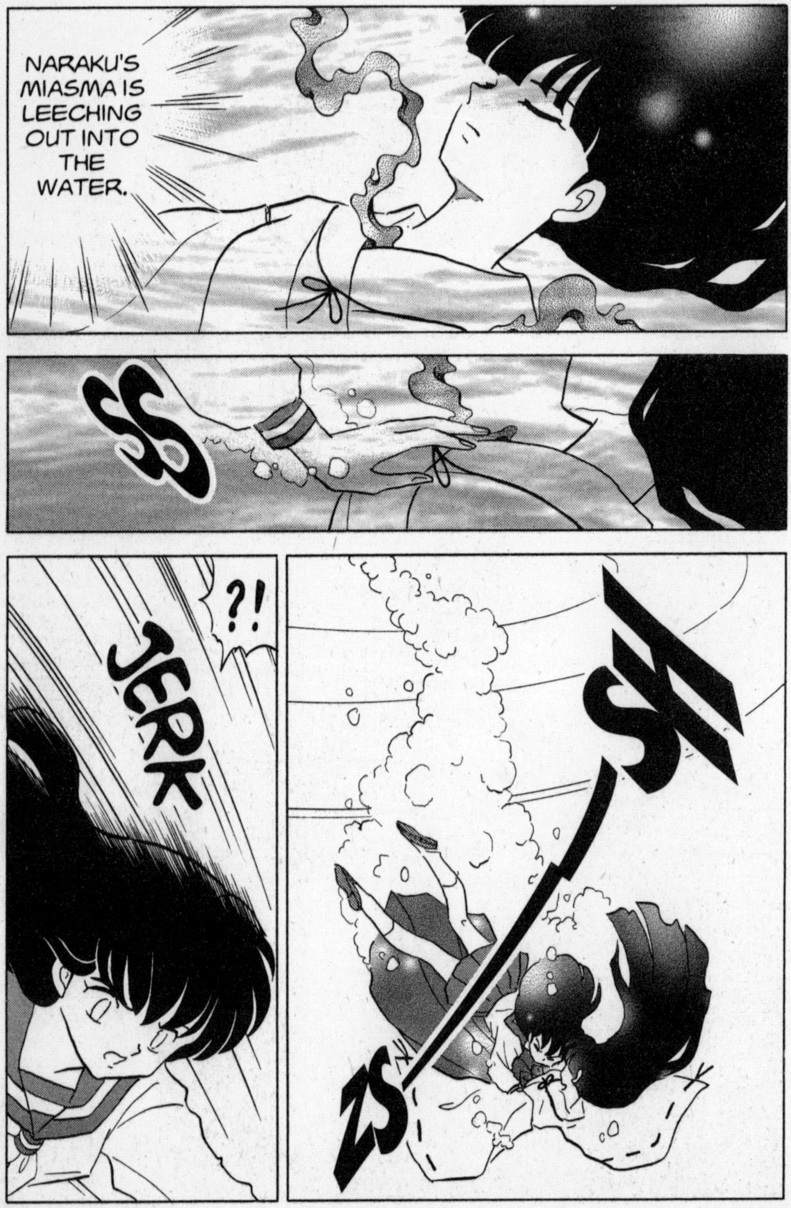
NARAKU'S MIASMA IS LEECHING OUT INTO THE WATER.
SS
?!
JERK

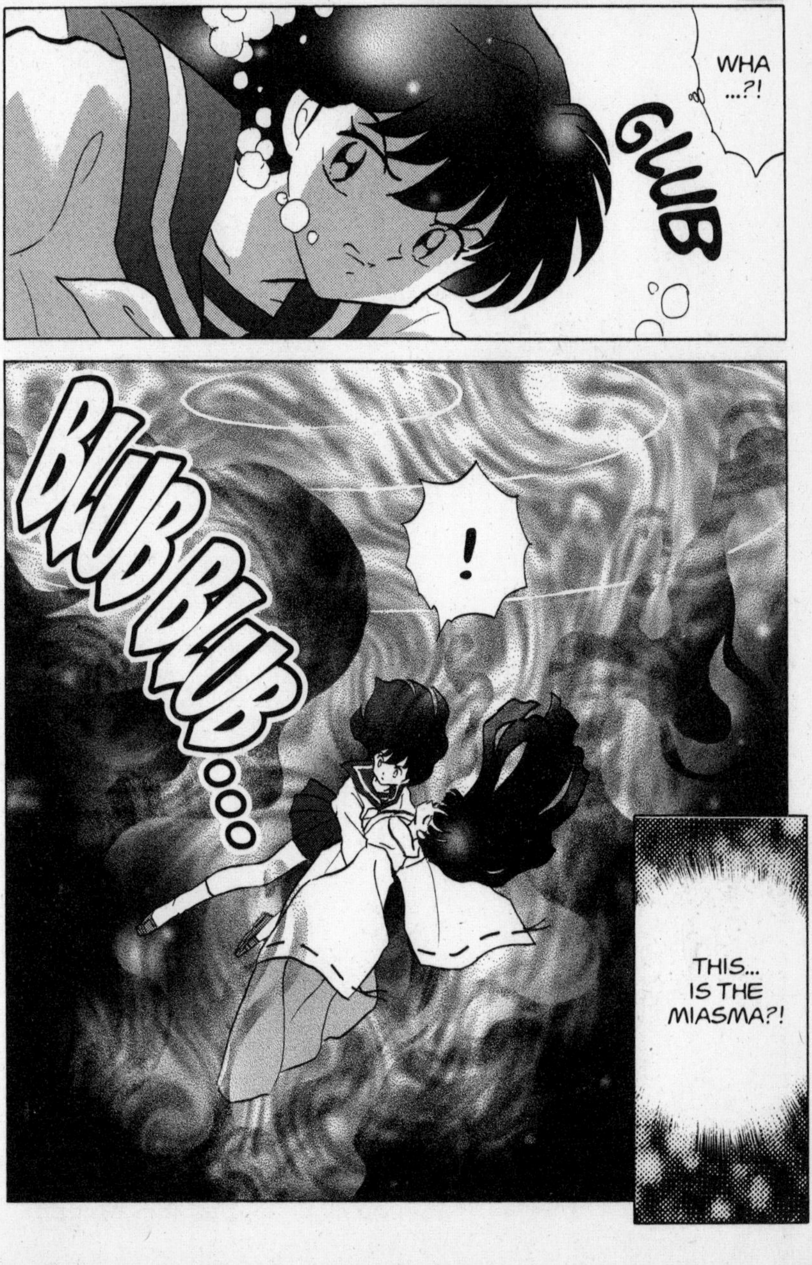
WHA ...?!
GLUB
BLUB BLUB BLUB...
!
THIS... IS THE MIASMA?!

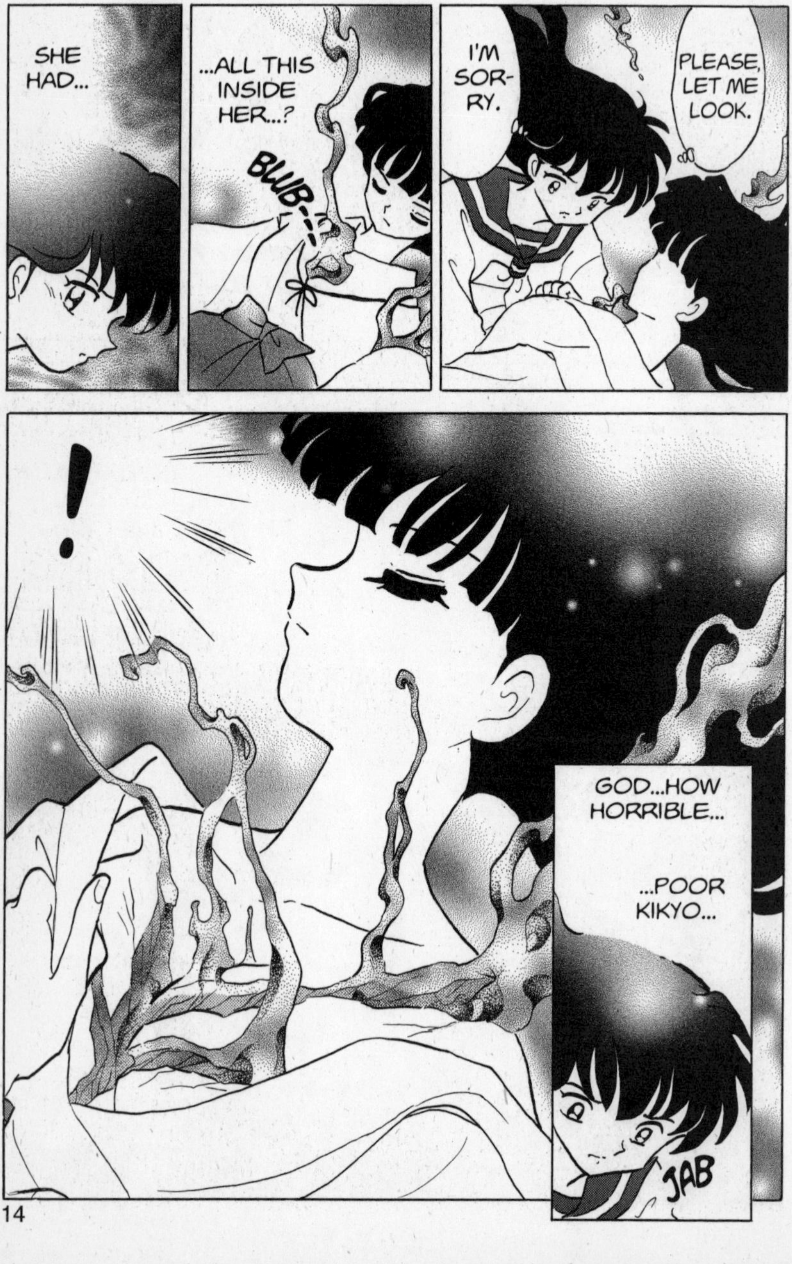
SHE HAD...
...ALL THIS INSIDE HER...?
BLUB-!!
I'M SOR-RY.
PLEASE, LET ME LOOK.
!
GOD...HOW HORRIBLE...
...POOR KIKYO...
JAB

GLINT

HUH ...?

TRICKLE....

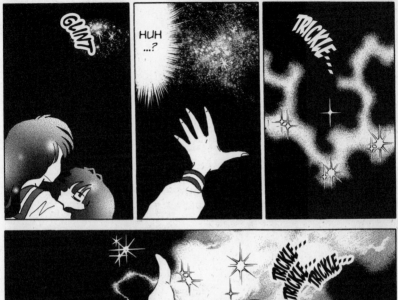

TRICKLE....
TRICKLE....
TRICKLE....

WHAT IS THIS...?

HER LADY-SHIP'S GRAVE SOIL.

YOUR TOUCH HAS PURIFIED IT.

PLACE IT IN THE HOLE IN HER CHEST.

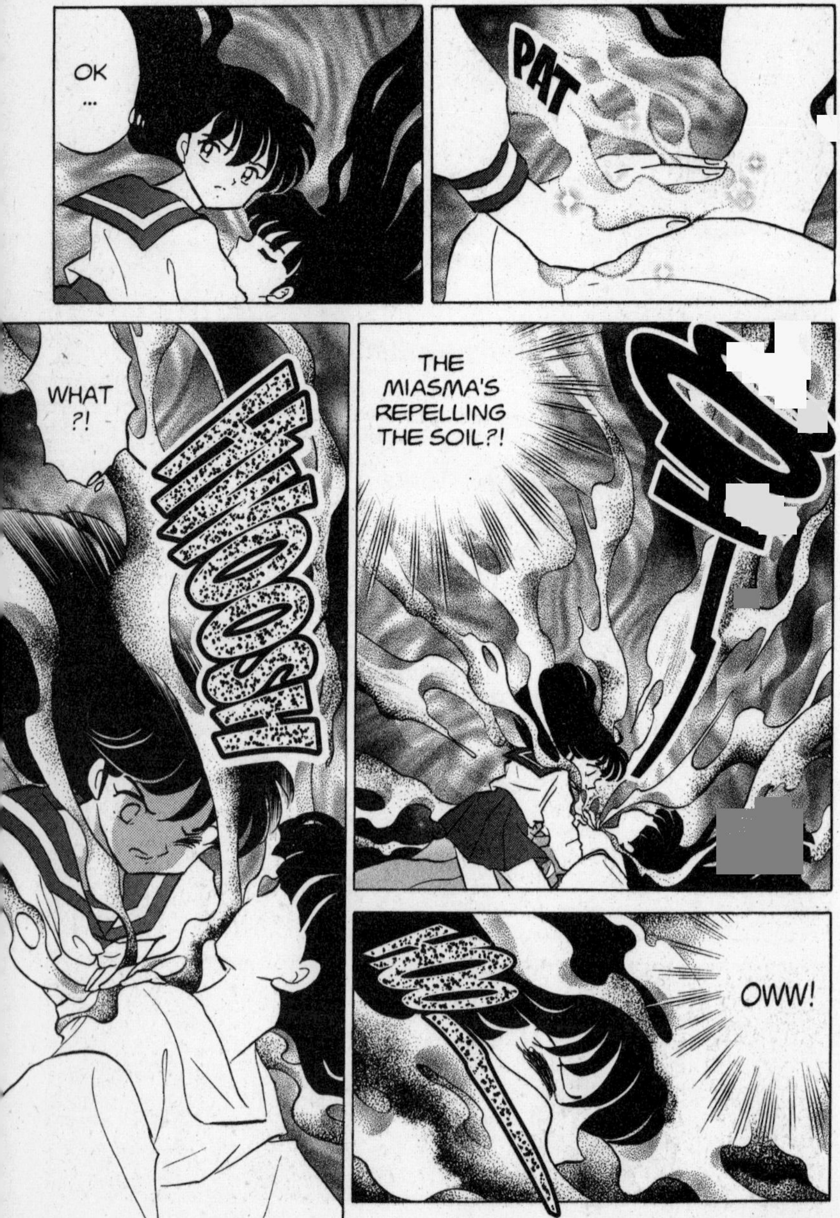
OK
...
PAT
WHAT
?!
WHOOSH!
THE
MIASMA'S
REPELLING
THE SOIL?!
OWW!

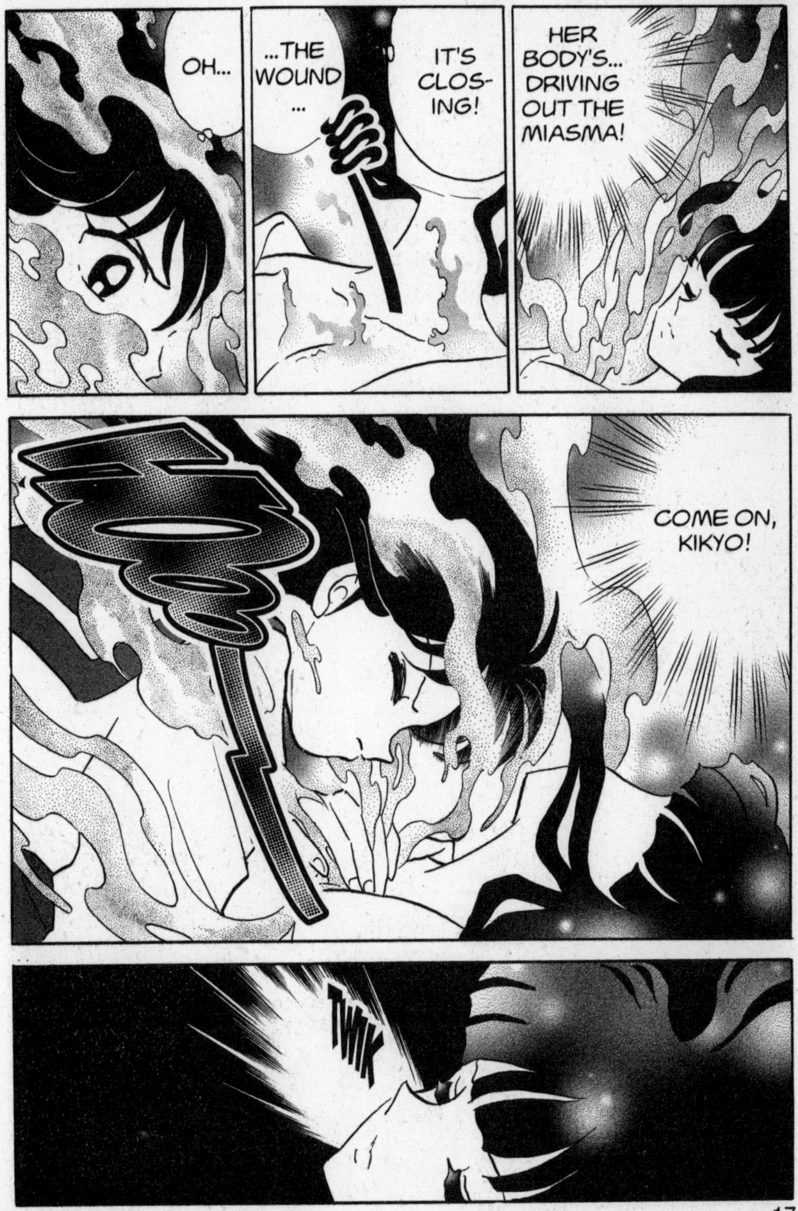
OH...
...THE WOUND ...
IT'S CLOS-ING!
HER BODY'S... DRIVING OUT THE MIASMA!
COME ON, KIKYO!
TWIK

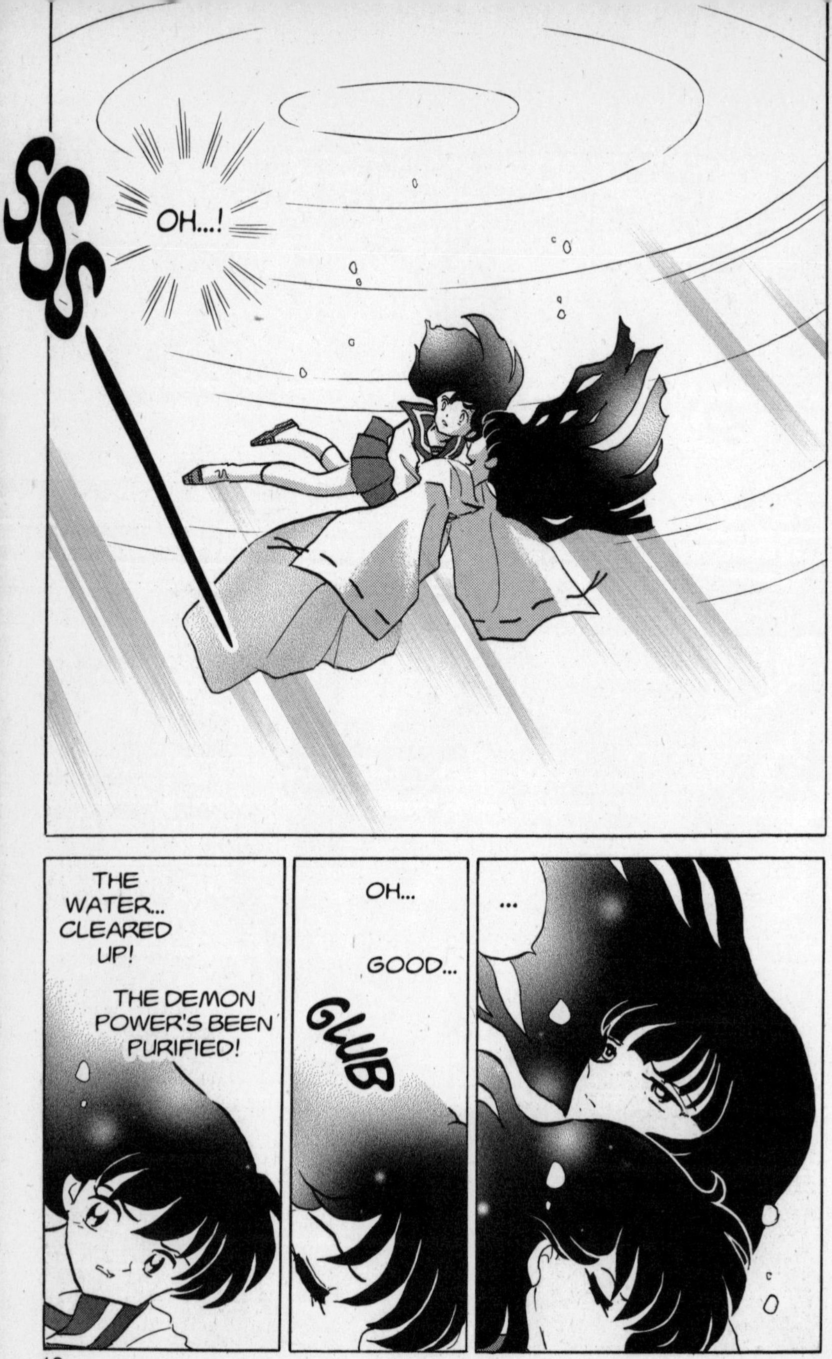
SSS
OH...!
THE WATER... CLEARED UP!
THE DEMON POWER'S BEEN PURIFIED!
OH...
GOOD...
GLUB
...

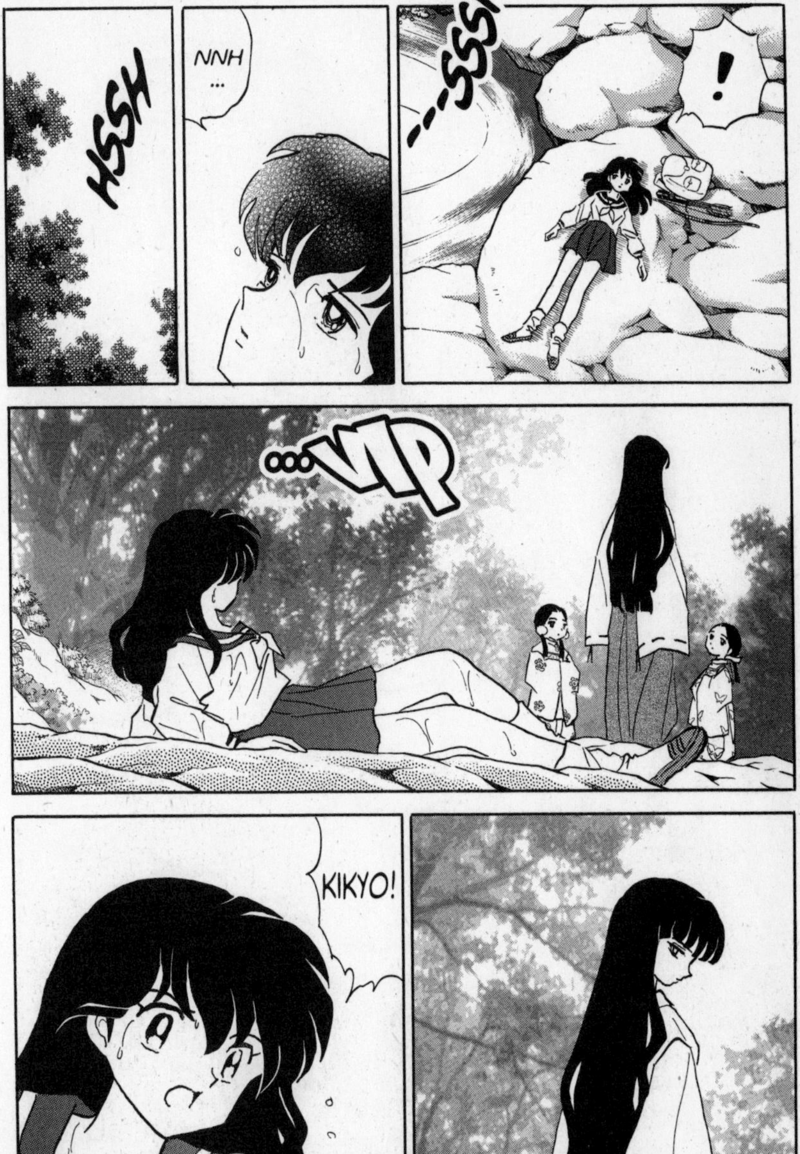
HSSH
NNH ...
...SSSH
!
...VIP
KIKYO!

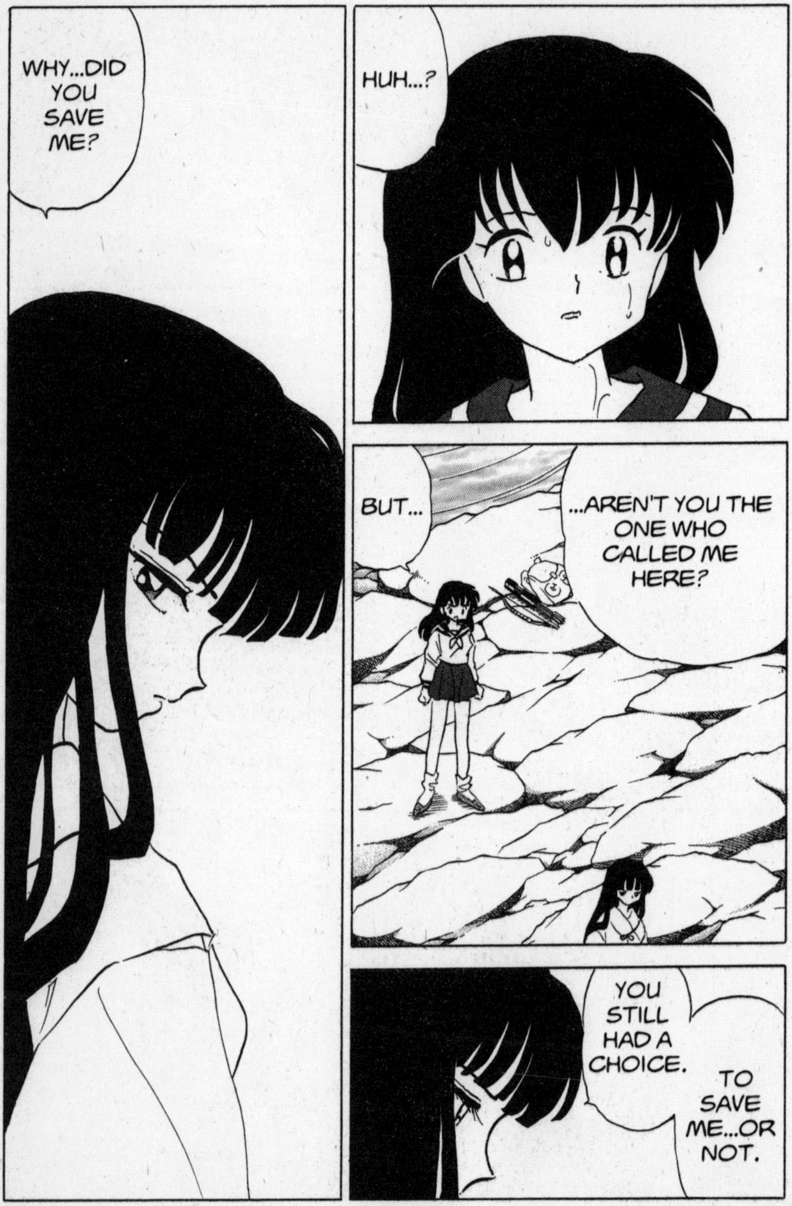
WHY...DID YOU SAVE ME?
HUH...?
BUT...
...AREN'T YOU THE ONE WHO CALLED ME HERE?
YOU STILL HAD A CHOICE.
TO SAVE ME...OR NOT.

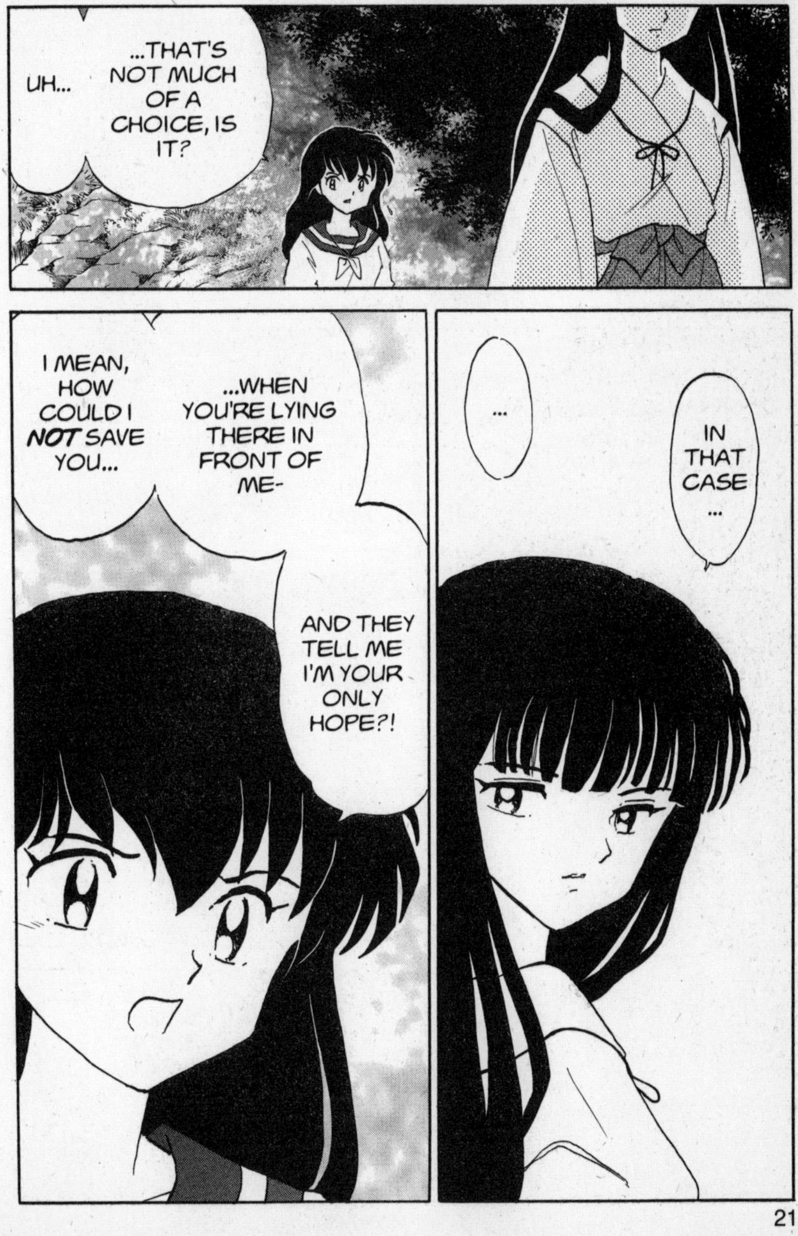
UH...
...THAT'S NOT MUCH OF A CHOICE, IS IT?
I MEAN, HOW COULD I ***NOT*** SAVE YOU...
...WHEN YOU'RE LYING THERE IN FRONT OF ME-
AND THEY TELL ME I'M YOUR ONLY HOPE?!
...
IN THAT CASE...

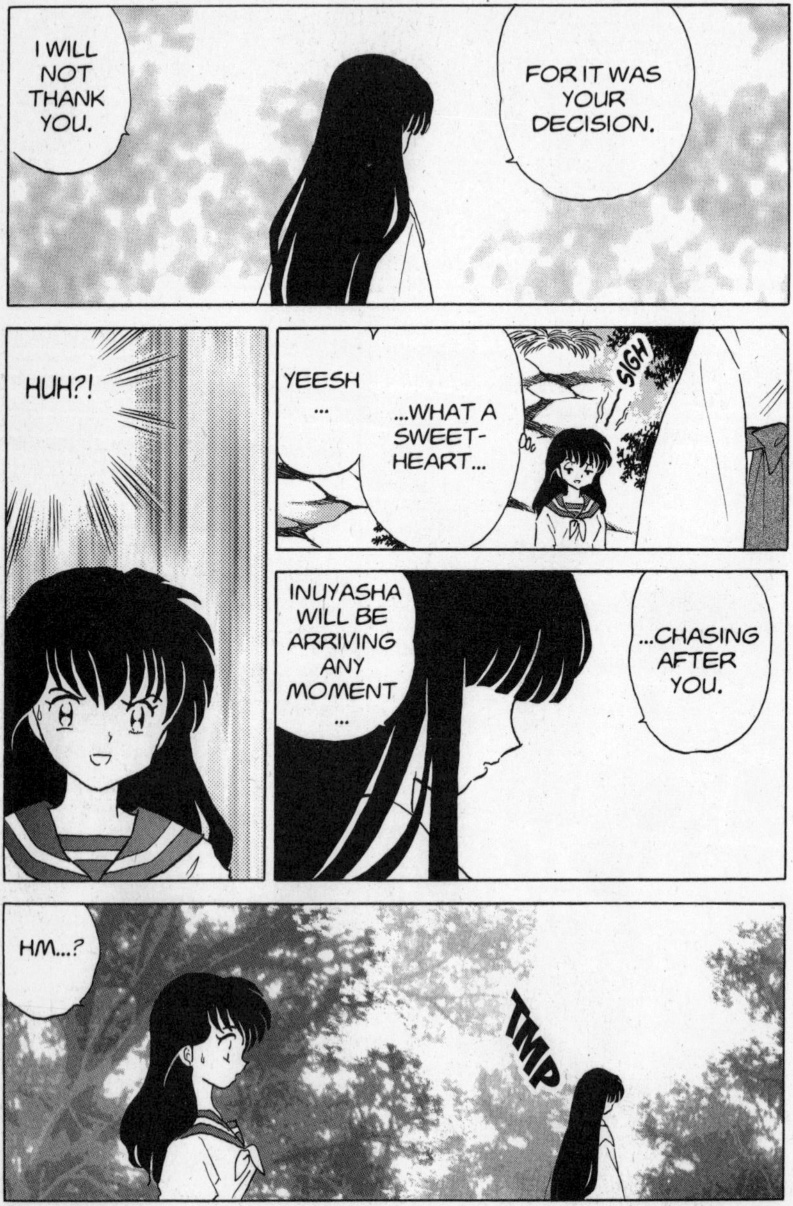
I WILL NOT THANK YOU.
FOR IT WAS YOUR DECISION.
HUH?!
YEESH ...
...WHAT A SWEET-HEART...
SIGH
INUYASHA WILL BE ARRIVING ANY MOMENT ...
...CHASING AFTER YOU.
HM...?
TMP

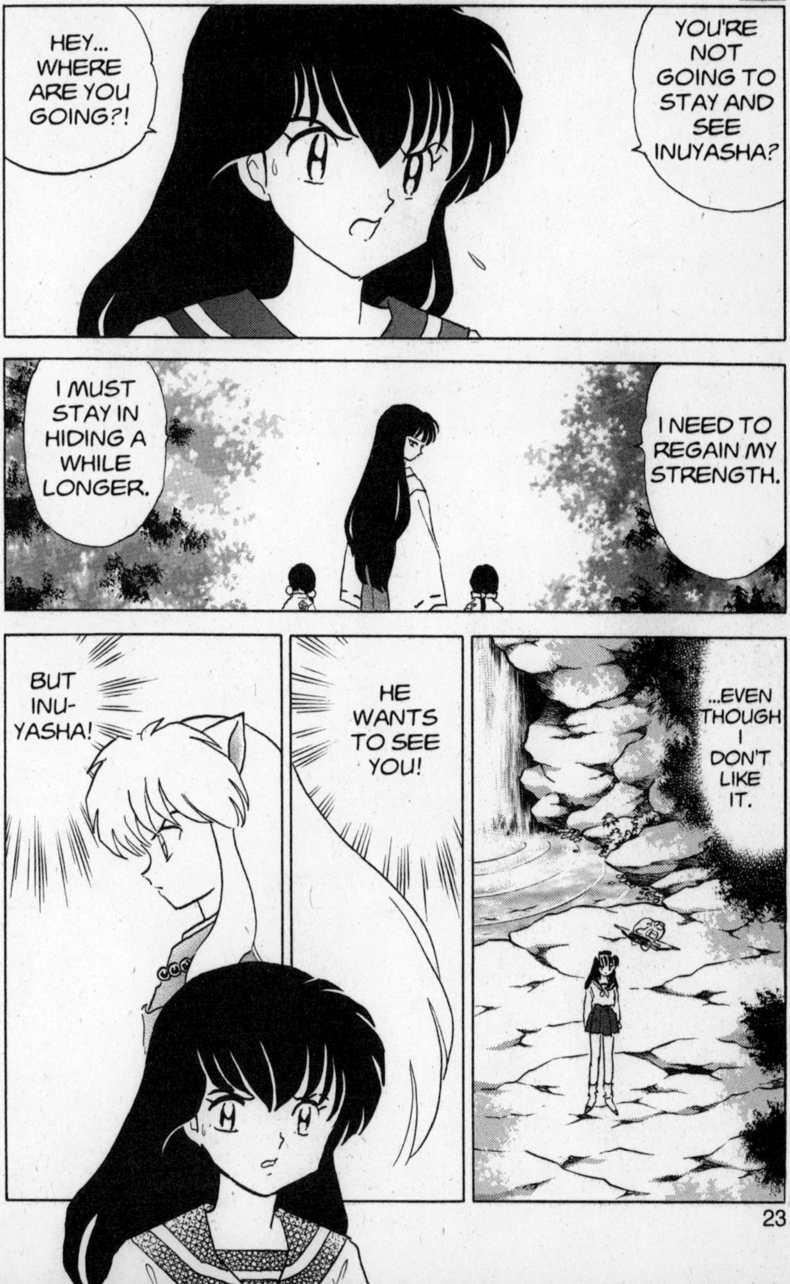
HEY... WHERE ARE YOU GOING?!
YOU'RE NOT GOING TO STAY AND SEE INUYASHA?
I MUST STAY IN HIDING A WHILE LONGER.
I NEED TO REGAIN MY STRENGTH.
BUT INU-YASHA!
HE WANTS TO SEE YOU!
...EVEN THOUGH I DON'T LIKE IT.

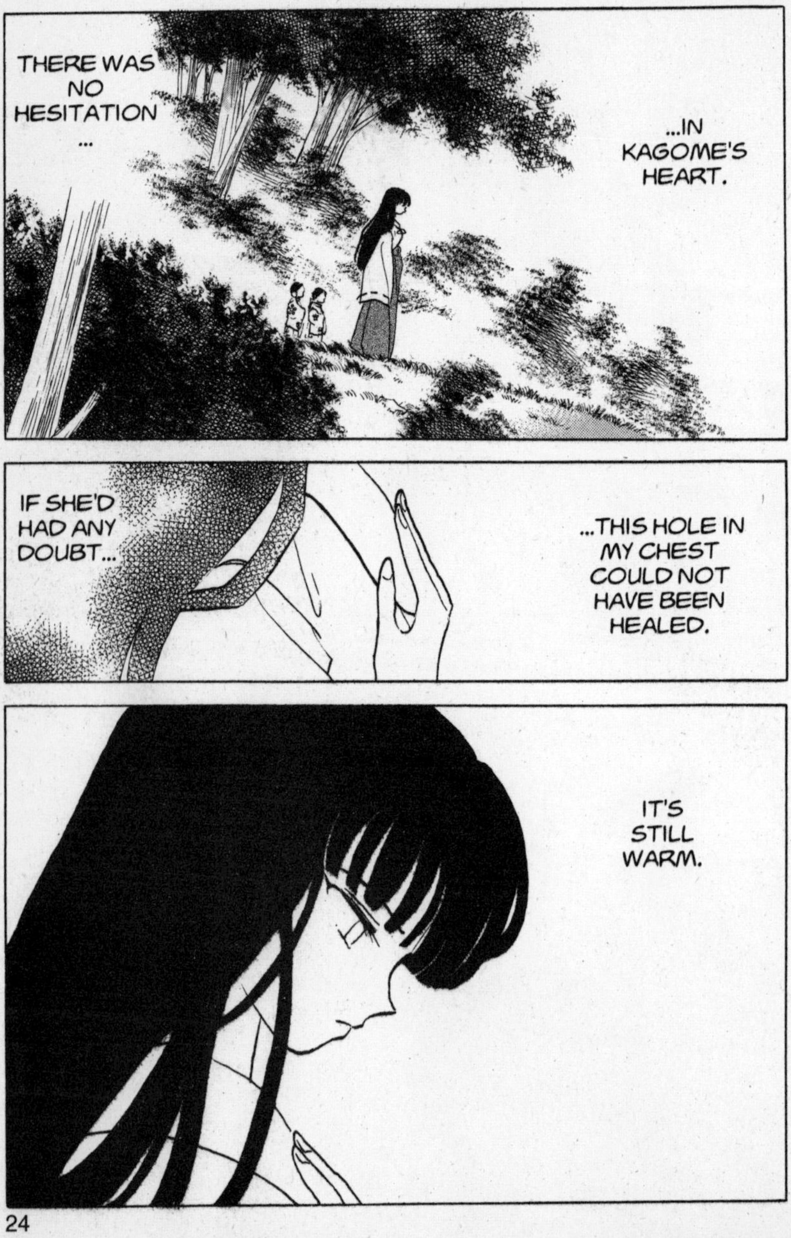
THERE WAS NO HESITATION ...
...IN KAGOME'S HEART.
IF SHE'D HAD ANY DOUBT...
...THIS HOLE IN MY CHEST COULD NOT HAVE BEEN HEALED.
IT'S STILL WARM.

SCROLL 2

THE ANGRY HEART

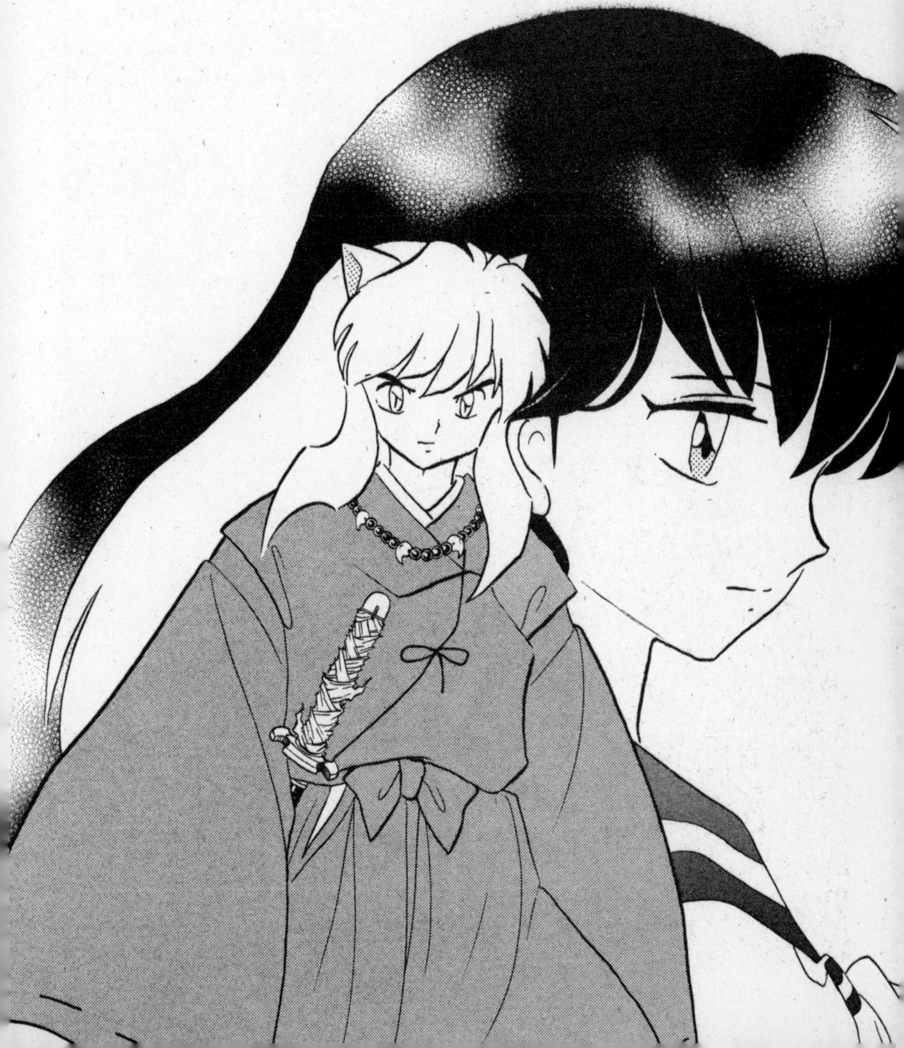

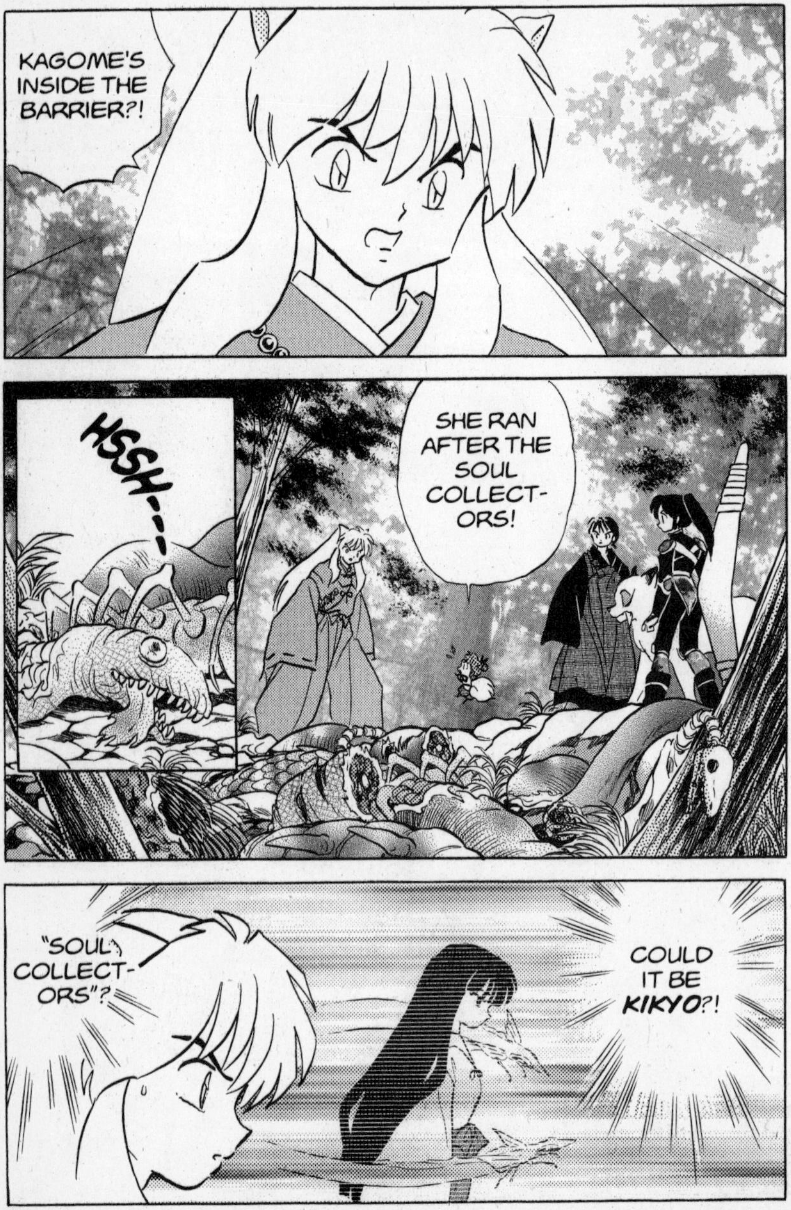
KAGOME'S INSIDE THE BARRIER?!
HSSH...
SHE RAN AFTER THE SOUL COLLECT-ORS!
"SOUL COLLECT-ORS"?
COULD IT BE **KIKYO**?!

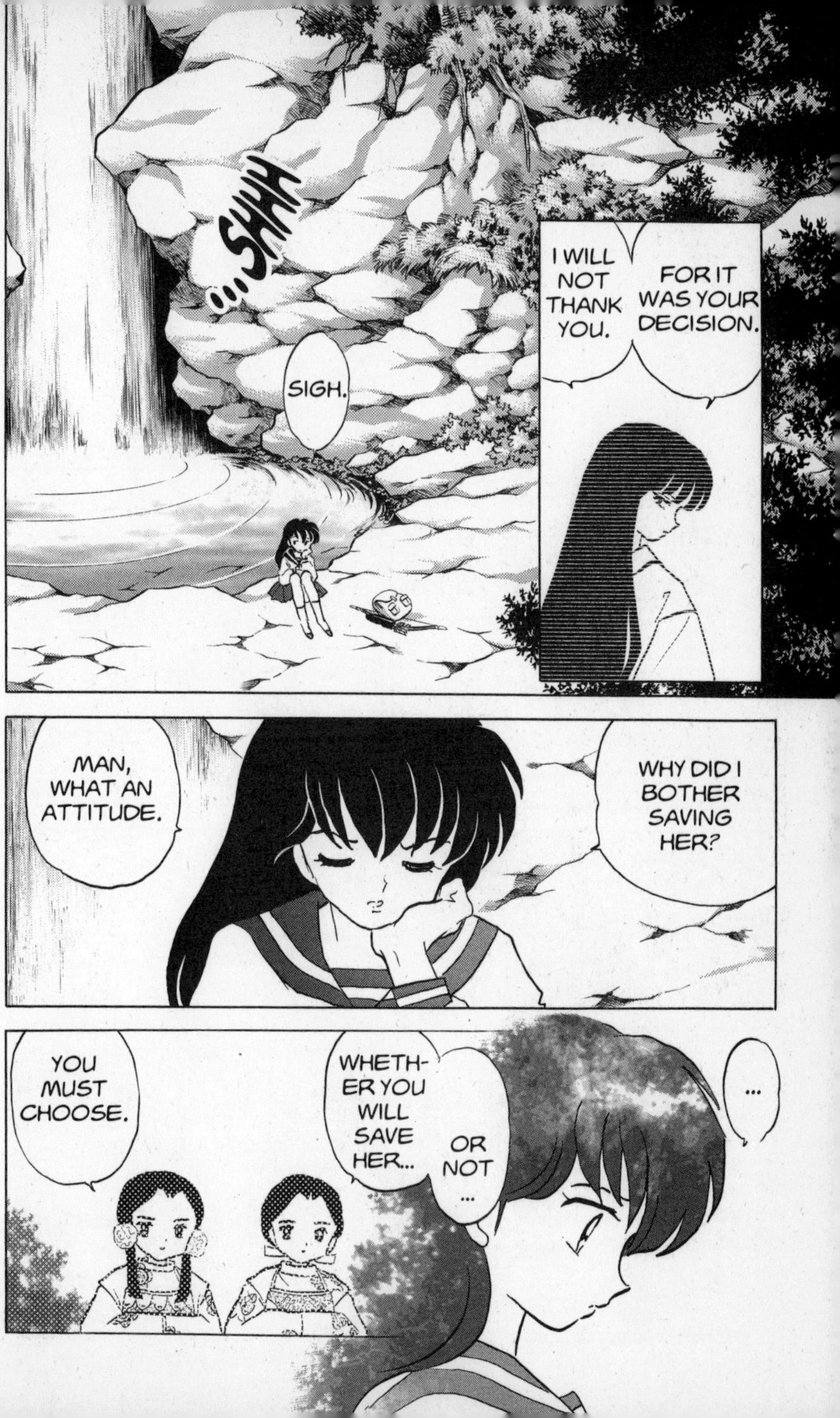
...SHHH
SIGH.
I WILL NOT THANK YOU.
FOR IT WAS YOUR DECISION.
MAN, WHAT AN ATTITUDE.
WHY DID I BOTHER SAVING HER?
YOU MUST CHOOSE.
WHETH-ER YOU WILL SAVE HER...
OR NOT ...
...

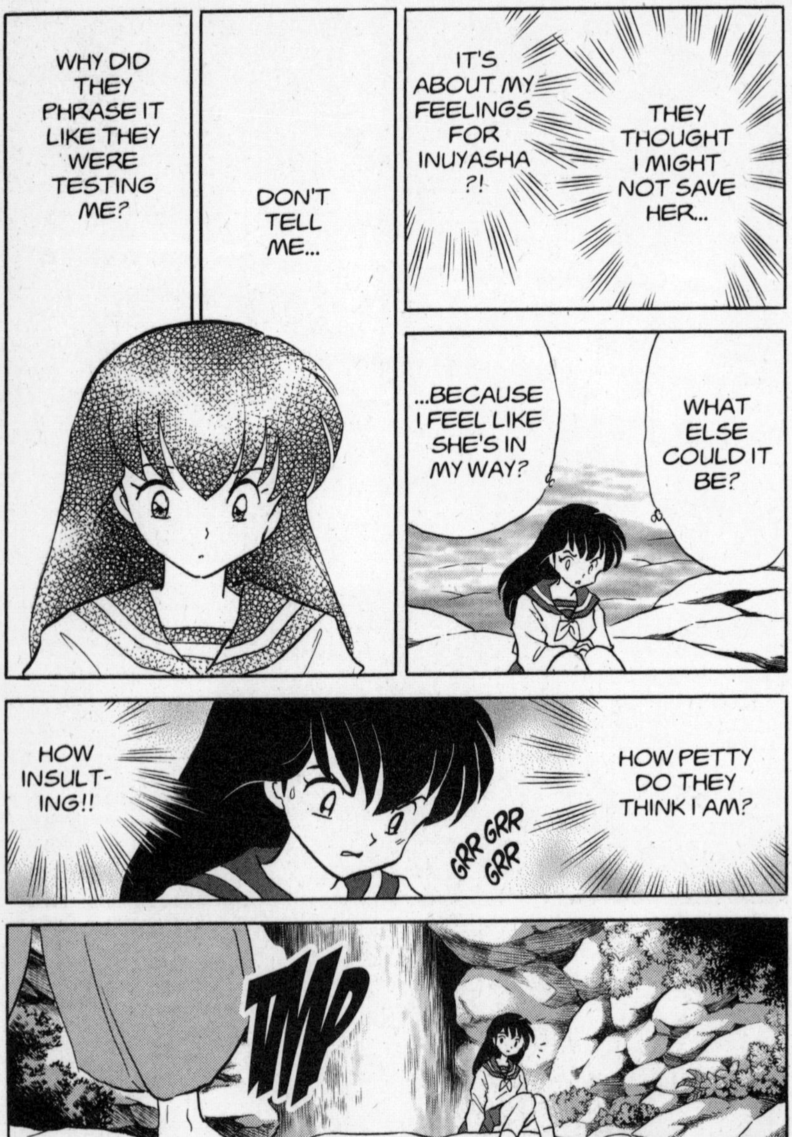
WHY DID THEY PHRASE IT LIKE THEY WERE TESTING ME?
DON'T TELL ME...
IT'S ABOUT MY FEELINGS FOR INUYASHA?!
THEY THOUGHT I MIGHT NOT SAVE HER...
...BECAUSE I FEEL LIKE SHE'S IN MY WAY?
WHAT ELSE COULD IT BE?
HOW INSULT-ING!!
GRR GRR GRR
HOW PETTY DO THEY THINK I AM?
TMP

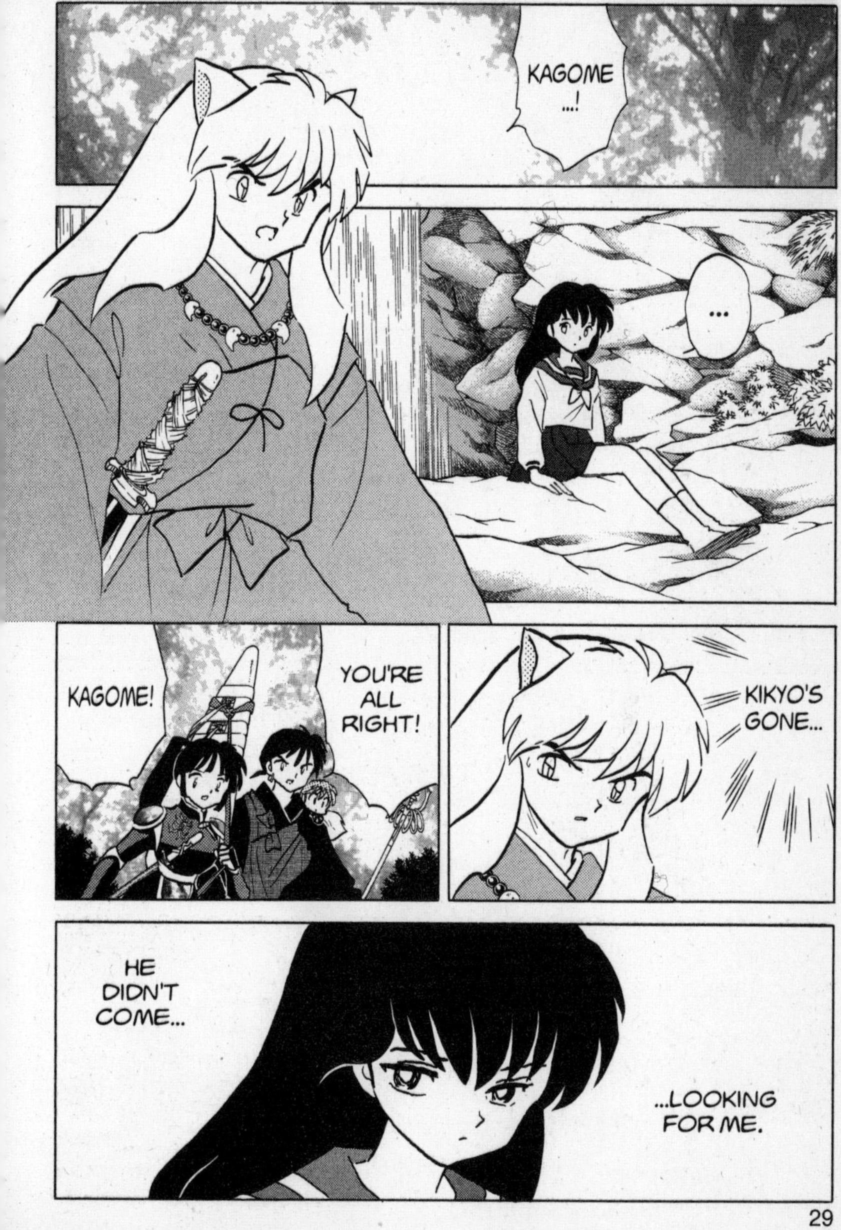
KAGOME ...!
...
KAGOME!
YOU'RE ALL RIGHT!
KIKYO'S GONE...
HE DIDN'T COME...
...LOOKING FOR ME.

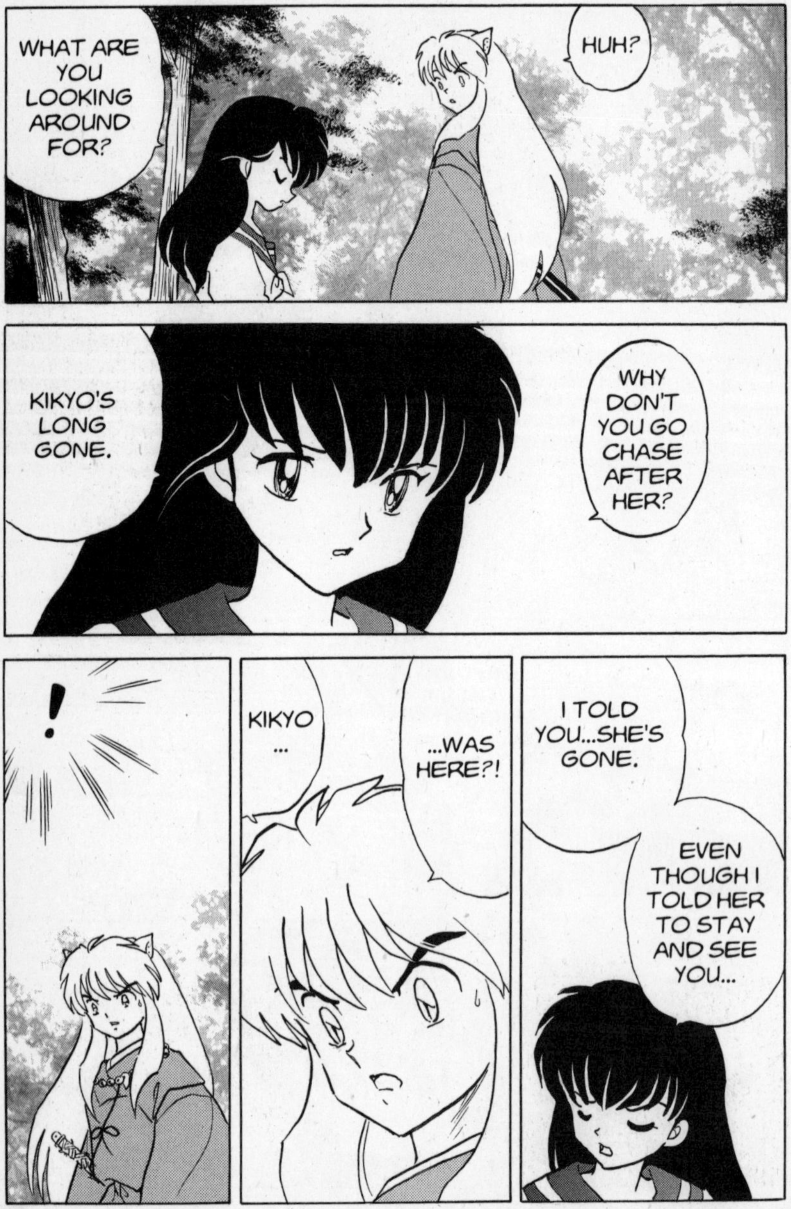
WHAT ARE YOU LOOKING AROUND FOR?
HUH?
KIKYO'S LONG GONE.
WHY DON'T YOU GO CHASE AFTER HER?
!
KIKYO ...
...WAS HERE?!
I TOLD YOU...SHE'S GONE.
EVEN THOUGH I TOLD HER TO STAY AND SEE YOU...

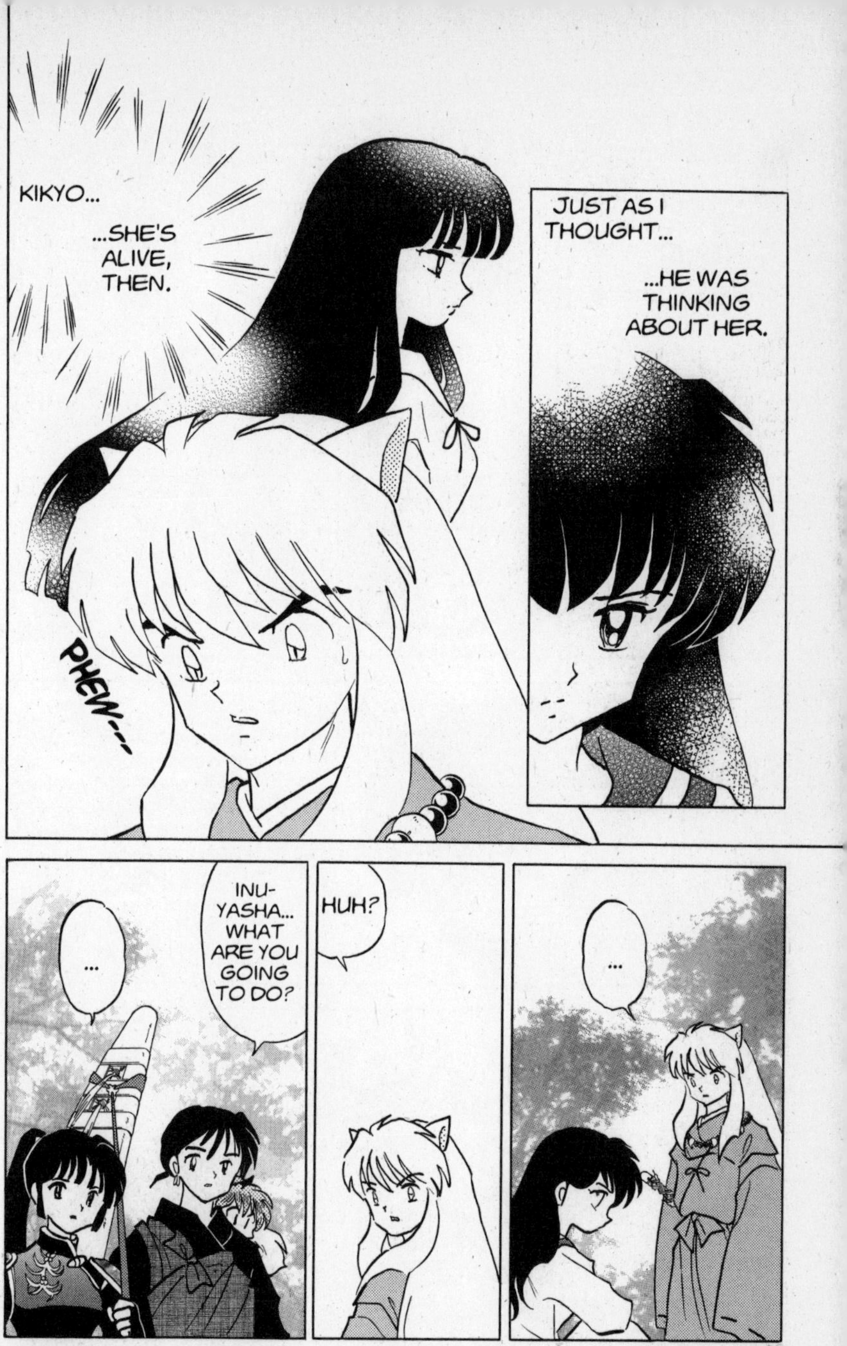
KIKYO...
...SHE'S ALIVE, THEN.
PHEW...
JUST AS I THOUGHT...
...HE WAS THINKING ABOUT HER.
...
INU-YASHA... WHAT ARE YOU GOING TO DO?
HUH?
...

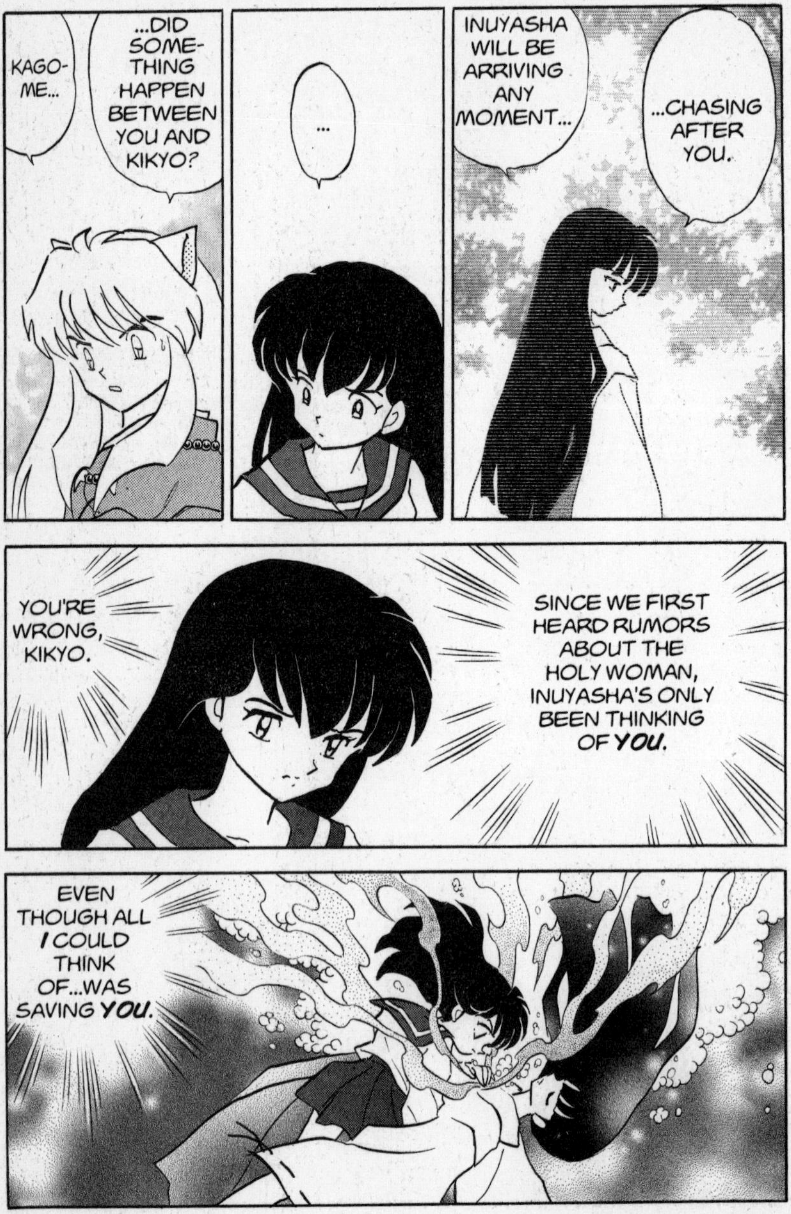
KAGO-ME...
...DID SOME-THING HAPPEN BETWEEN YOU AND KIKYO?
...
INUYASHA WILL BE ARRIVING ANY MOMENT...
...CHASING AFTER YOU.
YOU'RE WRONG, KIKYO.
SINCE WE FIRST HEARD RUMORS ABOUT THE HOLY WOMAN, INUYASHA'S ONLY BEEN THINKING OF *YOU*.
EVEN THOUGH ALL *I* COULD THINK OF...WAS SAVING *YOU*.

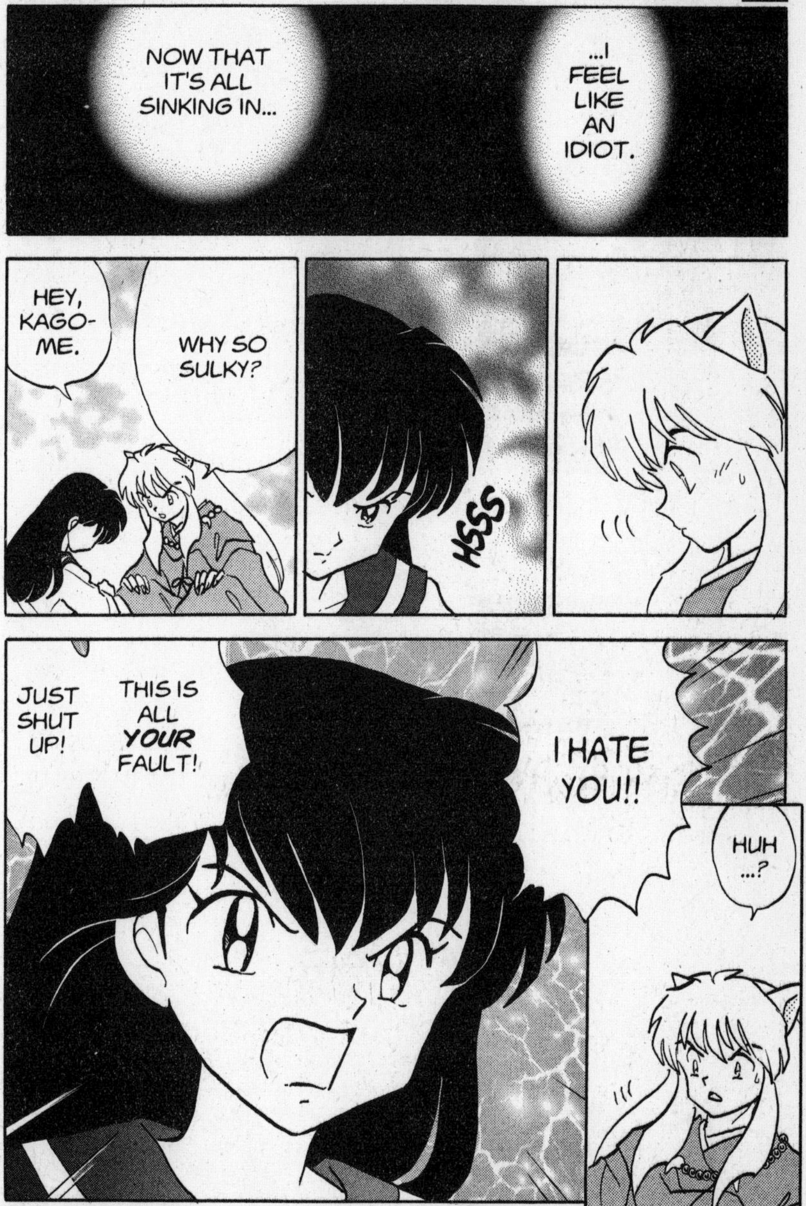
NOW THAT IT'S ALL SINKING IN...
...I FEEL LIKE AN IDIOT.
HEY, KAGOME.
WHY SO SULKY?
HSSS
JUST SHUT UP!
THIS IS ALL **YOUR** FAULT!
I HATE YOU!!
HUH ...?

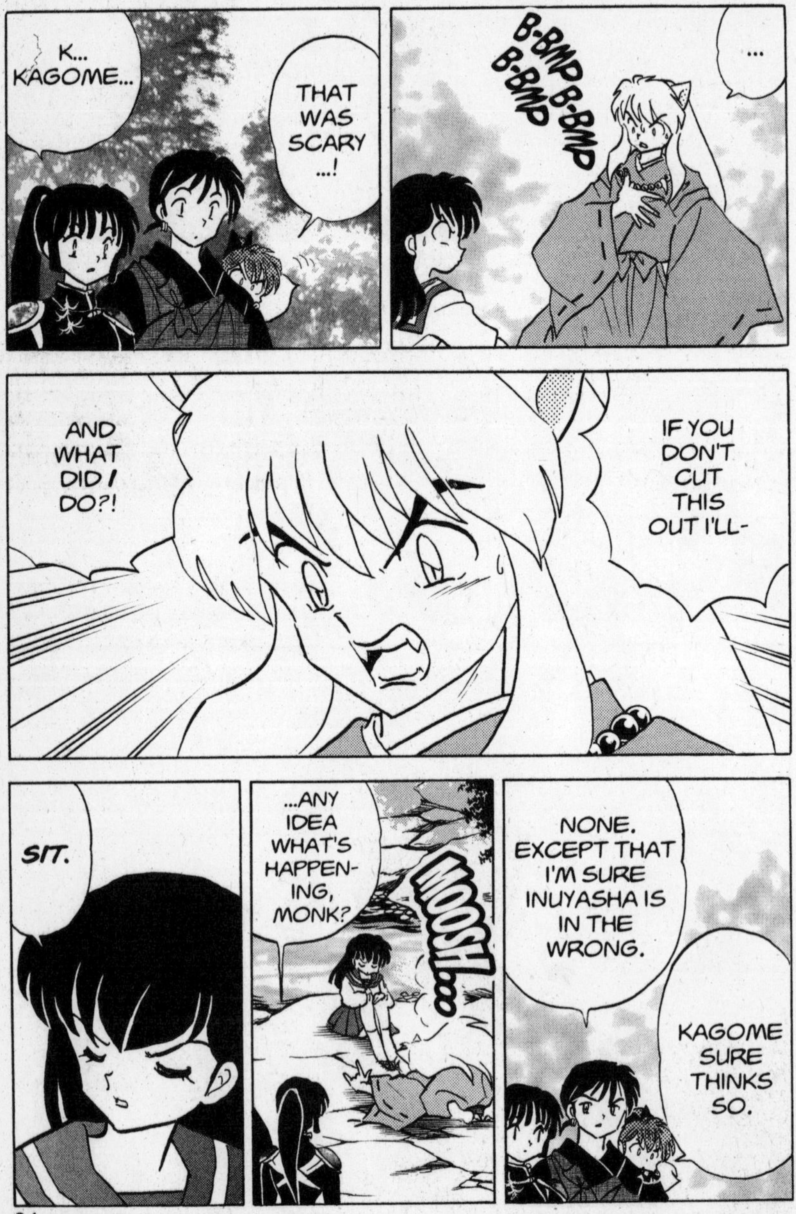
K... KAGOME...
THAT WAS SCARY ...!
B-BMP B-BMP B-BMP
...
AND WHAT DID I DO?!
IF YOU DON'T CUT THIS OUT I'LL-
SIT.
...ANY IDEA WHAT'S HAPPEN-ING, MONK?
WOOSH...
NONE. EXCEPT THAT I'M SURE INUYASHA IS IN THE WRONG.
KAGOME SURE THINKS SO.

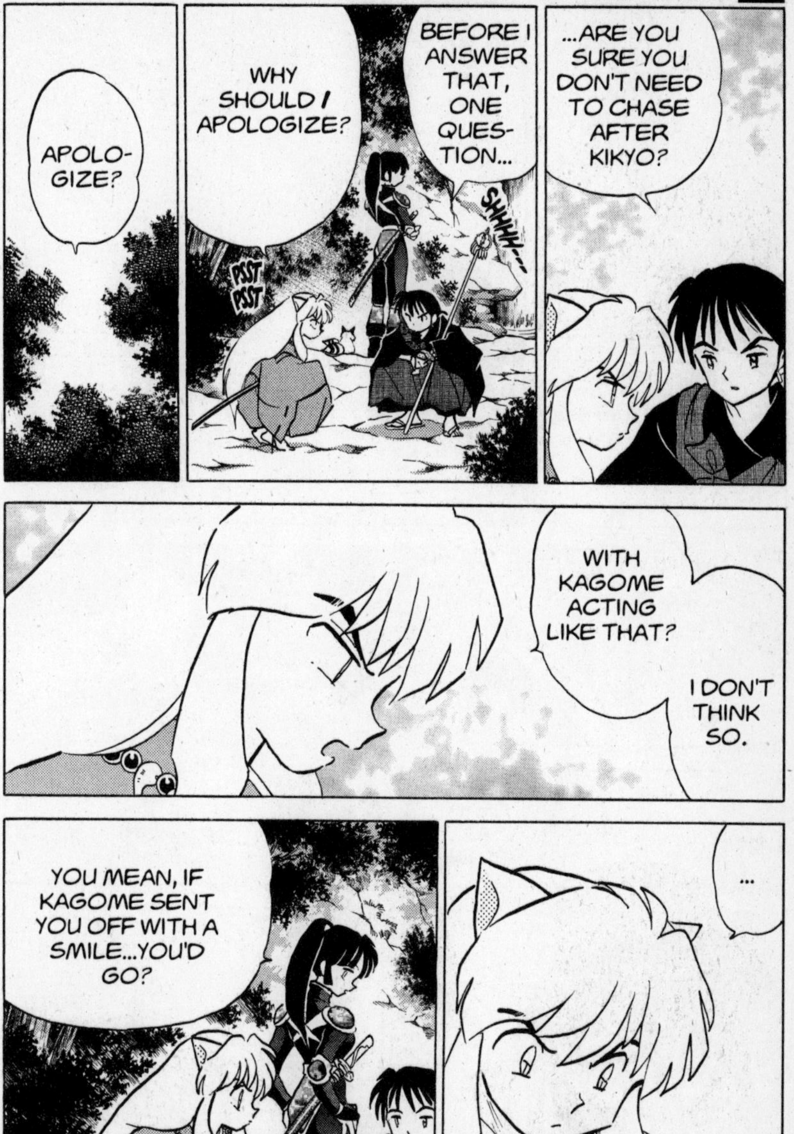
APOLO-GIZE?
WHY SHOULD I APOLOGIZE?
PSST PSST
BEFORE I ANSWER THAT, ONE QUES-TION...
SHHHH--!
...ARE YOU SURE YOU DON'T NEED TO CHASE AFTER KIKYO?
WITH KAGOME ACTING LIKE THAT?
I DON'T THINK SO.
YOU MEAN, IF KAGOME SENT YOU OFF WITH A SMILE...YOU'D GO?
...

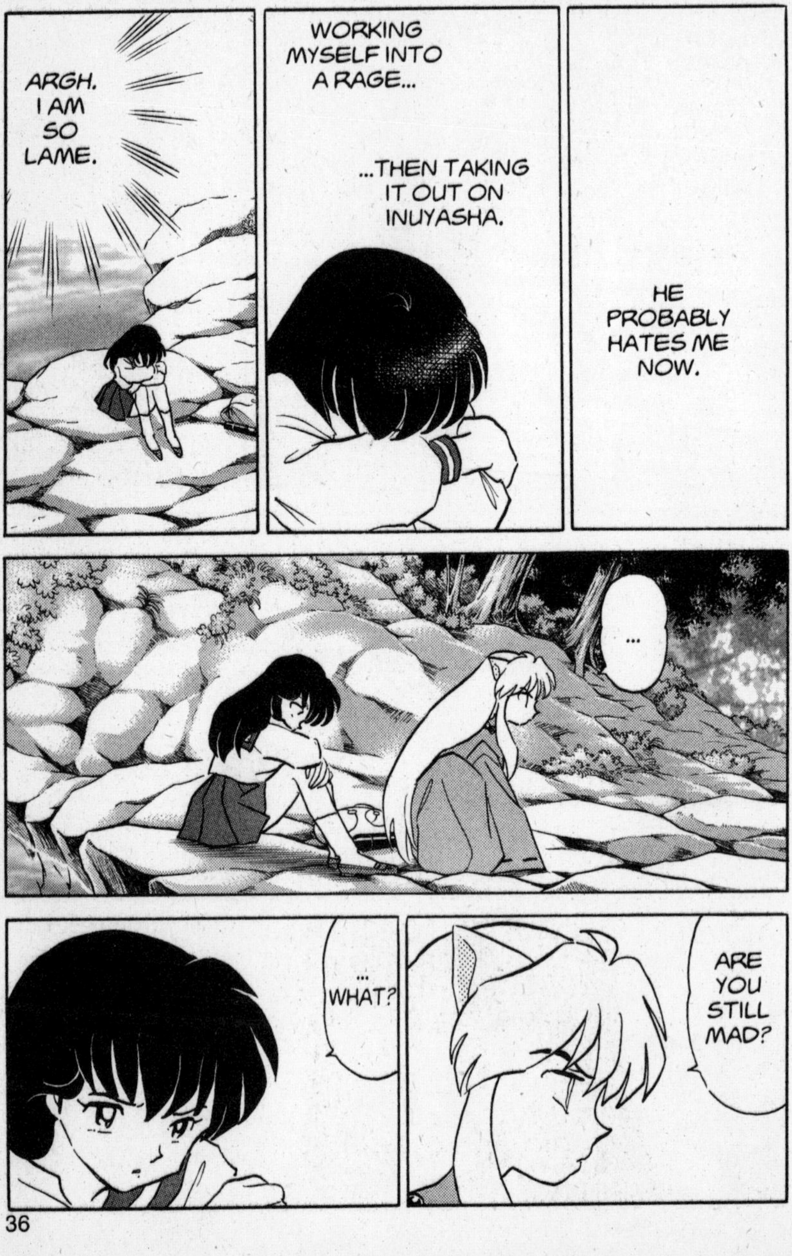
ARGH. I AM SO LAME.
WORKING MYSELF INTO A RAGE...
...THEN TAKING IT OUT ON INUYASHA.
HE PROBABLY HATES ME NOW.
...
... WHAT?
ARE YOU STILL MAD?

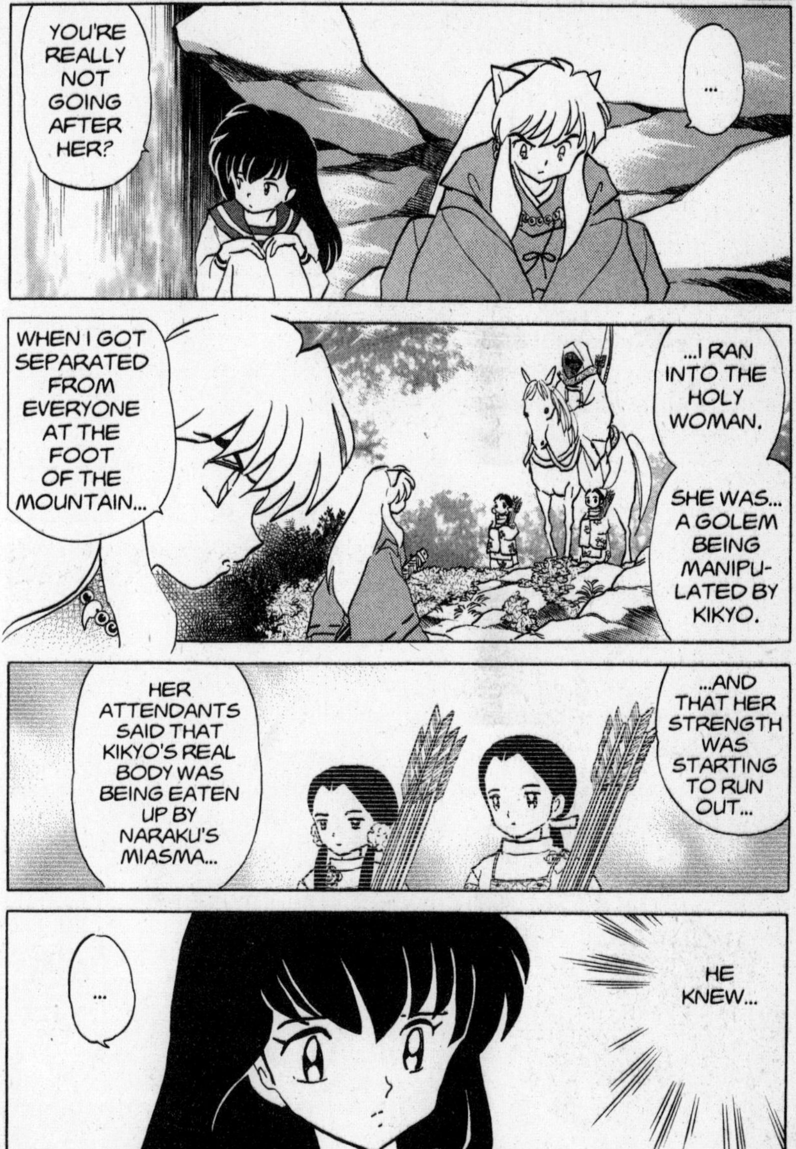
YOU'RE REALLY NOT GOING AFTER HER?
...
WHEN I GOT SEPARATED FROM EVERYONE AT THE FOOT OF THE MOUNTAIN...
...I RAN INTO THE HOLY WOMAN.
SHE WAS... A GOLEM BEING MANIPU-LATED BY KIKYO.
HER ATTENDANTS SAID THAT KIKYO'S REAL BODY WAS BEING EATEN UP BY NARAKU'S MIASMA...
...AND THAT HER STRENGTH WAS STARTING TO RUN OUT...
...
HE KNEW...

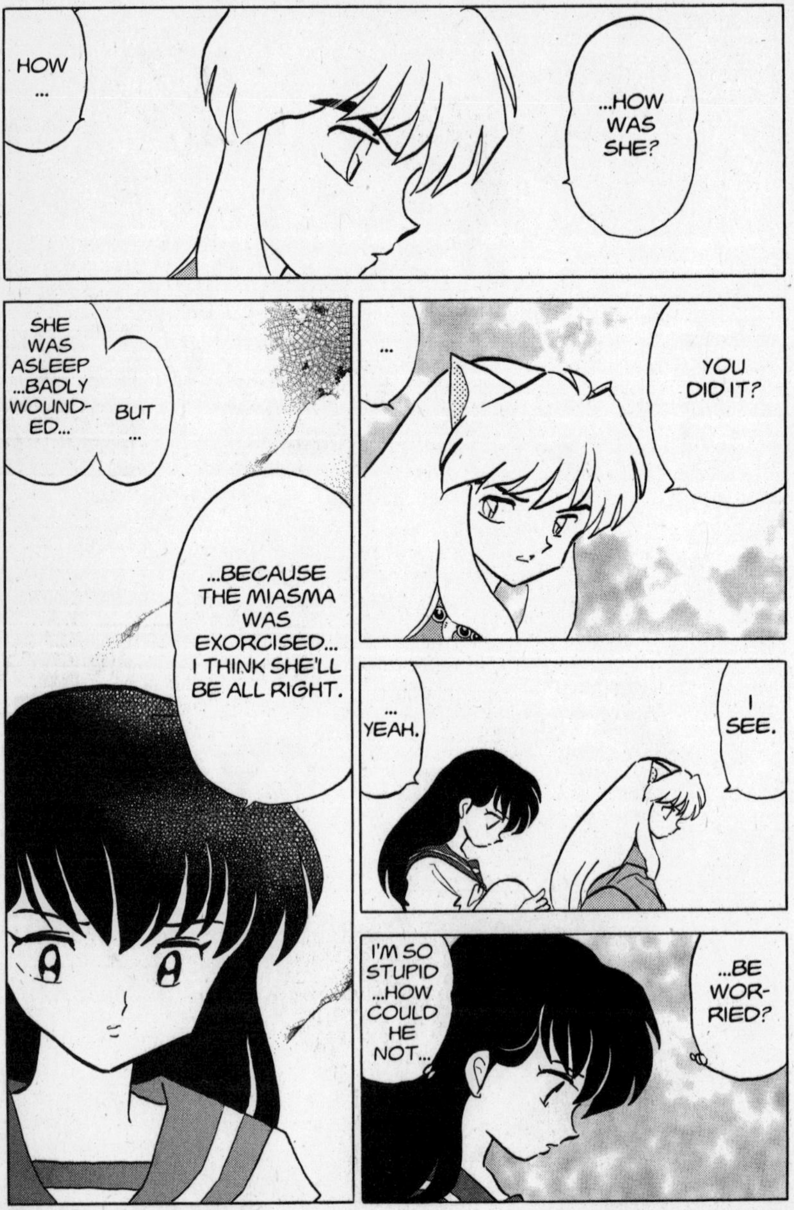
HOW ...
...HOW WAS SHE?
SHE WAS ASLEEP ...BADLY WOUND-ED...
BUT ...
...BECAUSE THE MIASMA WAS EXORCISED... I THINK SHE'LL BE ALL RIGHT.
...
YOU DID IT?
... YEAH.
I SEE.
I'M SO STUPID ...HOW COULD HE NOT...
...BE WOR-RIED?

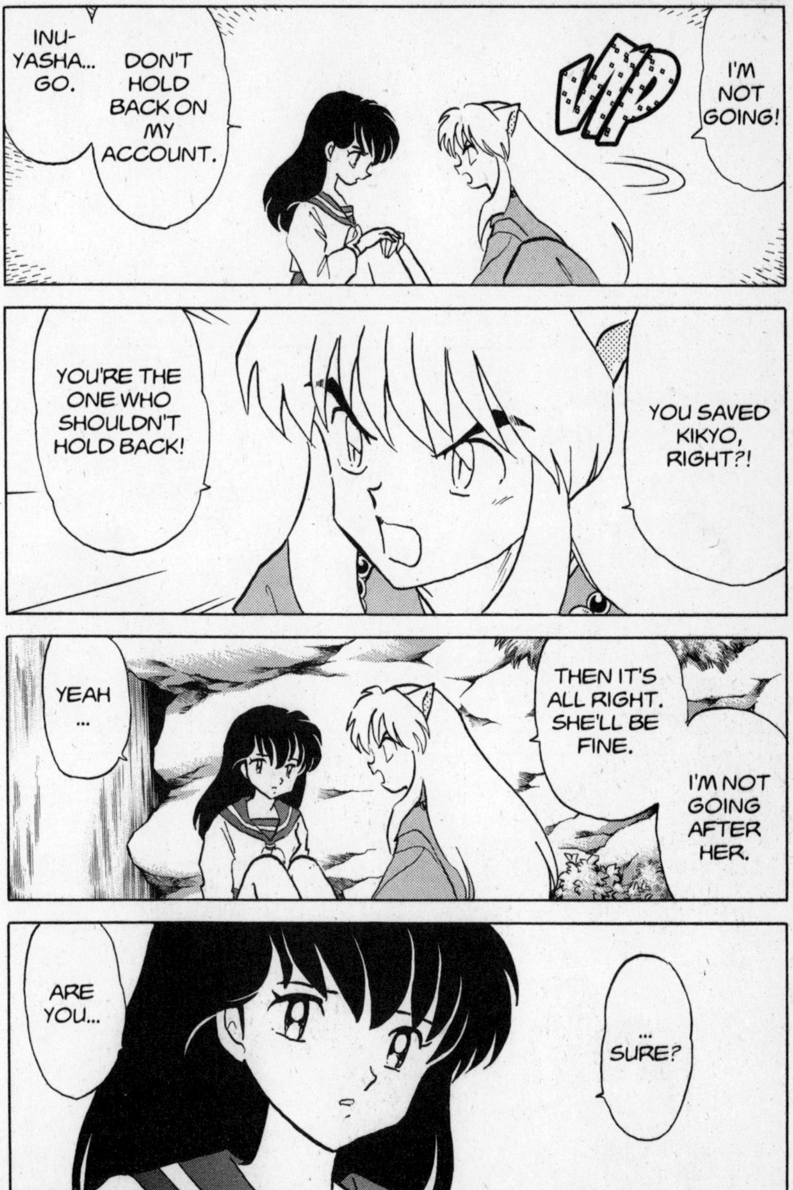
INU-YASHA... GO.
DON'T HOLD BACK ON MY ACCOUNT.
VIP
I'M NOT GOING!
YOU'RE THE ONE WHO SHOULDN'T HOLD BACK!
YOU SAVED KIKYO, RIGHT?!
YEAH ...
THEN IT'S ALL RIGHT. SHE'LL BE FINE.
I'M NOT GOING AFTER HER.
ARE YOU...
... SURE?

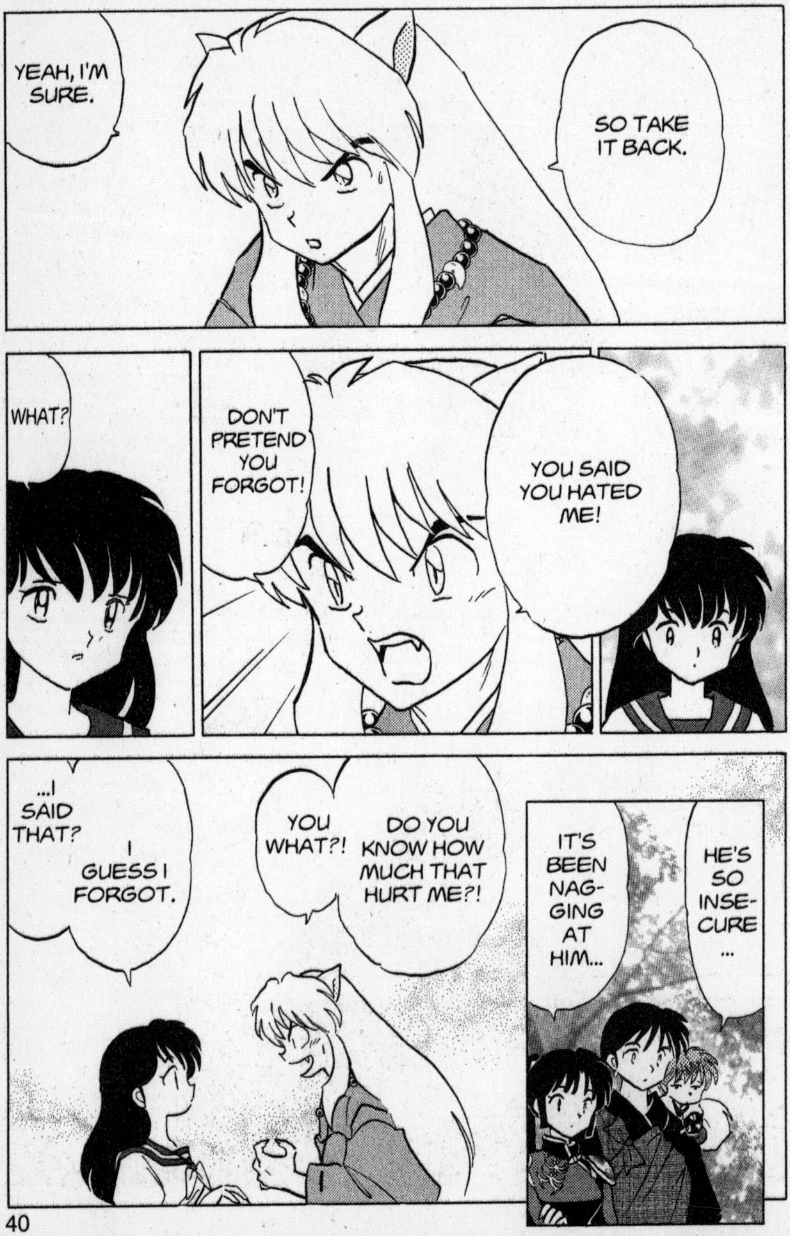
YEAH, I'M SURE.
SO TAKE IT BACK.
WHAT?
DON'T PRETEND YOU FORGOT!
YOU SAID YOU HATED ME!
...I SAID THAT?
I GUESS I FORGOT.
YOU WHAT?!
DO YOU KNOW HOW MUCH THAT HURT ME?!
IT'S BEEN NAG-GING AT HIM...
HE'S SO INSE-CURE...

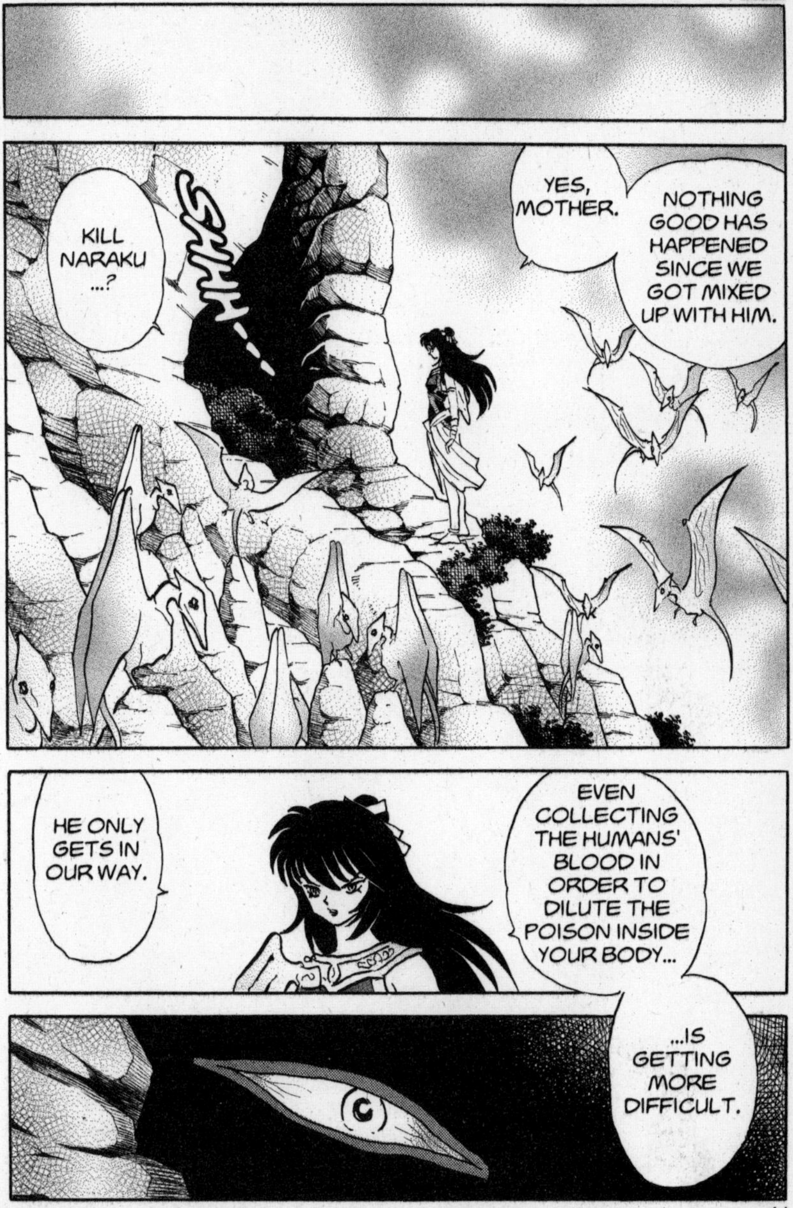
KILL NARAKU ...?
SHHH...
YES, MOTHER.
NOTHING GOOD HAS HAPPENED SINCE WE GOT MIXED UP WITH HIM.
HE ONLY GETS IN OUR WAY.
EVEN COLLECTING THE HUMANS' BLOOD IN ORDER TO DILUTE THE POISON INSIDE YOUR BODY...
...IS GETTING MORE DIFFICULT.

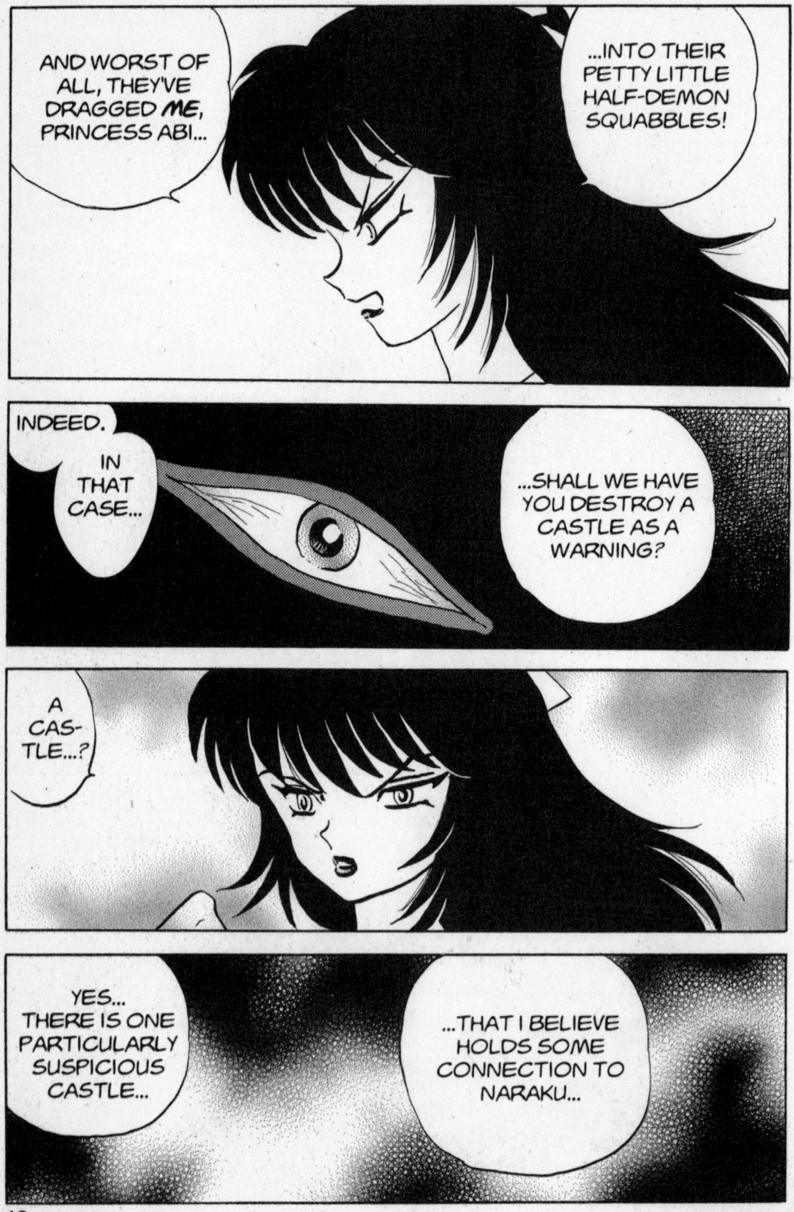

AND WORST OF ALL, THEY'VE DRAGGED *ME*, PRINCESS ABI...
...INTO THEIR PETTY LITTLE HALF-DEMON SQUABBLES!
INDEED.
IN THAT CASE...
...SHALL WE HAVE YOU DESTROY A CASTLE AS A WARNING?
A CAS-TLE...?
YES... THERE IS ONE PARTICULARLY SUSPICIOUS CASTLE...
...THAT I BELIEVE HOLDS SOME CONNECTION TO NARAKU...

SCROLL 3
THE CASTLE

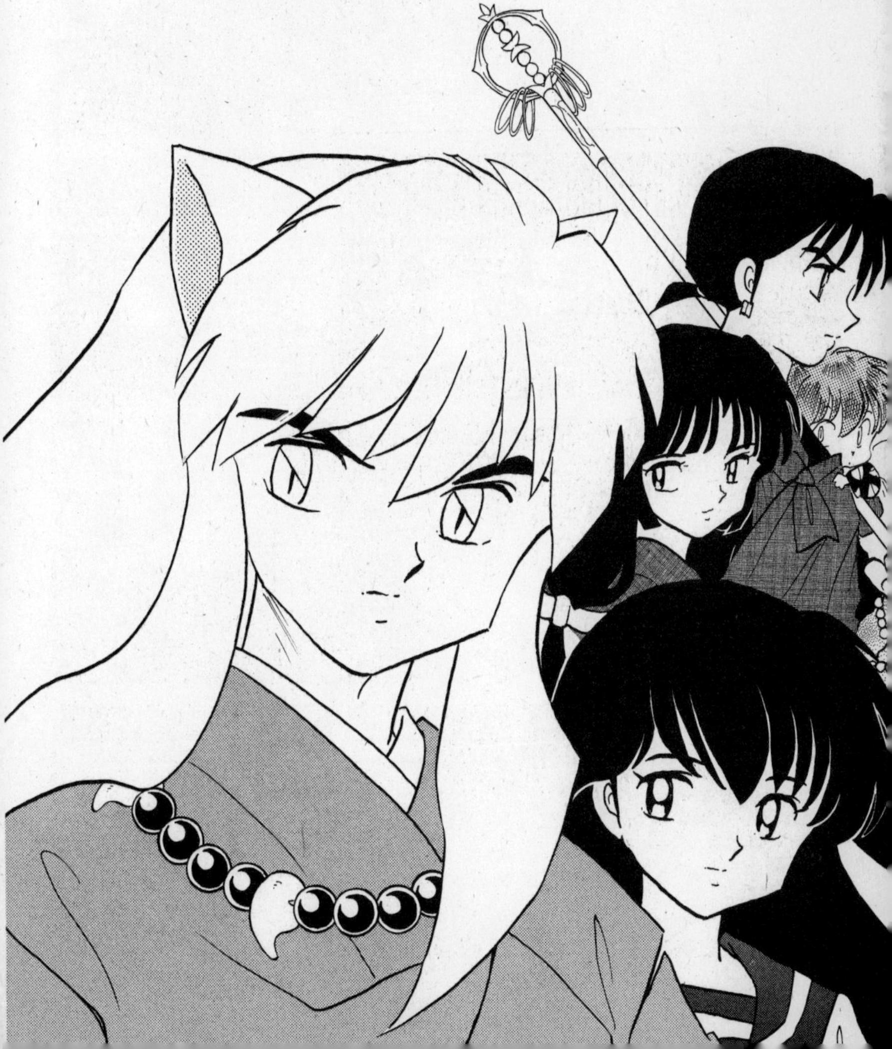

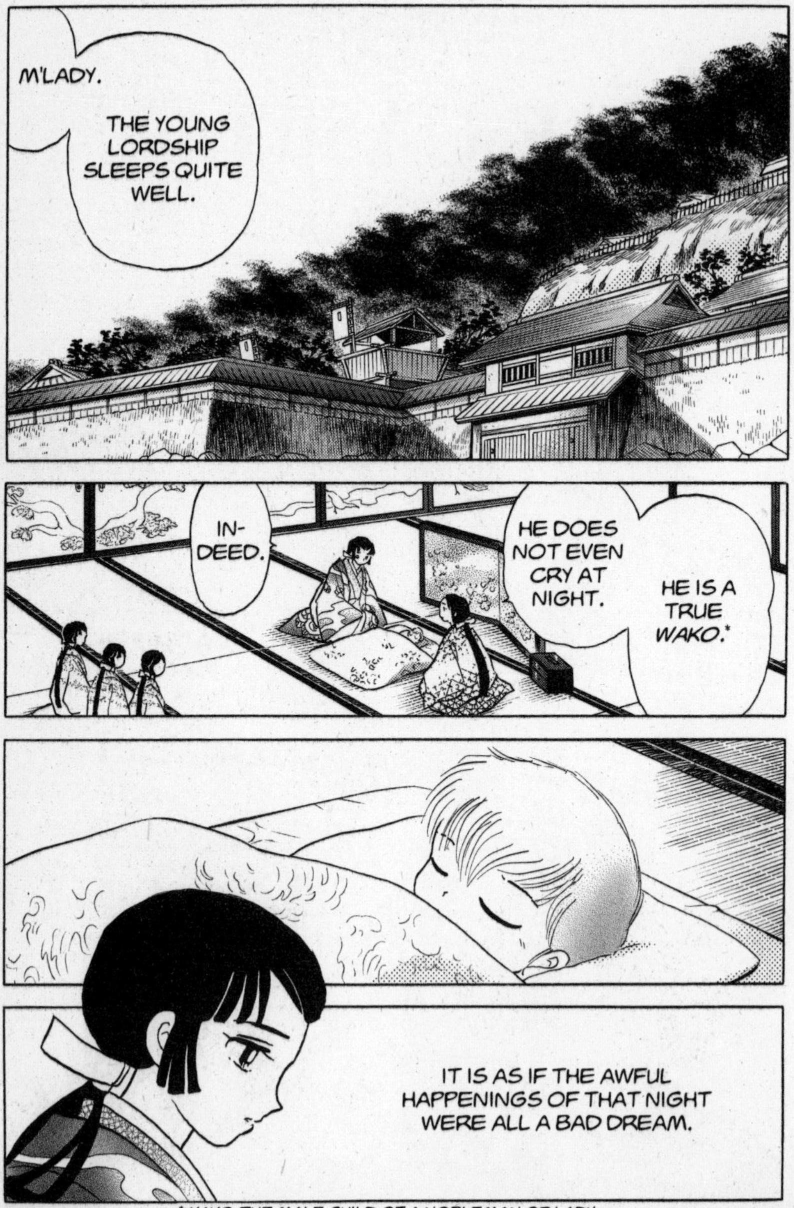
M'LADY.
THE YOUNG LORDSHIP SLEEPS QUITE WELL.
IN-DEED.
HE DOES NOT EVEN CRY AT NIGHT.
HE IS A TRUE WAKO.*
IT IS AS IF THE AWFUL HAPPENINGS OF THAT NIGHT WERE ALL A BAD DREAM.

*WAKO: THE MALE CHILD OF A NOBLEMAN OR LADY.

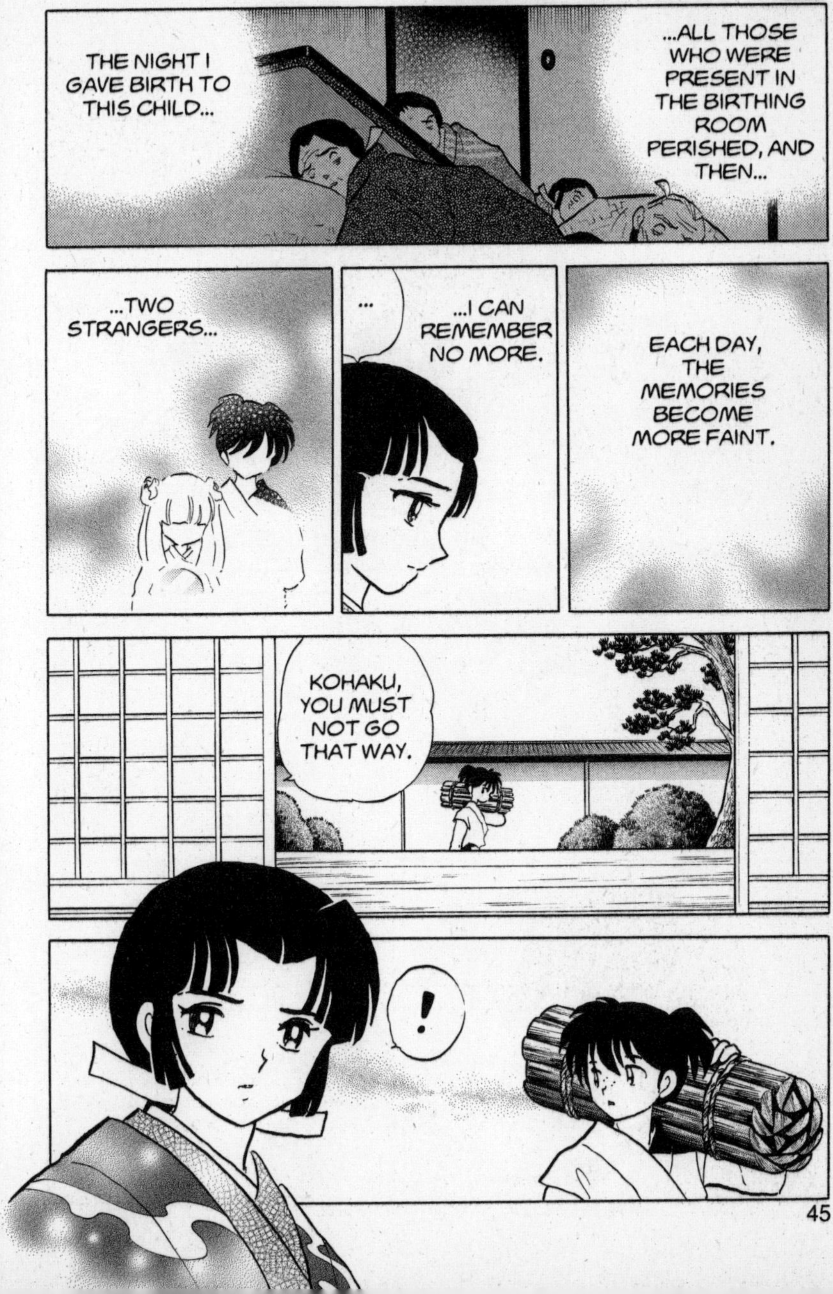
THE NIGHT I GAVE BIRTH TO THIS CHILD...
...ALL THOSE WHO WERE PRESENT IN THE BIRTHING ROOM PERISHED, AND THEN...
...TWO STRANGERS...
...
...I CAN REMEMBER NO MORE.
EACH DAY, THE MEMORIES BECOME MORE FAINT.
KOHAKU, YOU MUST NOT GO THAT WAY.
!

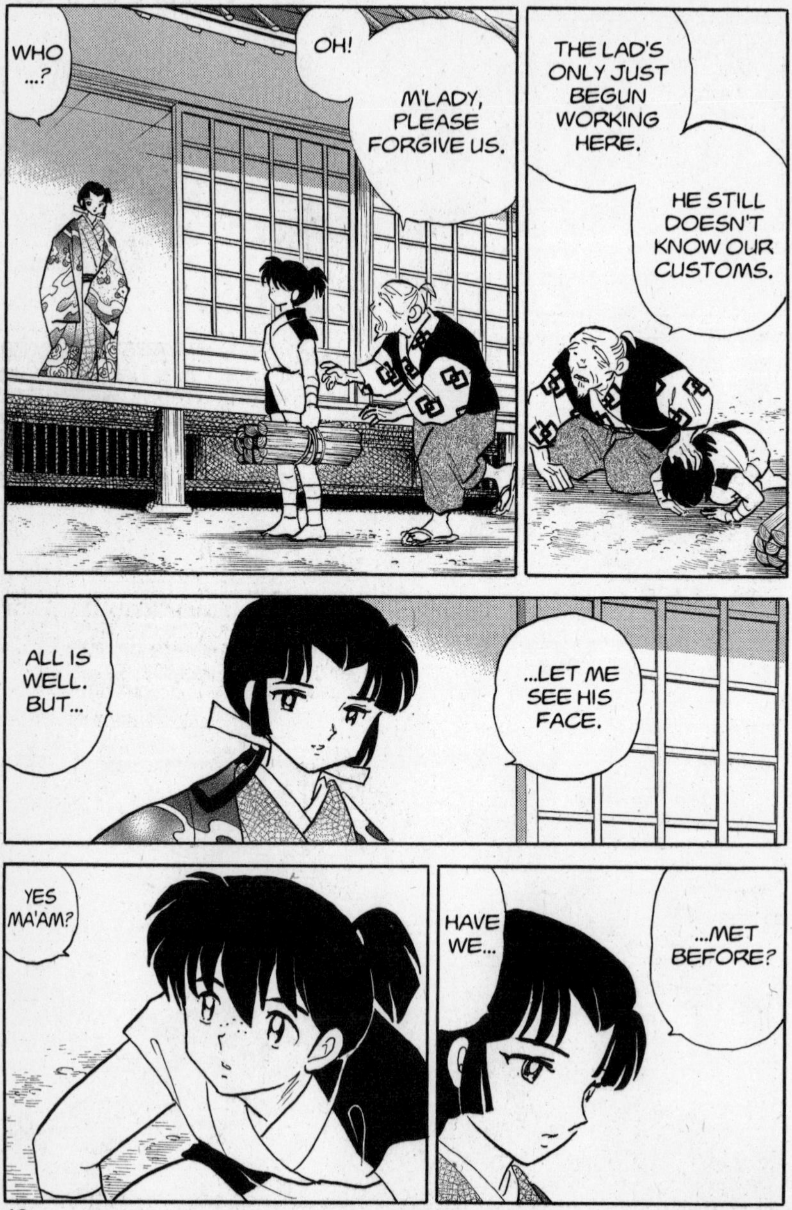
WHO ...?
OH!
M'LADY, PLEASE FORGIVE US.
THE LAD'S ONLY JUST BEGUN WORKING HERE.
HE STILL DOESN'T KNOW OUR CUSTOMS.
ALL IS WELL. BUT...
...LET ME SEE HIS FACE.
YES MA'AM?
HAVE WE...
...MET BEFORE?

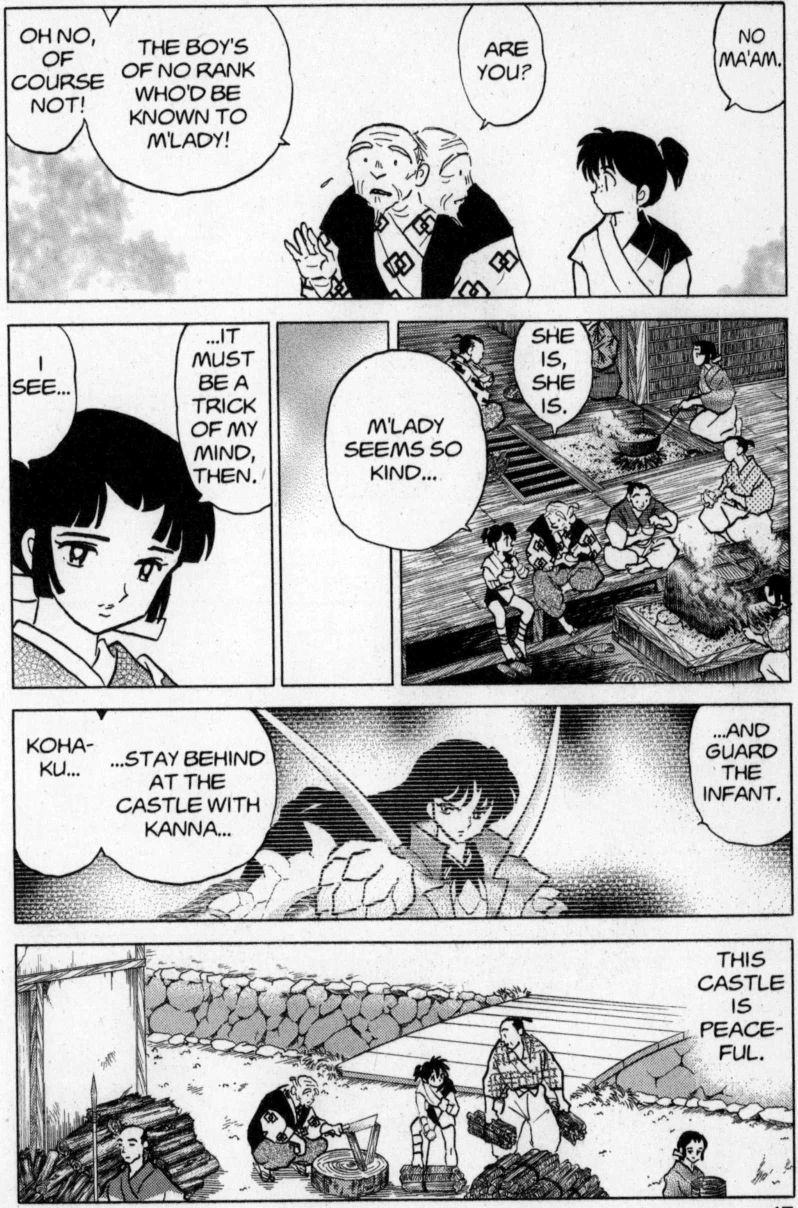
OH NO, OF COURSE NOT!
THE BOY'S OF NO RANK WHO'D BE KNOWN TO M'LADY!
ARE YOU?
NO MA'AM.
I SEE...
...IT MUST BE A TRICK OF MY MIND, THEN.
M'LADY SEEMS SO KIND...
SHE IS, SHE IS.
KOHA-KU...
...STAY BEHIND AT THE CASTLE WITH KANNA...
...AND GUARD THE INFANT.
THIS CASTLE IS PEACE-FUL.

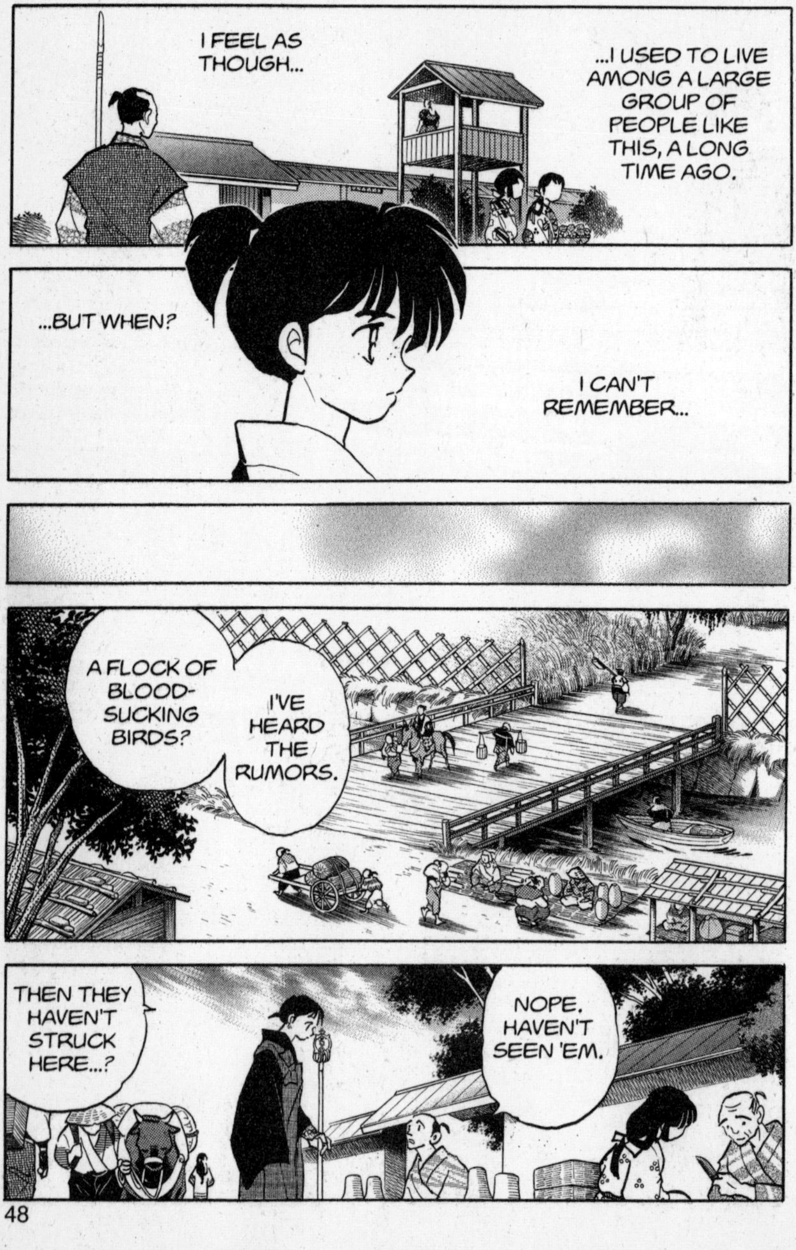
I FEEL AS THOUGH...
...I USED TO LIVE AMONG A LARGE GROUP OF PEOPLE LIKE THIS, A LONG TIME AGO.
...BUT WHEN?
I CAN'T REMEMBER...
A FLOCK OF BLOOD-SUCKING BIRDS?
I'VE HEARD THE RUMORS.
THEN THEY HAVEN'T STRUCK HERE...?
NOPE. HAVEN'T SEEN 'EM.

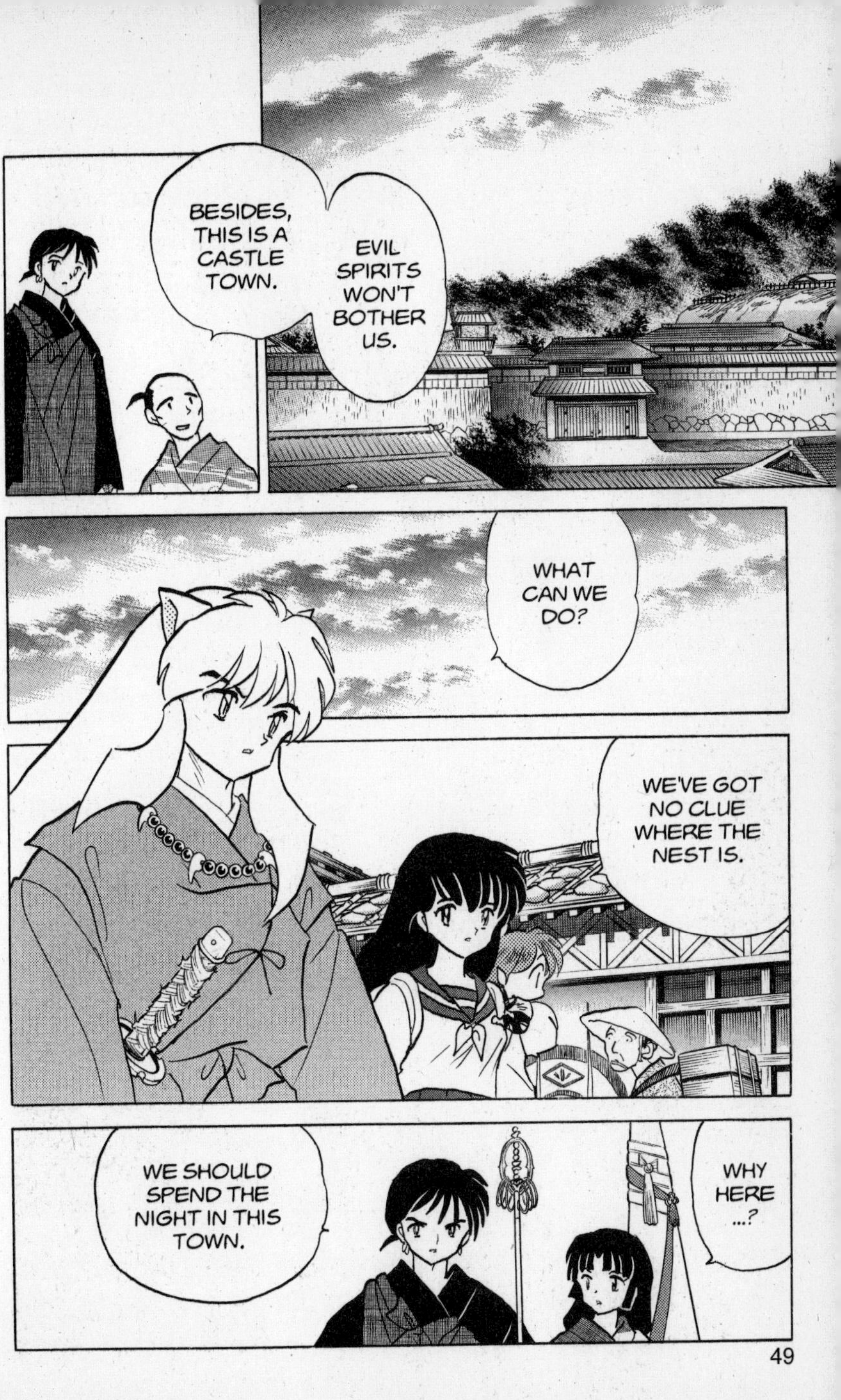
BESIDES, THIS IS A CASTLE TOWN.
EVIL SPIRITS WON'T BOTHER US.
WHAT CAN WE DO?
WE'VE GOT NO CLUE WHERE THE NEST IS.
WE SHOULD SPEND THE NIGHT IN THIS TOWN.
WHY HERE ...?

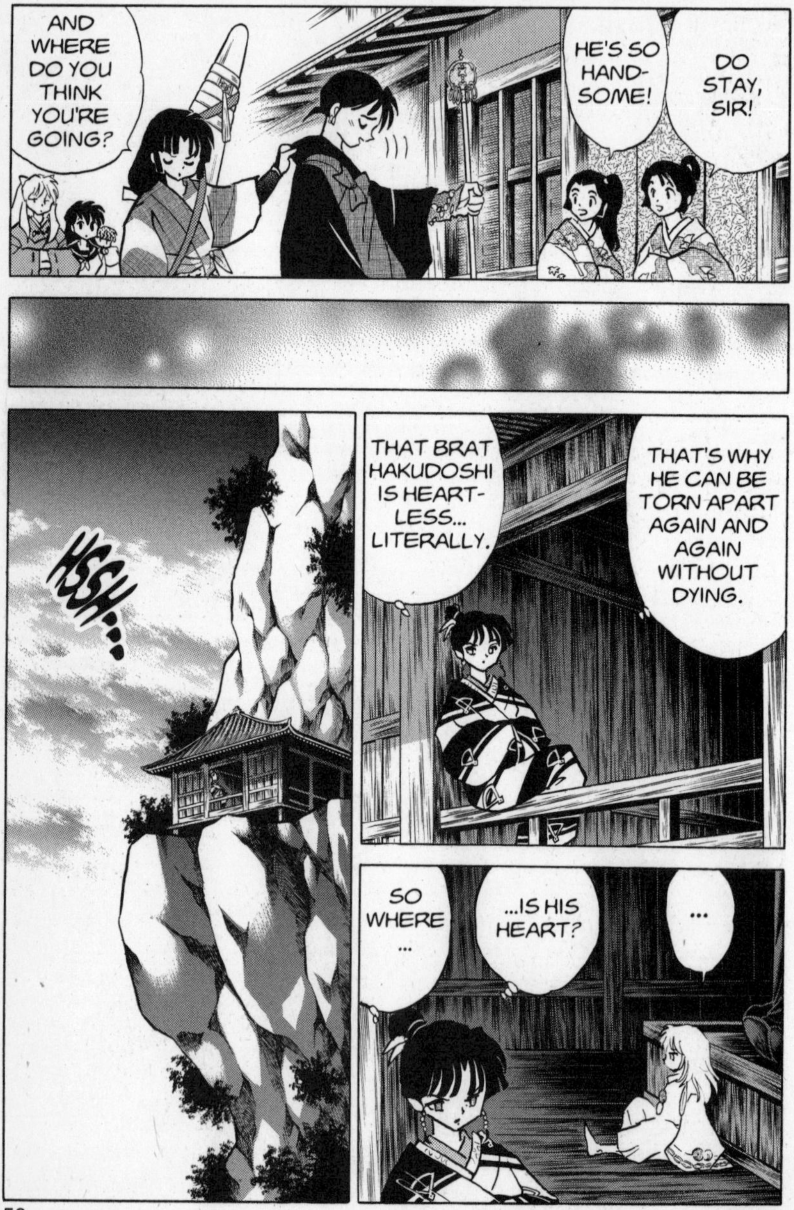
AND WHERE DO YOU THINK YOU'RE GOING?
HE'S SO HAND-SOME!
DO STAY, SIR!
HSSH...
THAT BRAT HAKUDOSHI IS HEART-LESS... LITERALLY.
THAT'S WHY HE CAN BE TORN APART AGAIN AND AGAIN WITHOUT DYING.
SO WHERE ...
...IS HIS HEART?
...

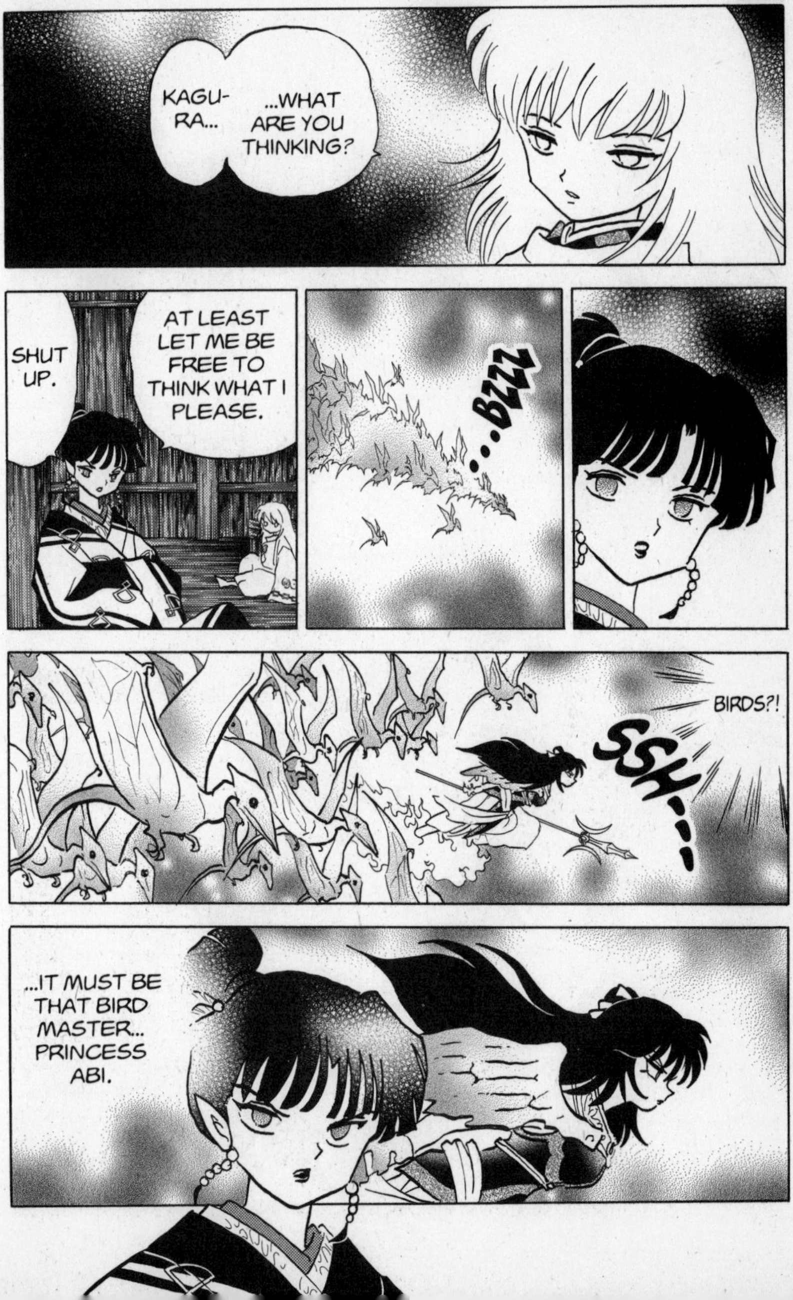
KAGU-RA...
...WHAT ARE YOU THINKING?
SHUT UP.
AT LEAST LET ME BE FREE TO THINK WHAT I PLEASE.
...BZZZ
BIRDS?!
SSH...
...IT MUST BE THAT BIRD MASTER... PRINCESS ABI.

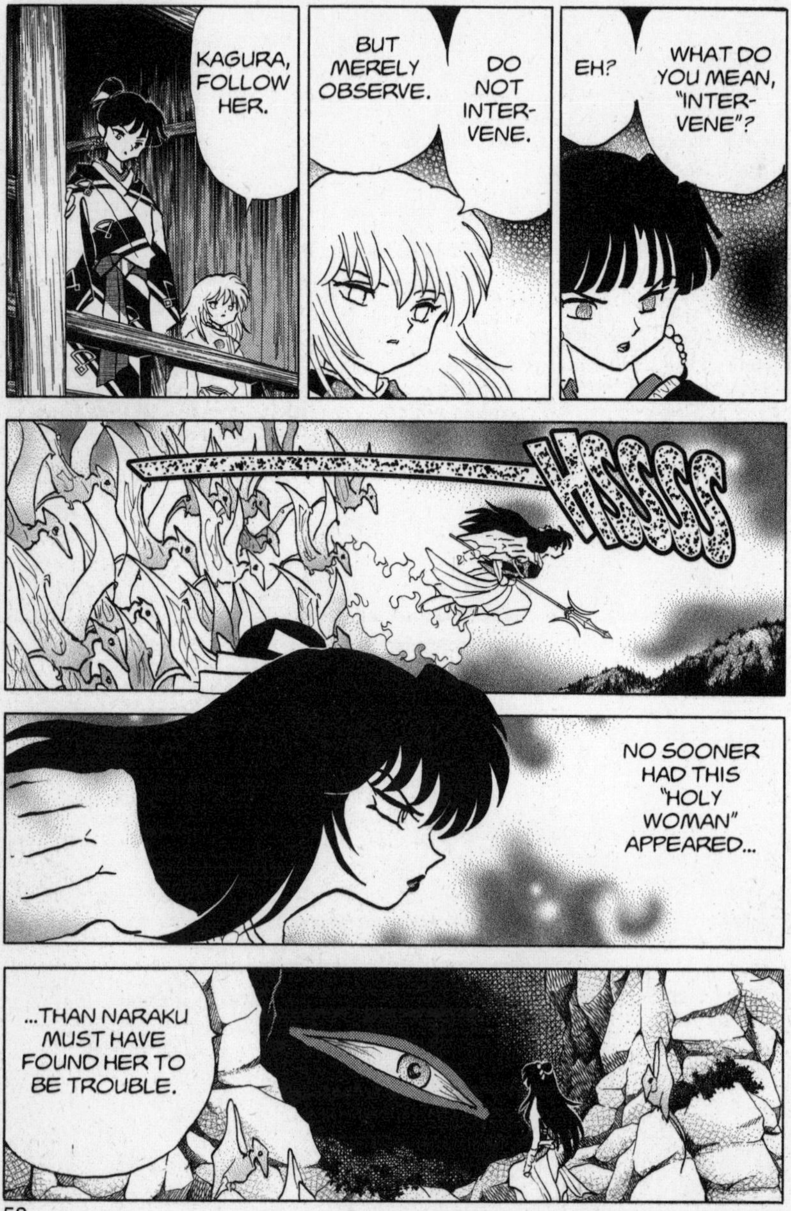
KAGURA, FOLLOW HER.
DO NOT INTER-VENE.
BUT MERELY OBSERVE.
EH?
WHAT DO YOU MEAN, "INTER-VENE"?
HSSSSS
NO SOONER HAD THIS "HOLY WOMAN" APPEARED...
...THAN NARAKU MUST HAVE FOUND HER TO BE TROUBLE.

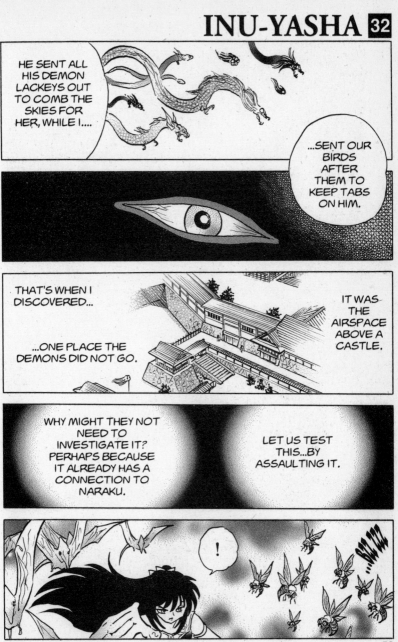

HE SENT ALL HIS DEMON LACKEYS OUT TO COMB THE SKIES FOR HER, WHILE I....

...SENT OUR BIRDS AFTER THEM TO KEEP TABS ON HIM.

THAT'S WHEN I DISCOVERED...

...ONE PLACE THE DEMONS DID NOT GO.

IT WAS THE AIRSPACE ABOVE A CASTLE.

WHY MIGHT THEY NOT NEED TO INVESTIGATE IT? PERHAPS BECAUSE IT ALREADY HAS A CONNECTION TO NARAKU.

LET US TEST THIS...BY ASSAULTING IT.

!

...BZZ ZZZ

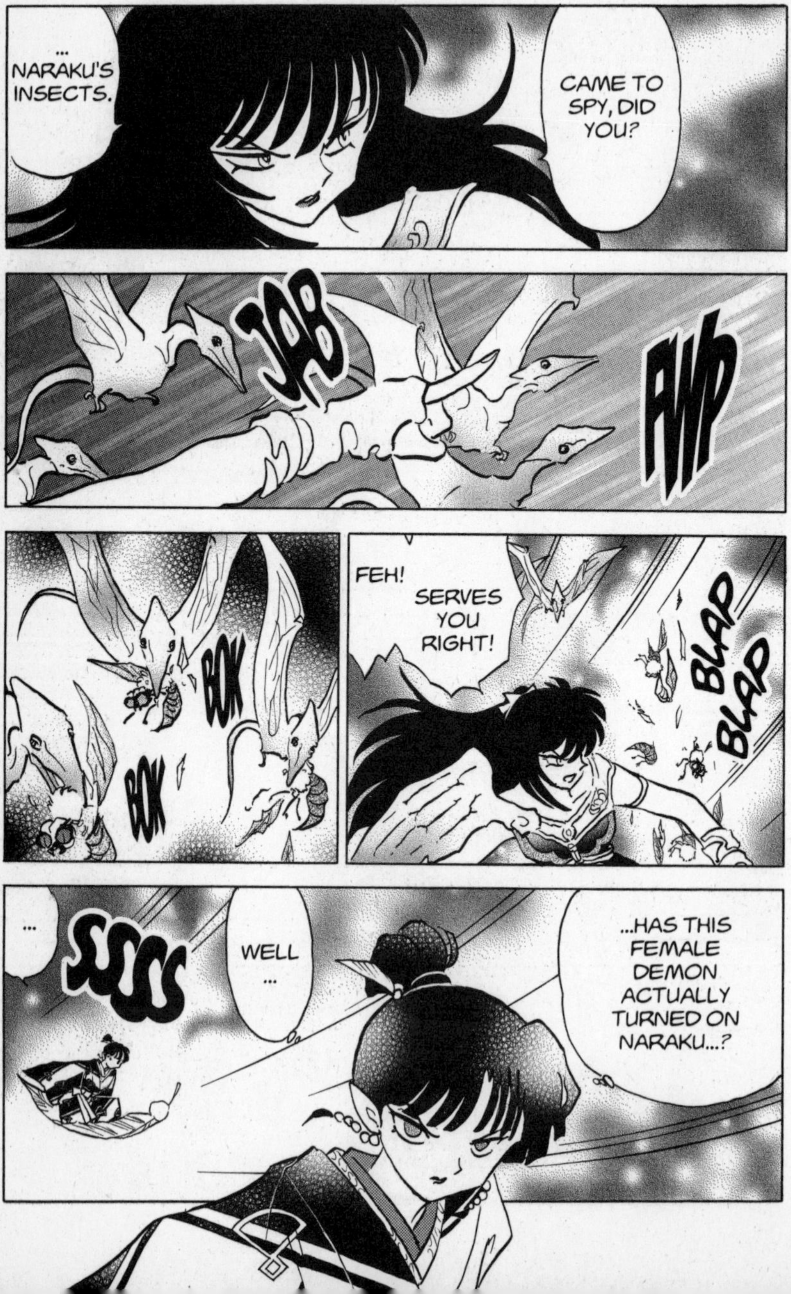

... NARAKU'S INSECTS.
CAME TO SPY, DID YOU?
JAB
FWP
BOK
BOK
FEH!
SERVES YOU RIGHT!
BLAP BLAP
...
SSSSS
WELL ...
...HAS THIS FEMALE DEMON ACTUALLY TURNED ON NARAKU...?

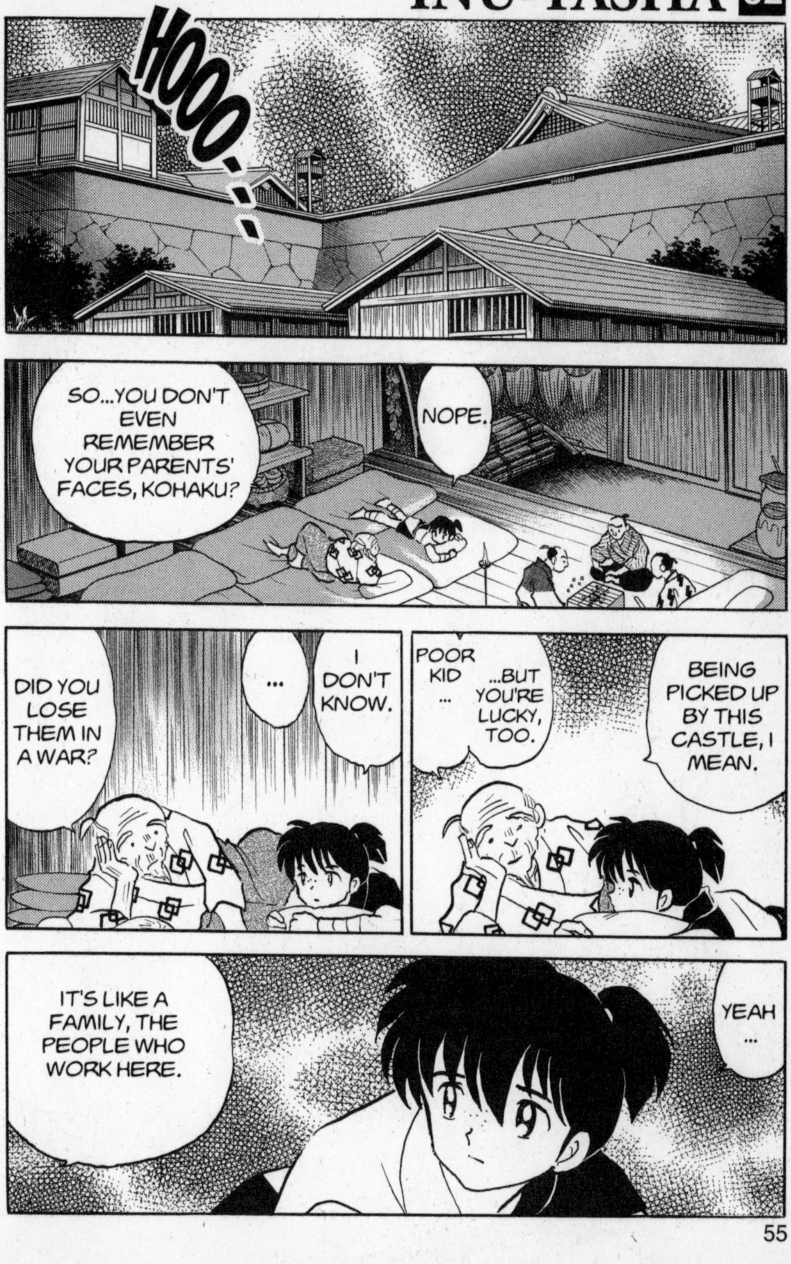
HOOO...
SO...YOU DON'T EVEN REMEMBER YOUR PARENTS' FACES, KOHAKU?
NOPE.
DID YOU LOSE THEM IN A WAR?
...
I DON'T KNOW.
POOR KID ...
...BUT YOU'RE LUCKY, TOO.
BEING PICKED UP BY THIS CASTLE, I MEAN.
IT'S LIKE A FAMILY, THE PEOPLE WHO WORK HERE.
YEAH ...

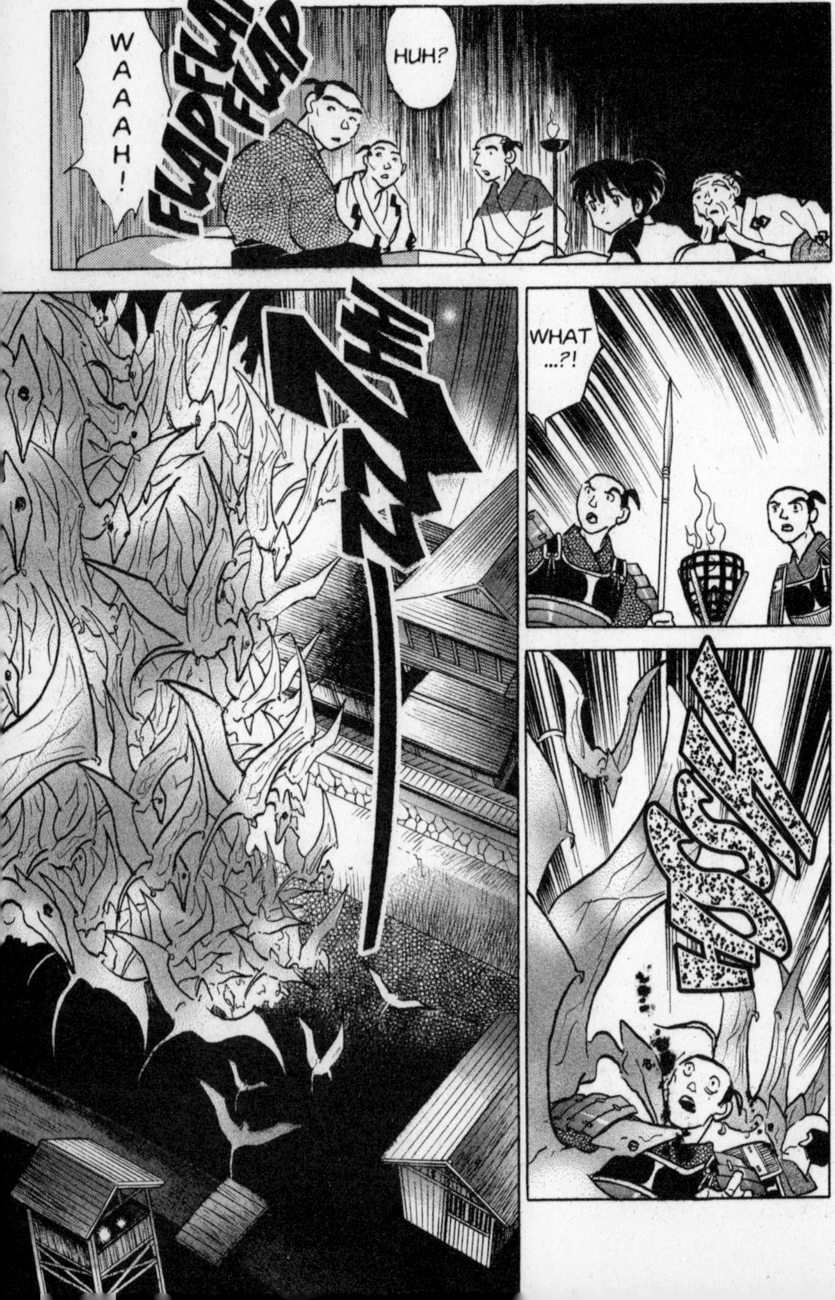
WAAAAH!
FLAPFLAP FLAP
HUH?
WHAT ...?!

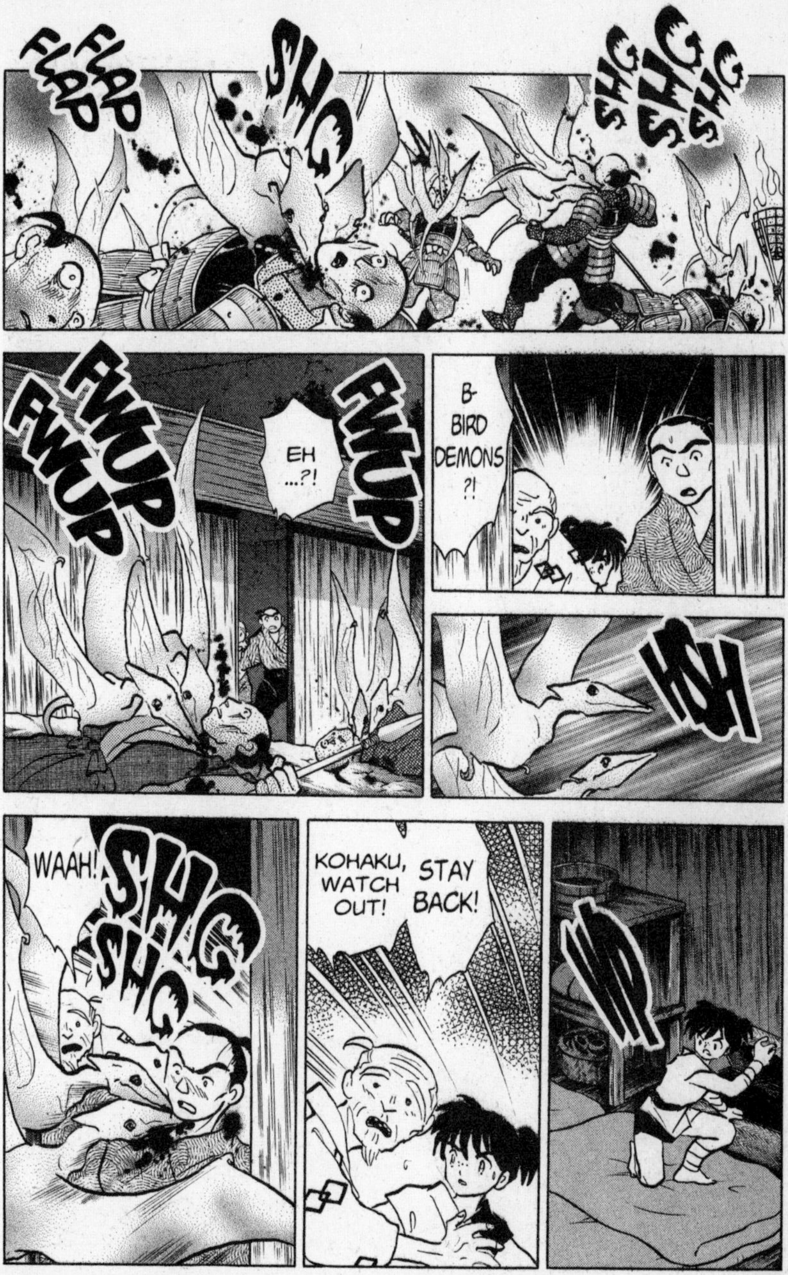
FLAP FLAP
SHG
SHG SHG SHG SHG
FWUP FWUP
FWUP
EH ...?!
B-BIRD DEMONS ?!
HSH
WAAH!
SHG SHG SHG
KOHAKU, WATCH OUT!
STAY BACK!
WHP

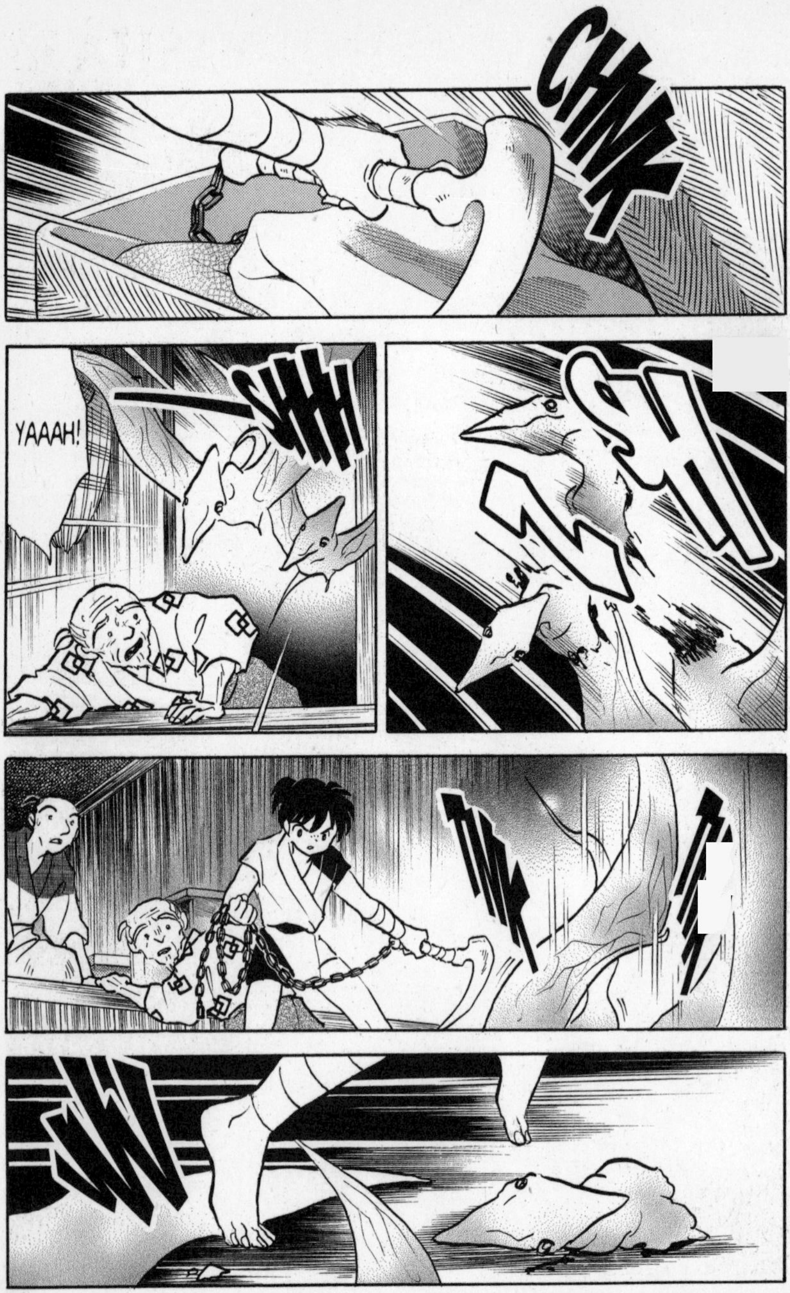
CHINK
YAAAH!
SHHH
TINK

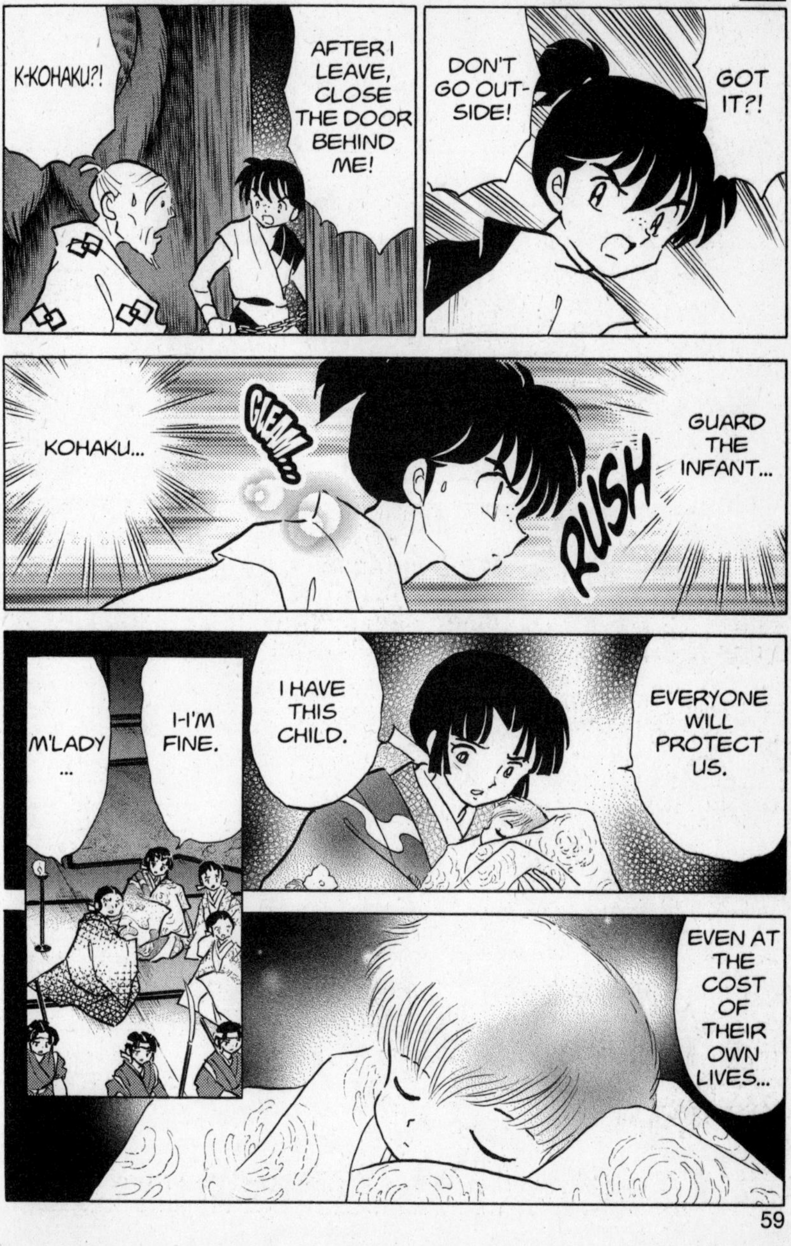
K-KOHAKU?!
AFTER I LEAVE, CLOSE THE DOOR BEHIND ME!
DON'T GO OUT-SIDE!
GOT IT?!
KOHAKU...
GLEAM...
RUSH
GUARD THE INFANT...
M'LADY ...
I-I'M FINE.
I HAVE THIS CHILD.
EVERYONE WILL PROTECT US.
EVEN AT THE COST OF THEIR OWN LIVES...

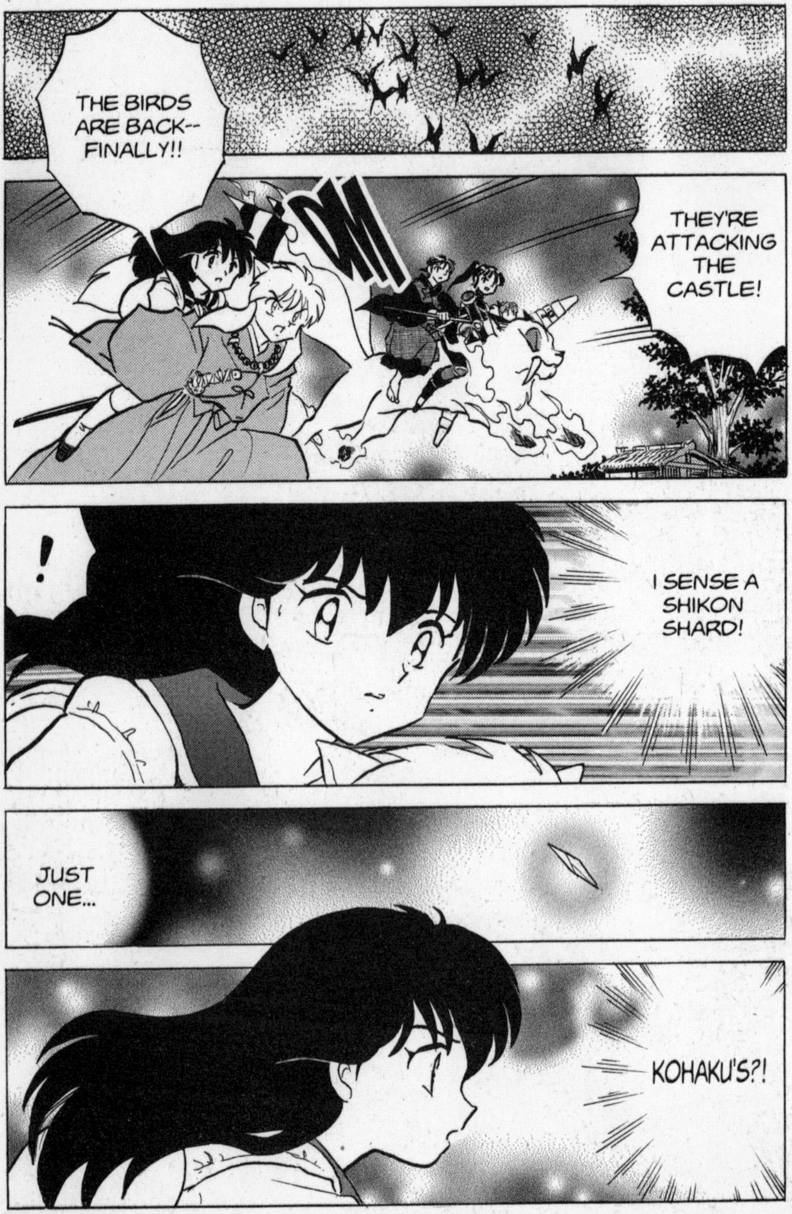
THE BIRDS ARE BACK-- FINALLY!!
THEY'RE ATTACKING THE CASTLE!
!
I SENSE A SHIKON SHARD!
JUST ONE...
KOHAKU'S?!

SCROLL 4
ORDERS

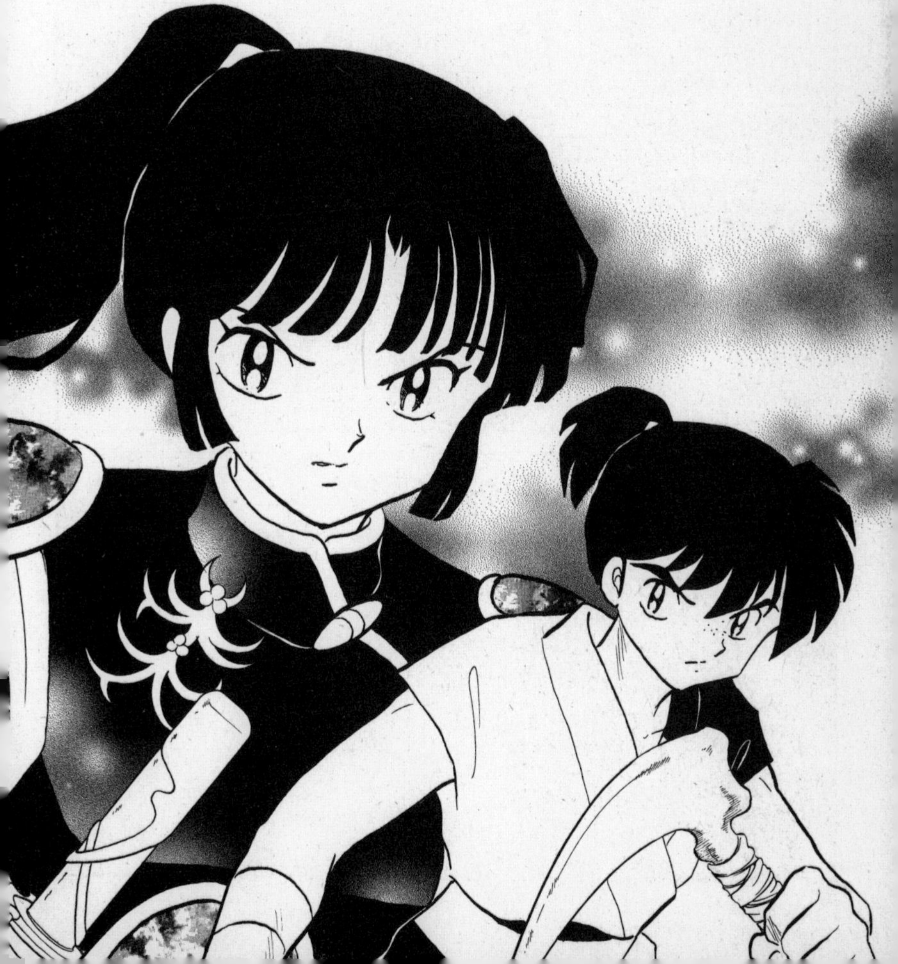

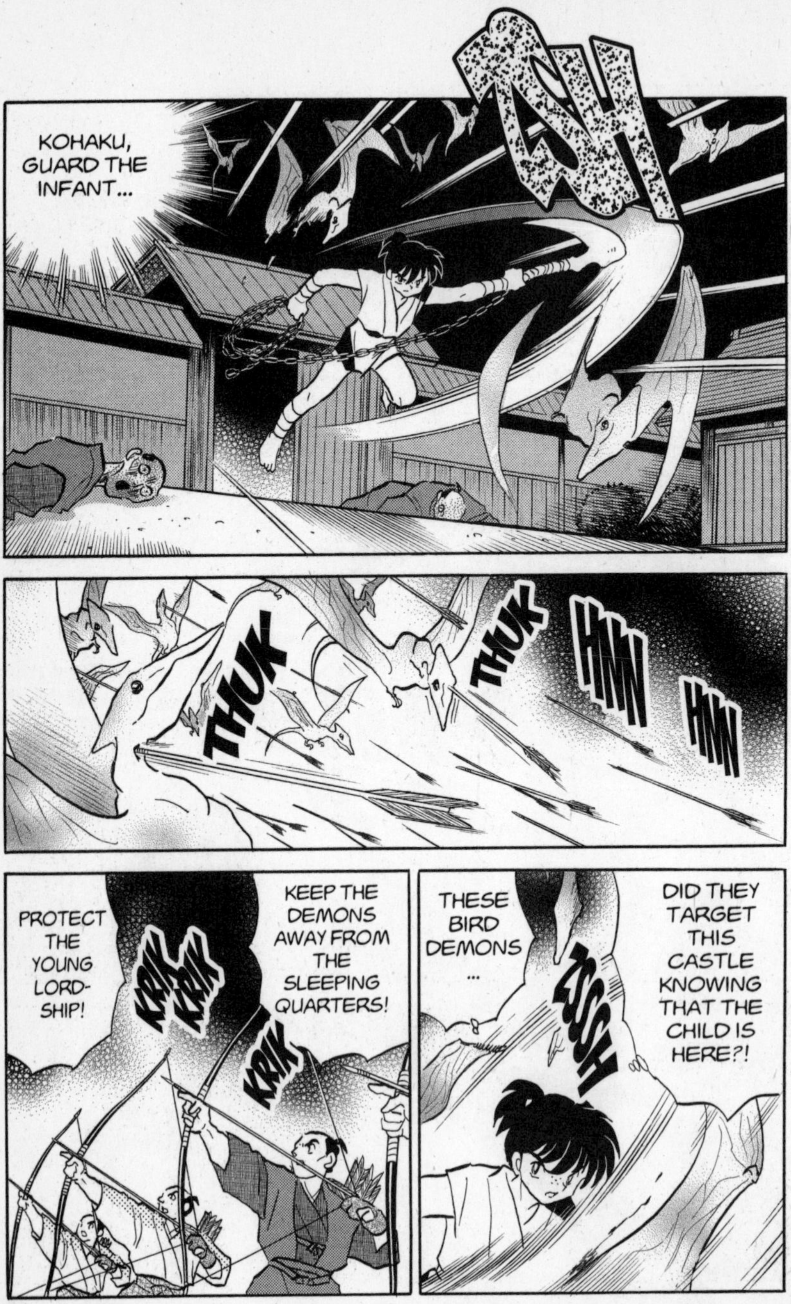
KOHAKU, GUARD THE INFANT...
ZSH
THUK
THUK
HMN
HMN
PROTECT THE YOUNG LORD-SHIP!
KRIK KRIK
KEEP THE DEMONS AWAY FROM THE SLEEPING QUARTERS!
KRIK
THESE BIRD DEMONS ...
ZSSH
DID THEY TARGET THIS CASTLE KNOWING THAT THE CHILD IS HERE?!

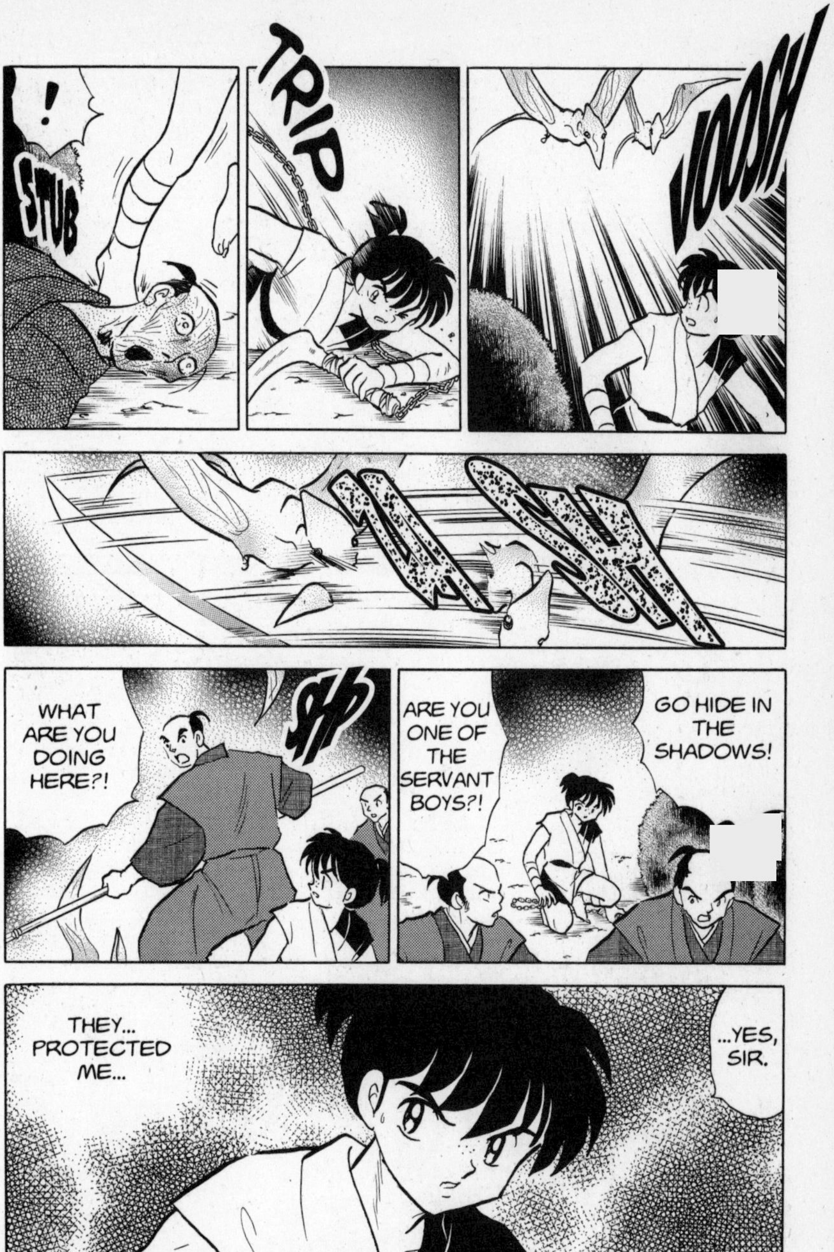
!
STUB
TRIP
VOOSH
WHAT ARE YOU DOING HERE?!
ARE YOU ONE OF THE SERVANT BOYS?!
GO HIDE IN THE SHADOWS!
THEY... PROTECTED ME...
...YES, SIR.

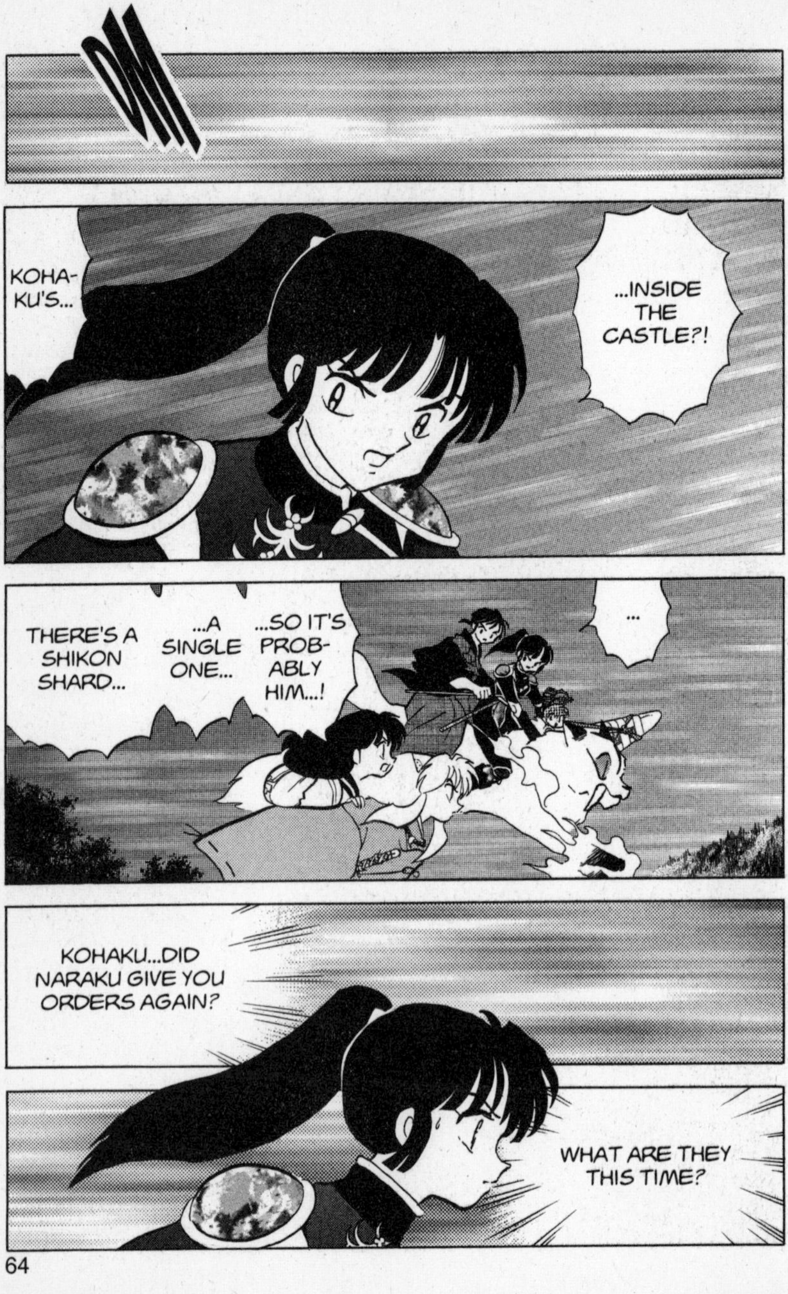

KOHA-KU'S...
...INSIDE THE CASTLE?!
THERE'S A SHIKON SHARD...
...A SINGLE ONE...
...SO IT'S PROBABLY HIM...!
...
KOHAKU...DID NARAKU GIVE YOU ORDERS AGAIN?
WHAT ARE THEY THIS TIME?

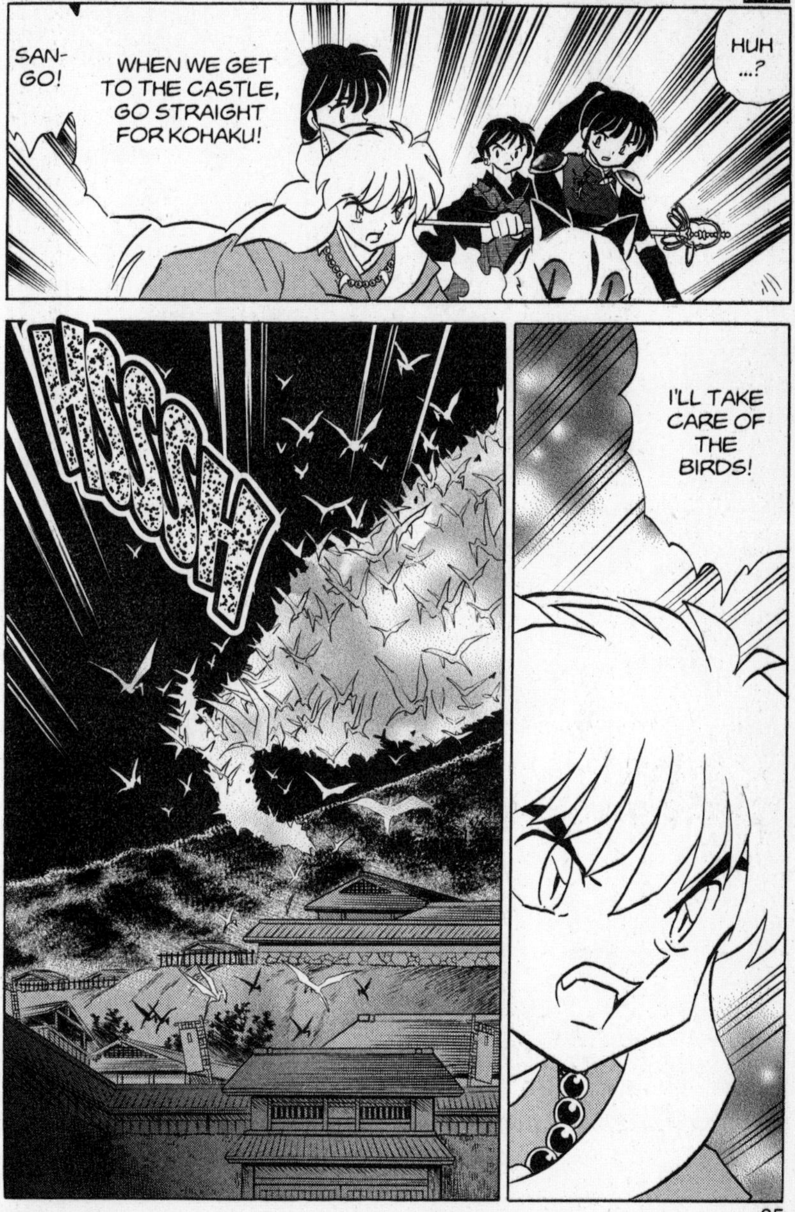
SAN-GO!
WHEN WE GET TO THE CASTLE, GO STRAIGHT FOR KOHAKU!
HUH ...?
HSSSH
I'LL TAKE CARE OF THE BIRDS!

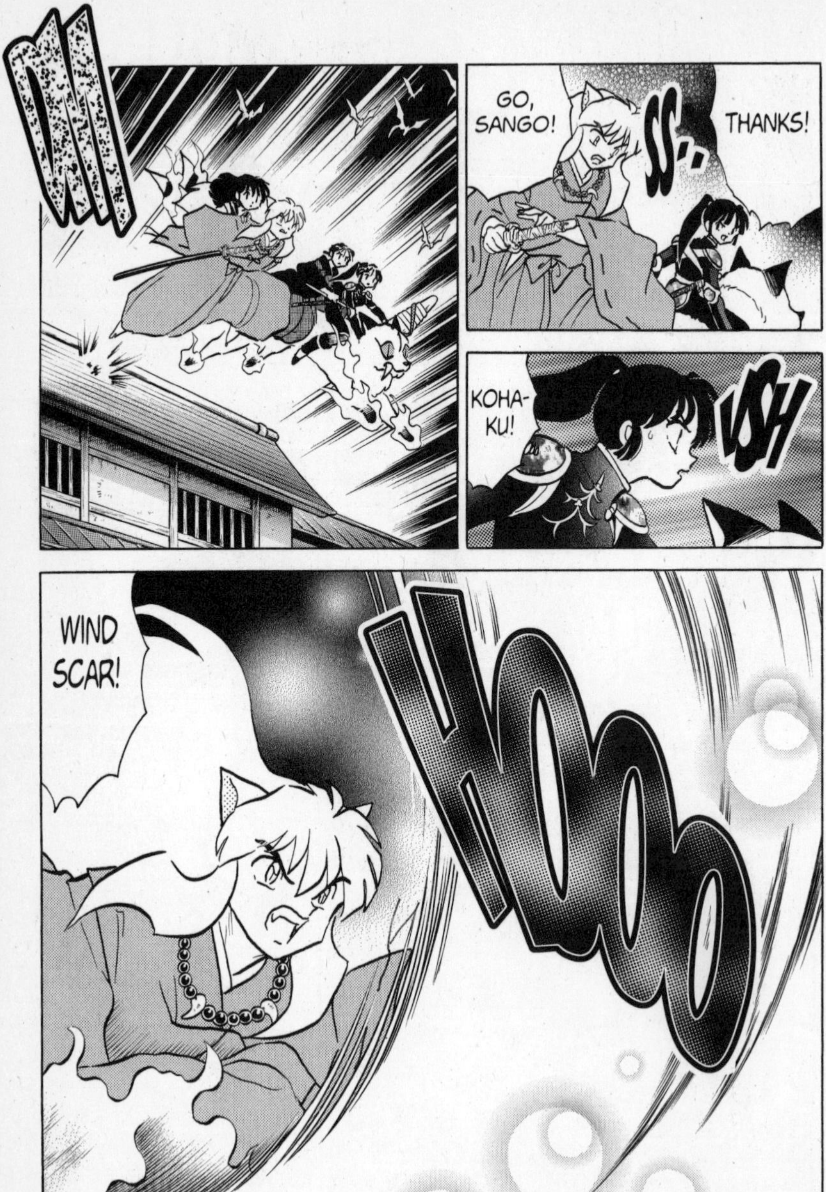

OM
GO, SANGO!
SS..
THANKS!
KOHA-KU!
VSH
WIND SCAR!
HOOOO

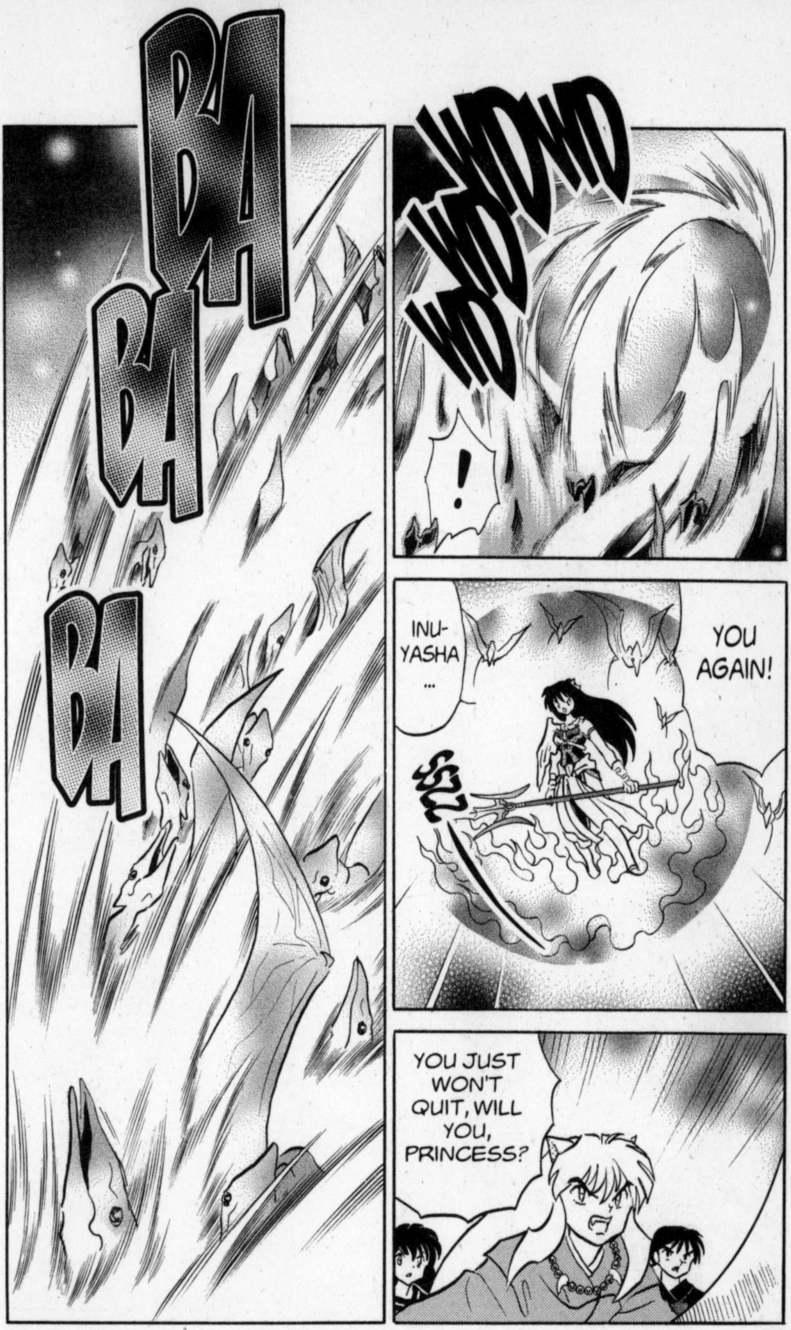
BA
BA
BA
!
INU-YASHA ...
YOU AGAIN!
YOU JUST WON'T QUIT, WILL YOU, PRINCESS?

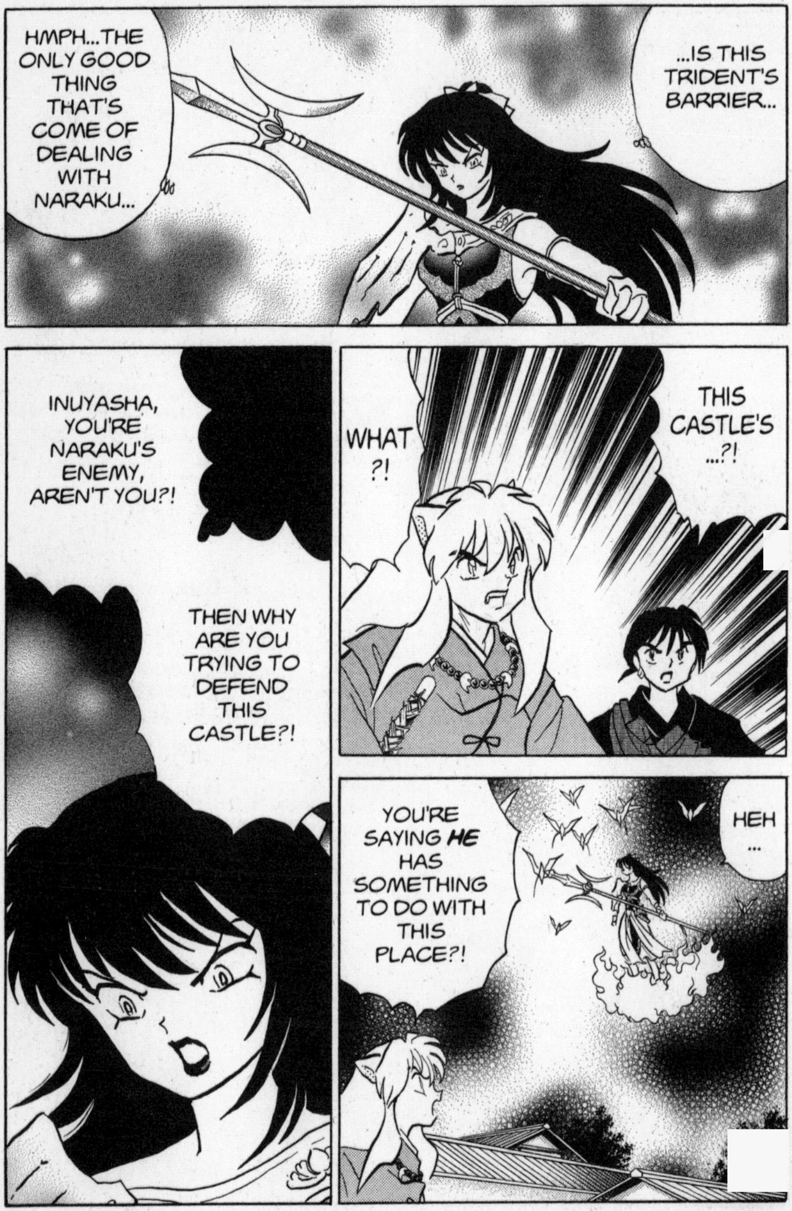
HMPH...THE ONLY GOOD THING THAT'S COME OF DEALING WITH NARAKU...
...IS THIS TRIDENT'S BARRIER...
INUYASHA, YOU'RE NARAKU'S ENEMY, AREN'T YOU?!
THEN WHY ARE YOU TRYING TO DEFEND THIS CASTLE?!
WHAT?!
THIS CASTLE'S ...?!
YOU'RE SAYING HE HAS SOMETHING TO DO WITH THIS PLACE?!
HEH ...

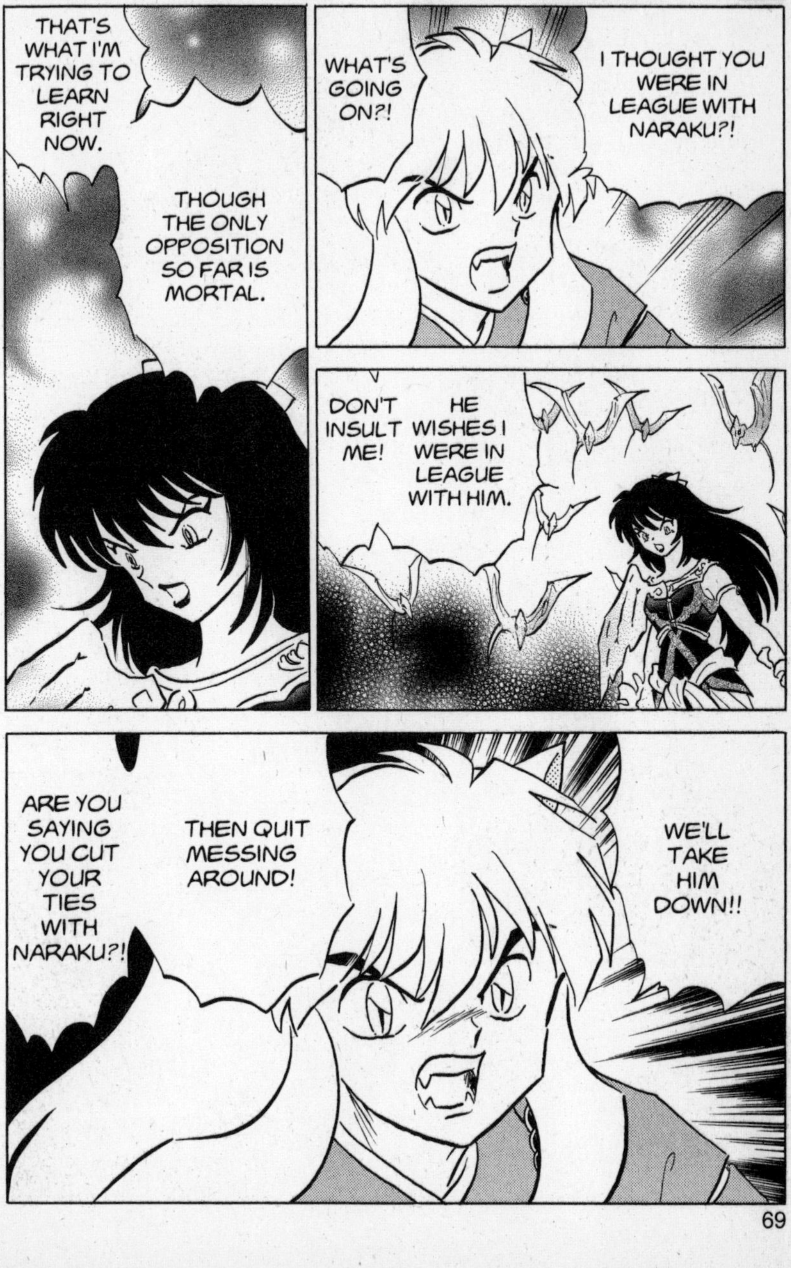
THAT'S WHAT I'M TRYING TO LEARN RIGHT NOW.
THOUGH THE ONLY OPPOSITION SO FAR IS MORTAL.
WHAT'S GOING ON?!
I THOUGHT YOU WERE IN LEAGUE WITH NARAKU?!
DON'T INSULT ME!
HE WISHES I WERE IN LEAGUE WITH HIM.
ARE YOU SAYING YOU CUT YOUR TIES WITH NARAKU?!
THEN QUIT MESSING AROUND!
WE'LL TAKE HIM DOWN!!

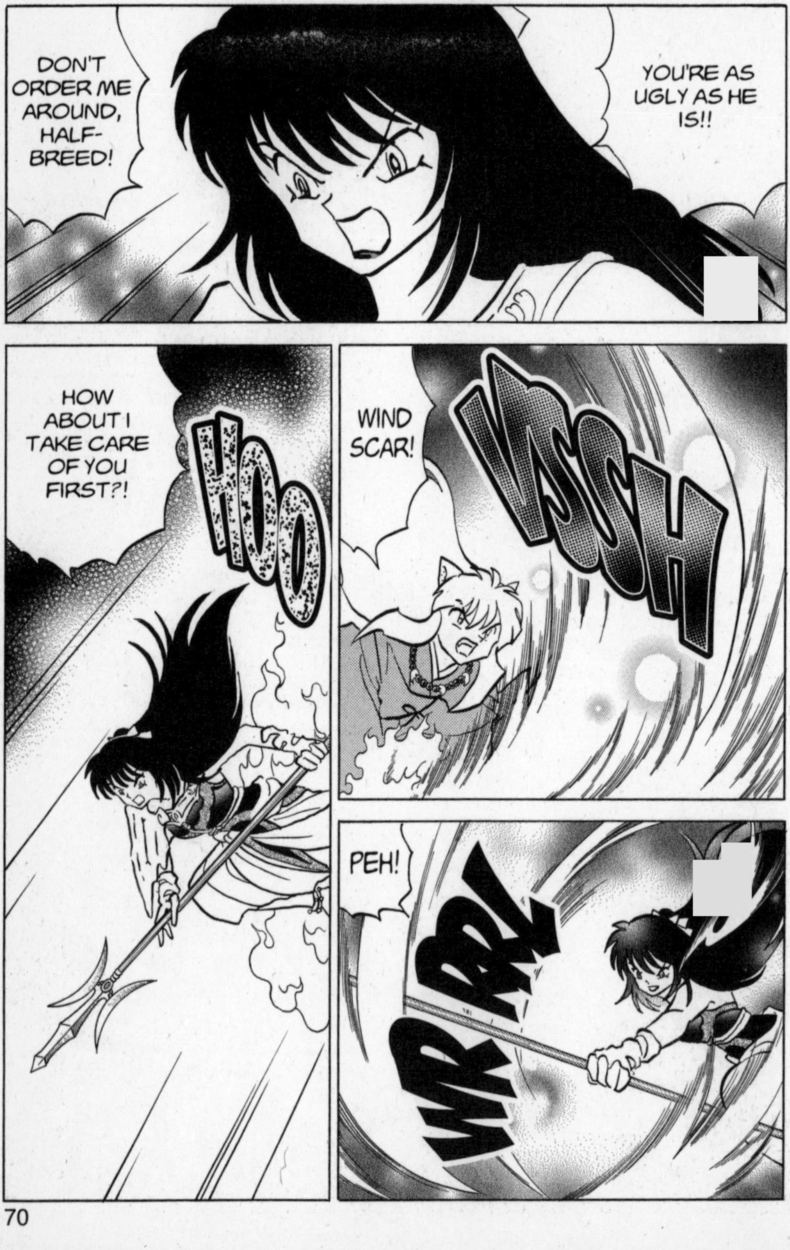
DON'T ORDER ME AROUND, HALF-BREED!
YOU'RE AS UGLY AS HE IS!!
HOW ABOUT I TAKE CARE OF YOU FIRST?!
HOO
WIND SCAR!
VSSCH
PEH!
WRRL

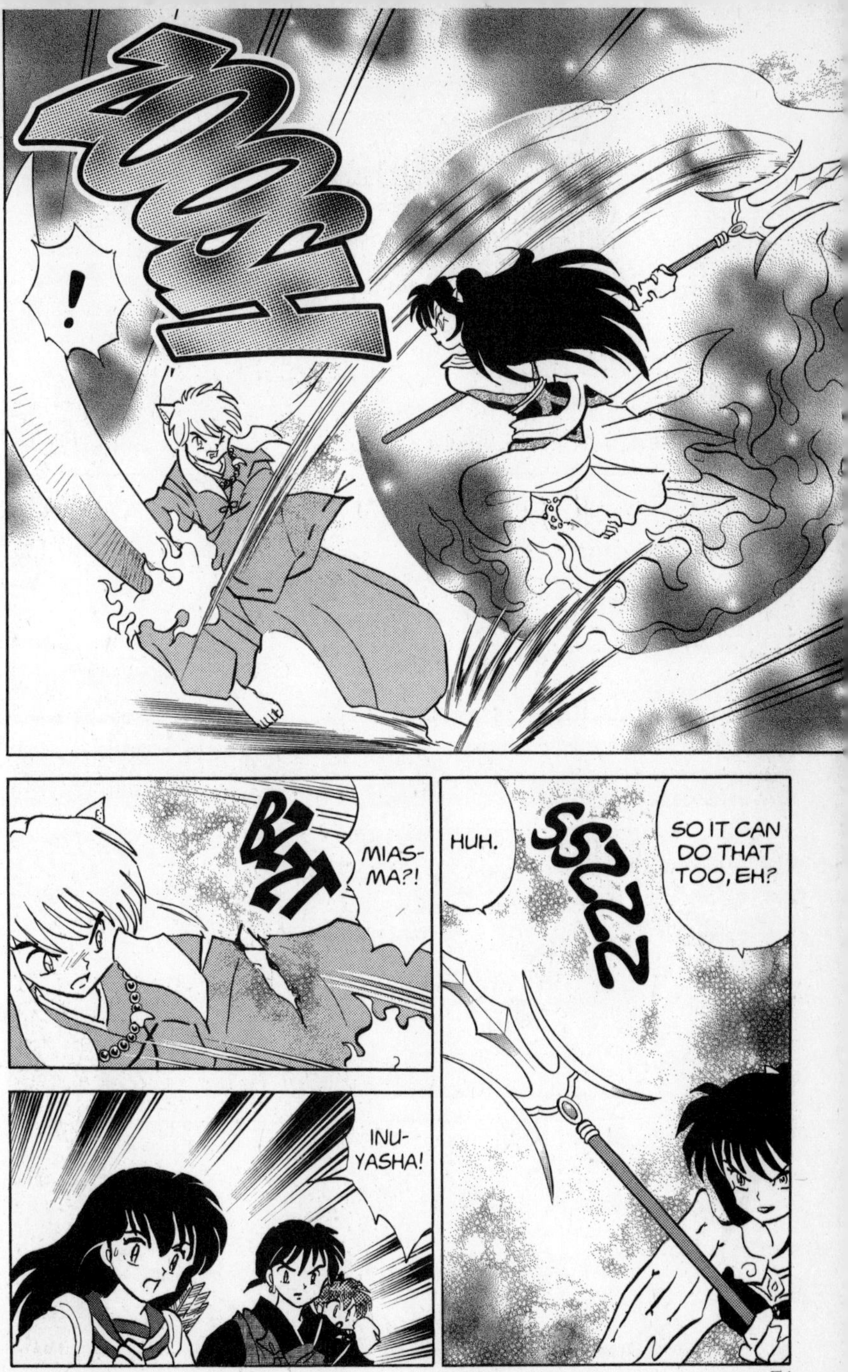
WOOSH
!
BZZT
MIAS-
MA?!
HUH.
SSZZZ
SO IT CAN
DO THAT
TOO, EH?
INU-
YASHA!

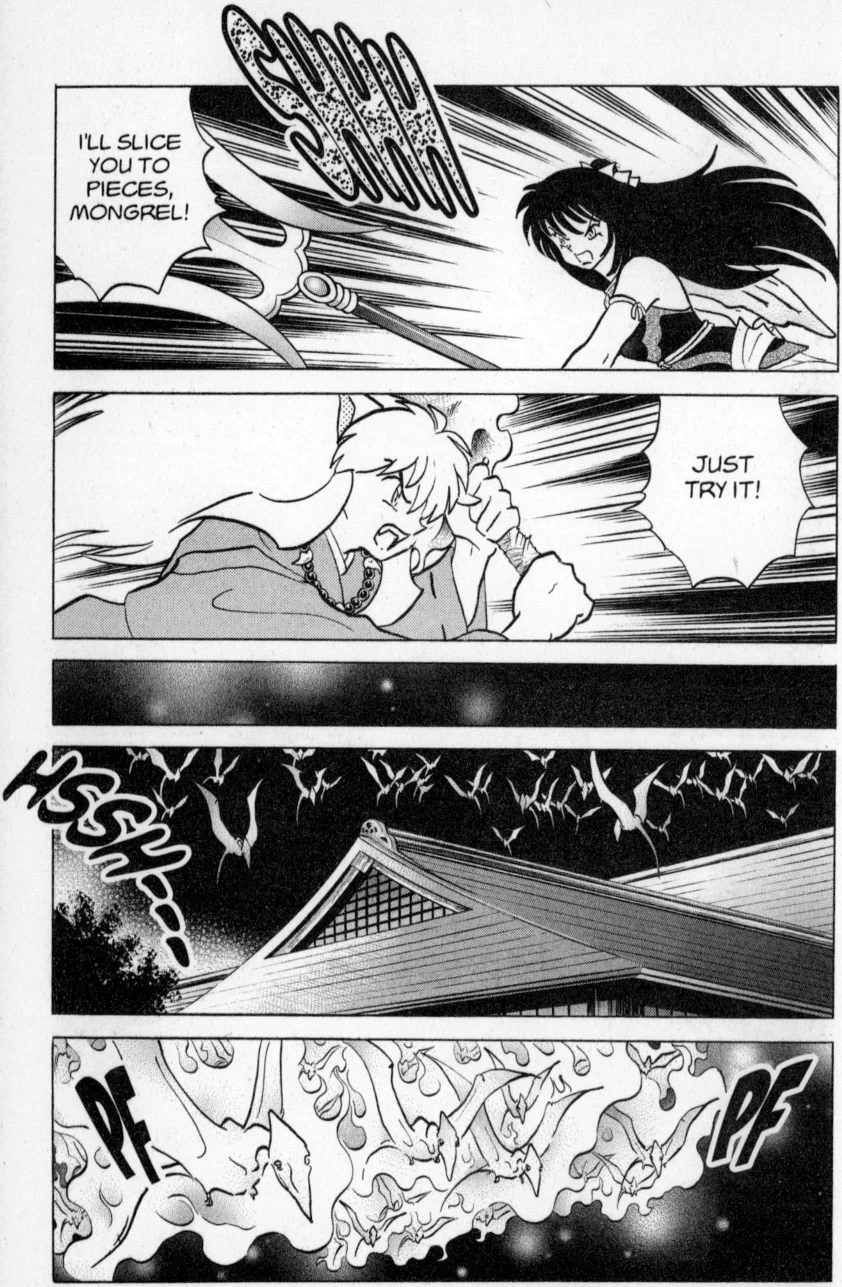
SHHH
I'LL SLICE YOU TO PIECES, MONGREL!
JUST TRY IT!
HSSSH...
PF
PF

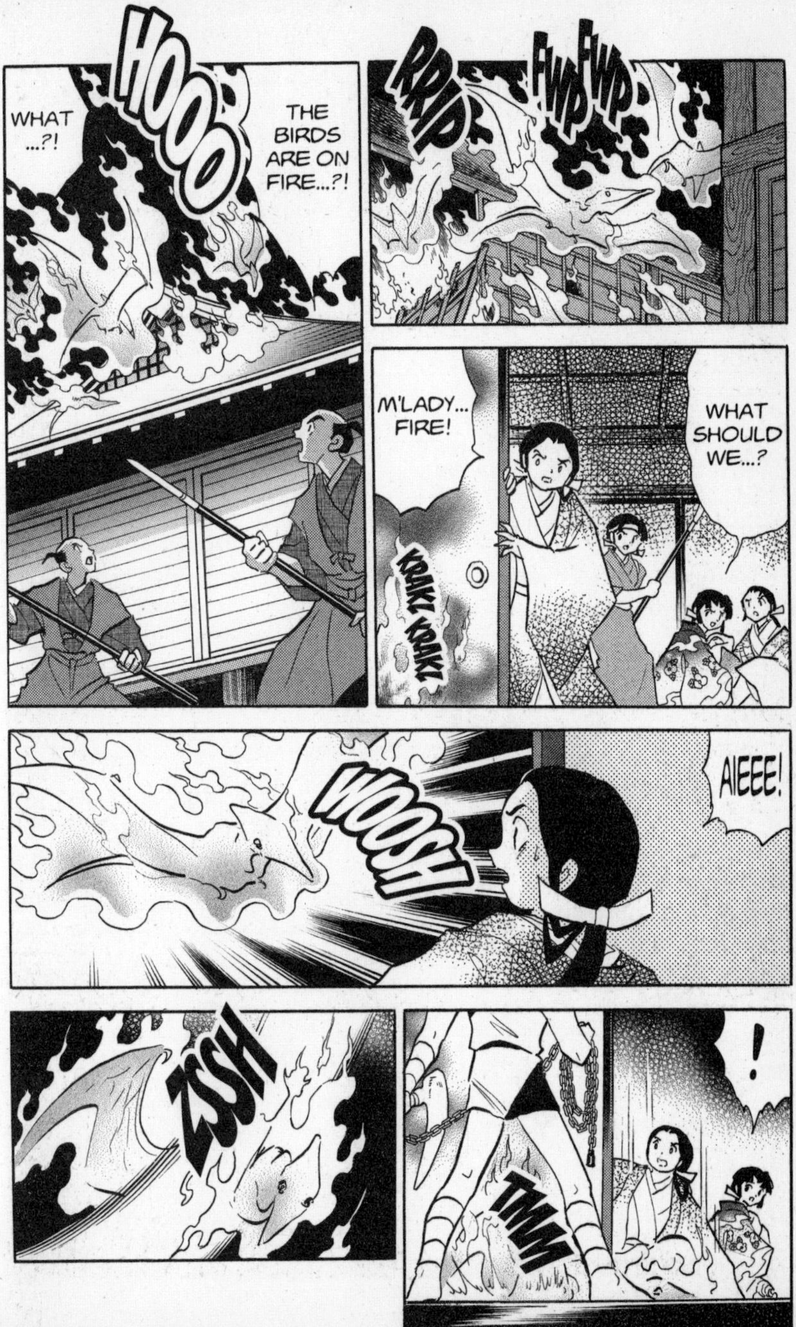
HOOO
WHAT ...?!
THE BIRDS ARE ON FIRE...?!
RRIP
FWP FWP
M'LADY... FIRE!
WHAT SHOULD WE...?
KRAKL KRAKL
WOOSH!
AIEEE!
ZSH
!
TMM

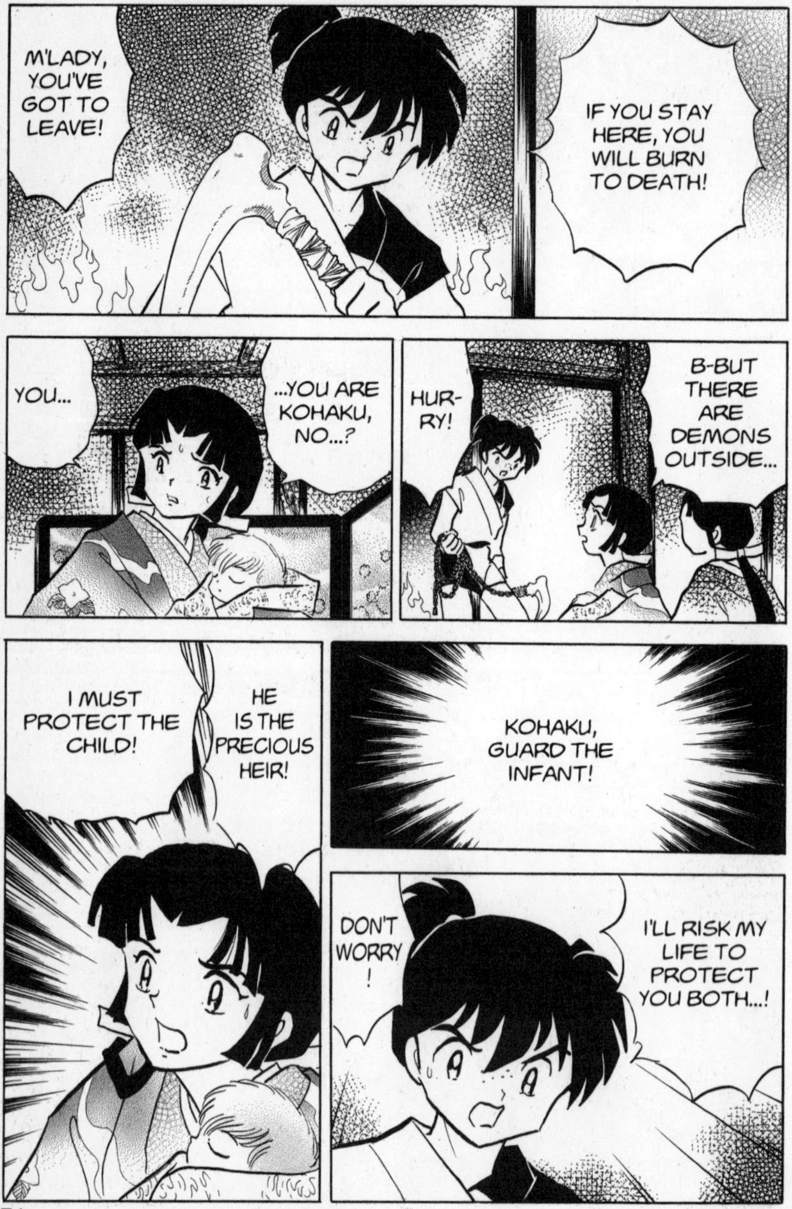
M'LADY, YOU'VE GOT TO LEAVE!
IF YOU STAY HERE, YOU WILL BURN TO DEATH!
YOU...
...YOU ARE KOHAKU, NO...?
HUR-RY!
B-BUT THERE ARE DEMONS OUTSIDE...
I MUST PROTECT THE CHILD!
HE IS THE PRECIOUS HEIR!
KOHAKU, GUARD THE INFANT!
DON'T WORRY!
I'LL RISK MY LIFE TO PROTECT YOU BOTH...!

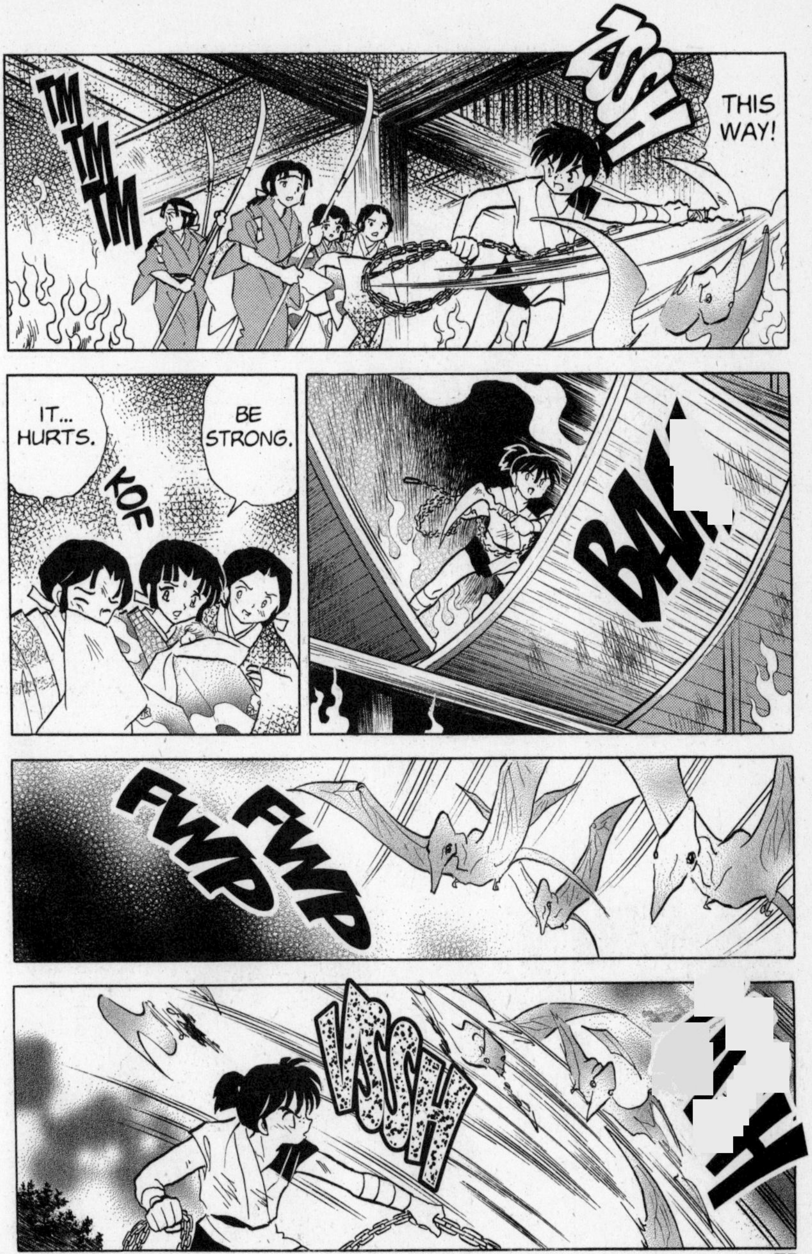
TM TM TM
ZASSH!!
THIS WAY!
IT... HURTS.
BE STRONG.
KOF
FWP
FWP
VSSH

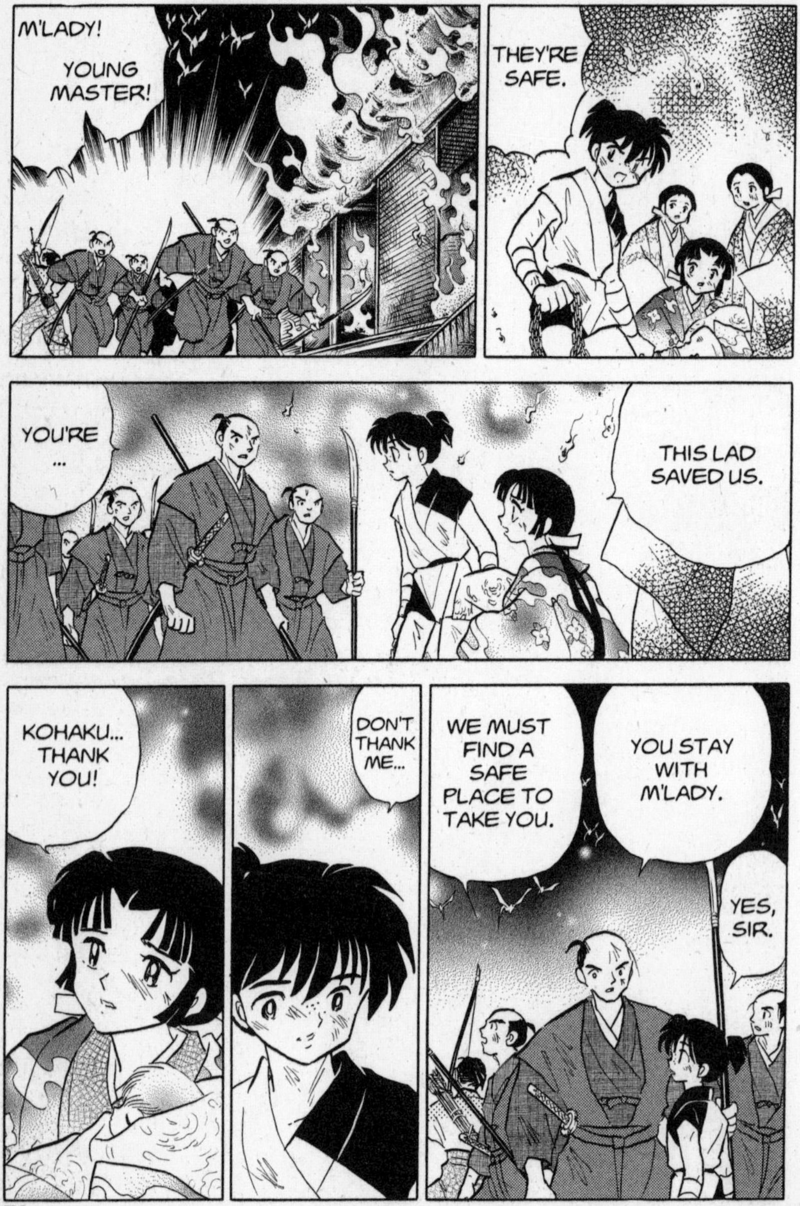
M'LADY!
YOUNG MASTER!
THEY'RE SAFE.
YOU'RE ...
THIS LAD SAVED US.
KOHAKU... THANK YOU!
DON'T THANK ME...
WE MUST FIND A SAFE PLACE TO TAKE YOU.
YOU STAY WITH M'LADY.
YES, SIR.

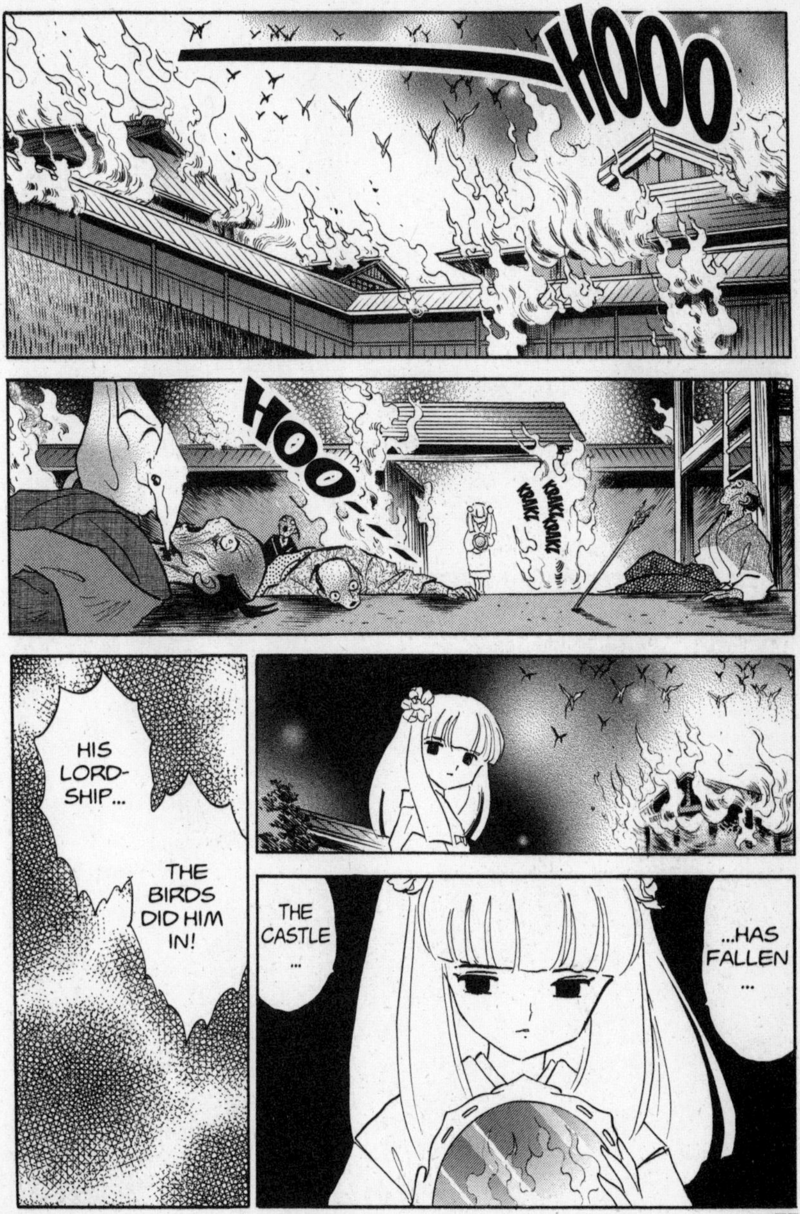
HOOO
HOO...
KRAK! KRAK!
KRAK!
HIS LORDSHIP...
THE BIRDS DID HIM IN!
THE CASTLE ...
...HAS FALLEN ...

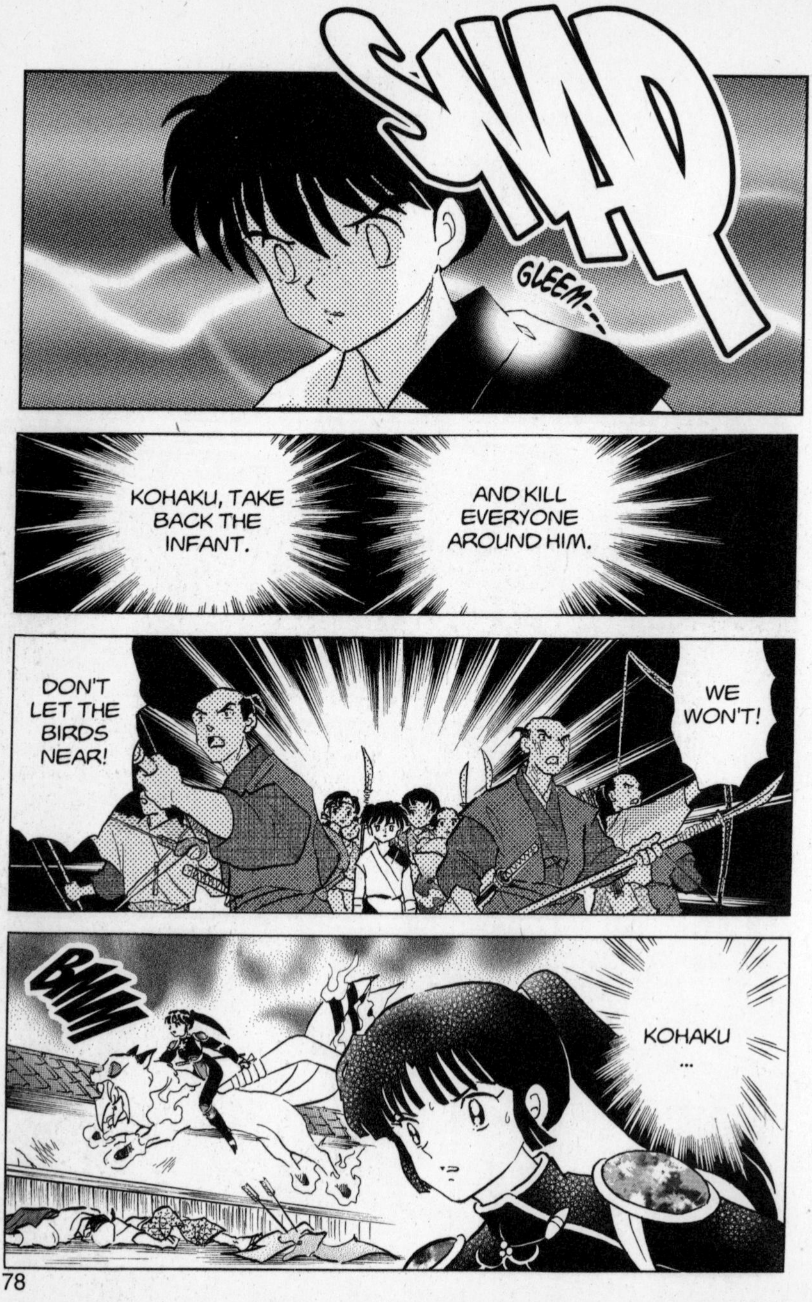
SNAP
GLEEM---
KOHAKU, TAKE BACK THE INFANT.
AND KILL EVERYONE AROUND HIM.
DON'T LET THE BIRDS NEAR!
WE WON'T!
BMM
KOHAKU ...

SCROLL 5

RESTORED MEMORY

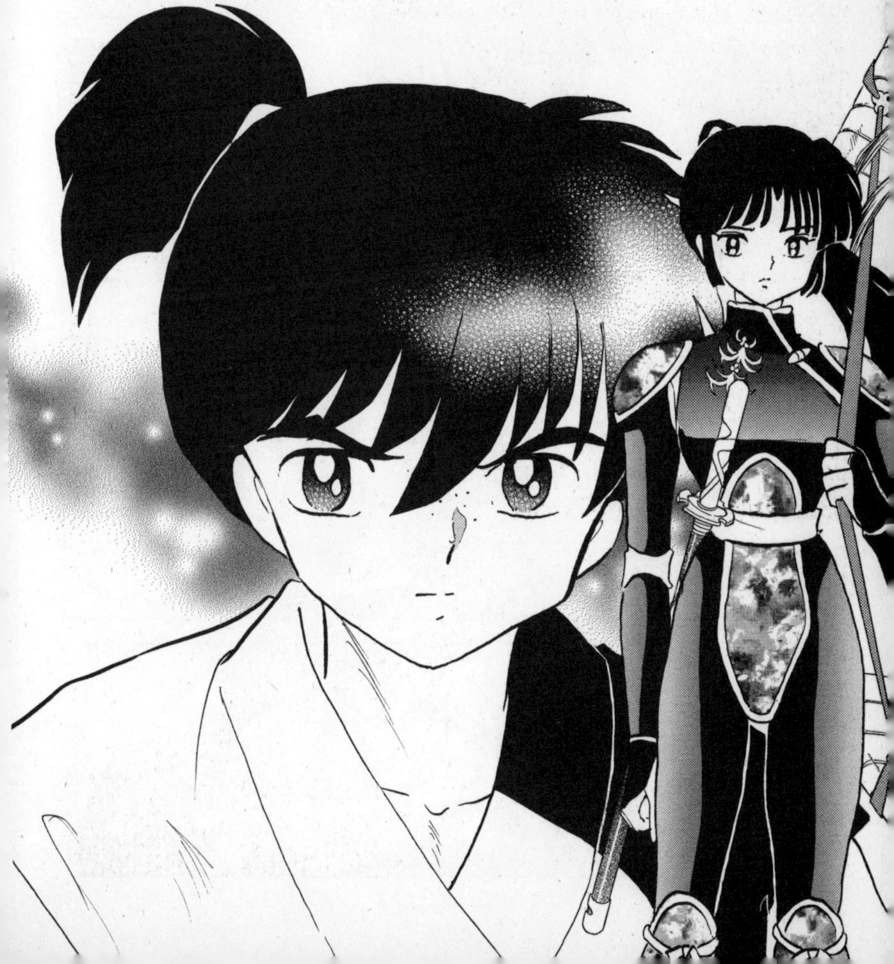

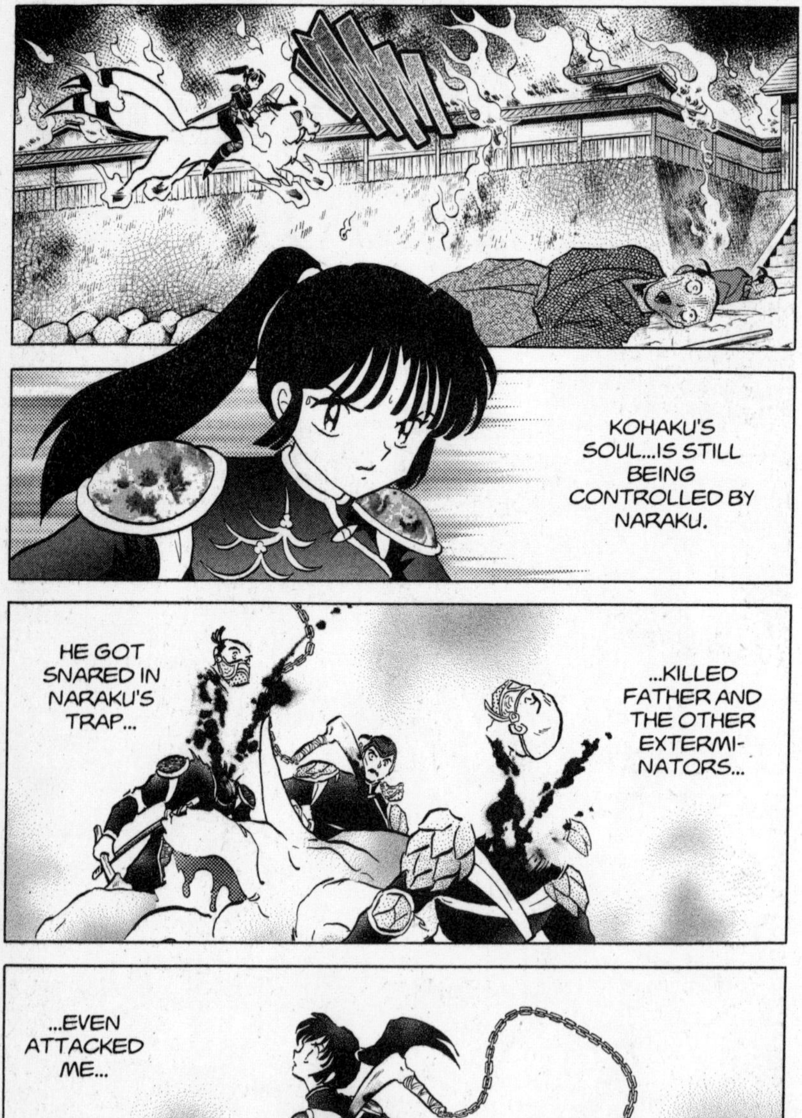
KOHAKU'S SOUL...IS STILL BEING CONTROLLED BY NARAKU.
HE GOT SNARED IN NARAKU'S TRAP...
...KILLED FATHER AND THE OTHER EXTERMI-NATORS...
...EVEN ATTACKED ME...

...HE HAS RESISTED RECALLING THE EVENTS OF THAT HEINOUS DAY...

...AND WITHOUT HIS MEMORIES HAS CONTINUED SERVING NARAKU.

AND YET...HE IS MY ONLY BROTHER.

PLEASE...

...DON'T ADD TO YOUR CRIMES.

ZASH

THOK

THE BIRDS-- THERE ARE FEWER OF THEM!

BE STRONG JUST A LITTLE LONGER, M'LADY!

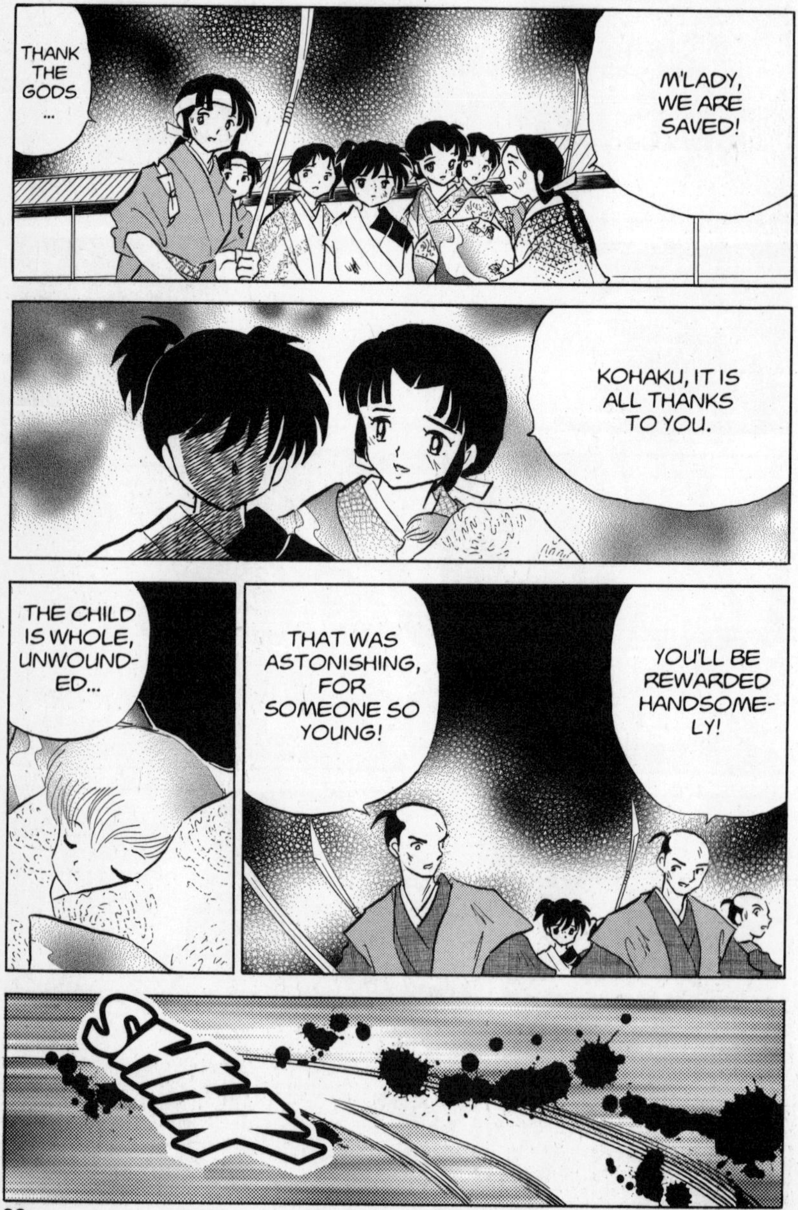
THANK THE GODS ...
M'LADY, WE ARE SAVED!
KOHAKU, IT IS ALL THANKS TO YOU.
THE CHILD IS WHOLE, UNWOUND-ED...
THAT WAS ASTONISHING, FOR SOMEONE SO YOUNG!
YOU'LL BE REWARDED HANDSOME-LY!

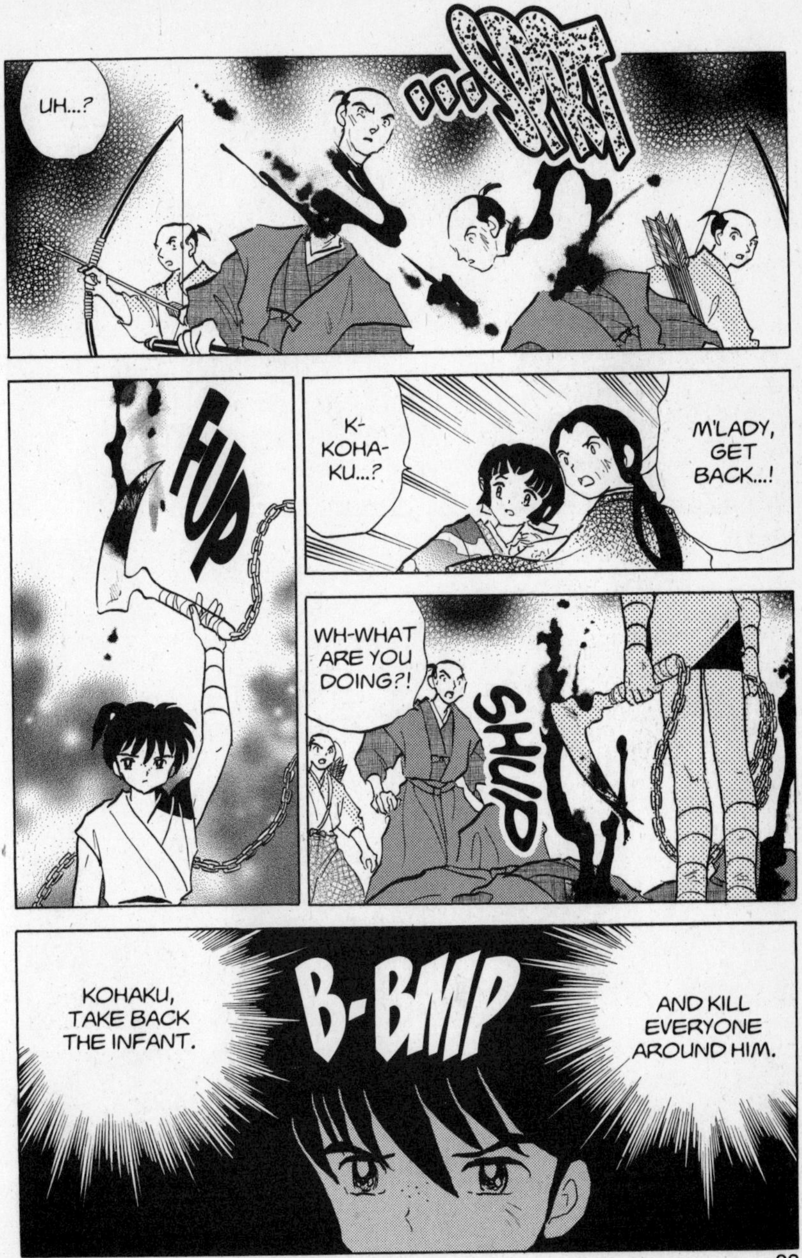
UH...?
...SPRT
FUP
K-KOHAKU...?
M'LADY, GET BACK...!
WH-WHAT ARE YOU DOING?!
SHUP
KOHAKU, TAKE BACK THE INFANT.
B-BMP
AND KILL EVERYONE AROUND HIM.

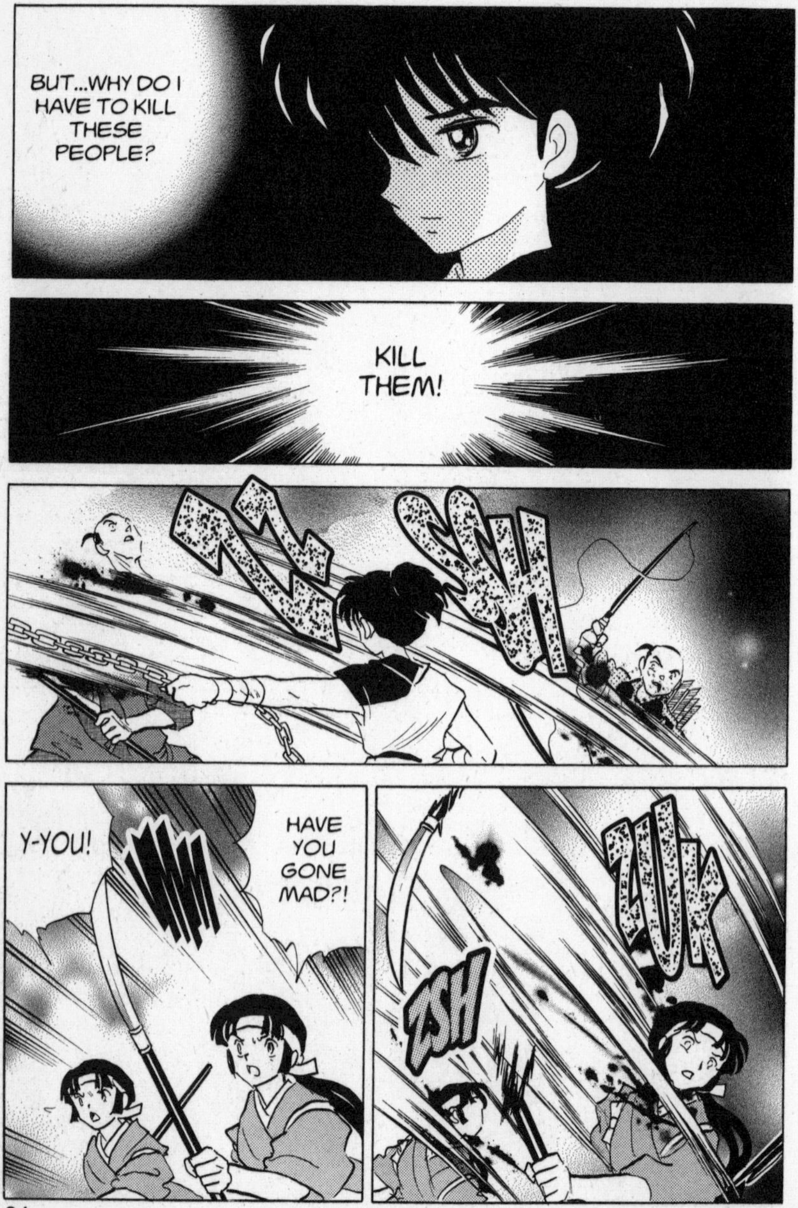
BUT...WHY DO I HAVE TO KILL THESE PEOPLE?
KILL THEM!
Y-YOU!
HAVE YOU GONE MAD?!
ZUK
ZSH

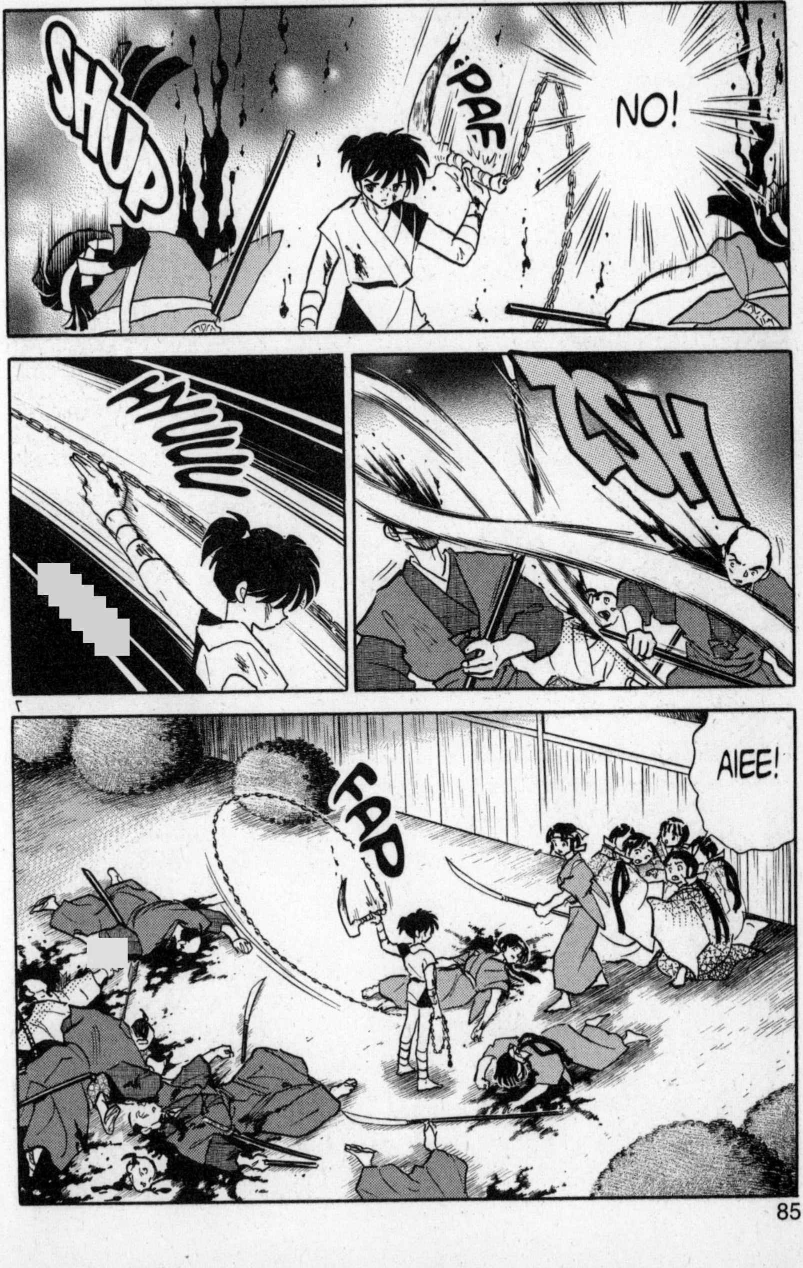
SHUP
PAF
NO!
HYUUU
ZSH
FAP
AIEE!

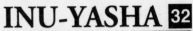

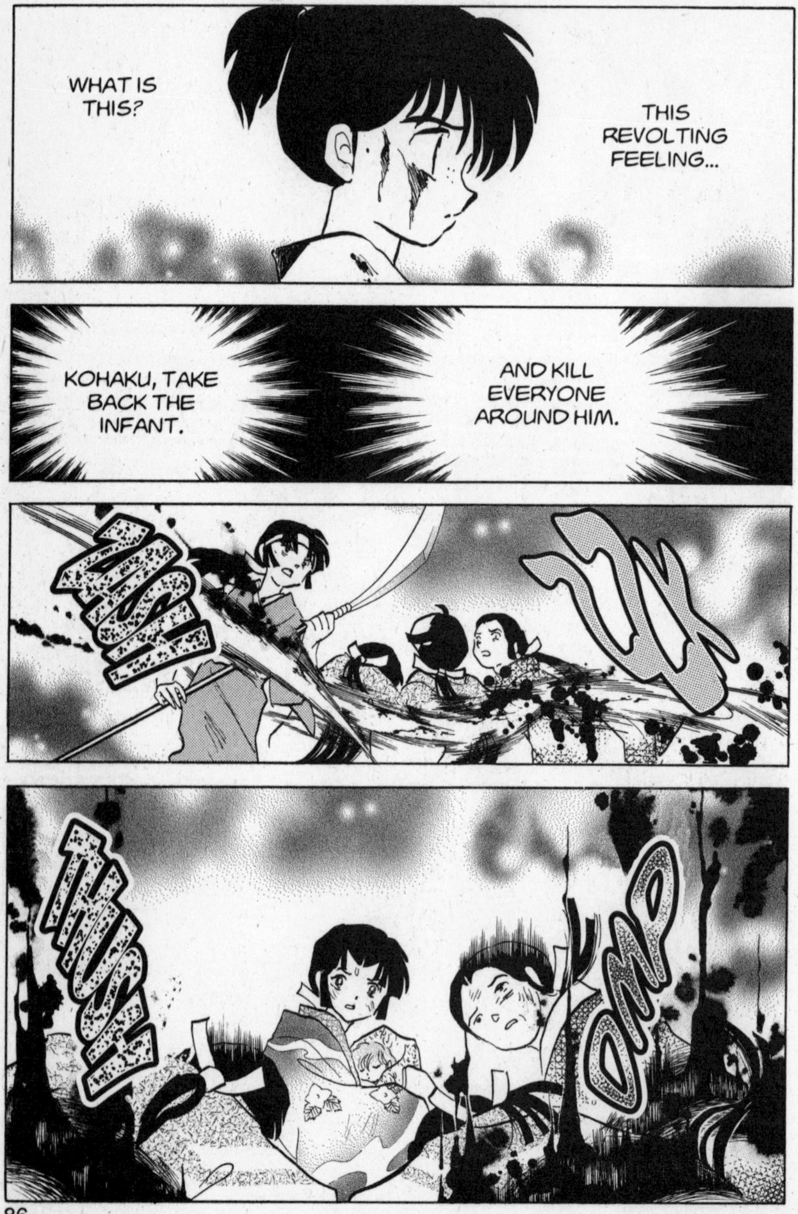
WHAT IS THIS?
THIS REVOLTING FEELING...
KOHAKU, TAKE BACK THE INFANT.
AND KILL EVERYONE AROUND HIM.
ZASH!
THUSH!

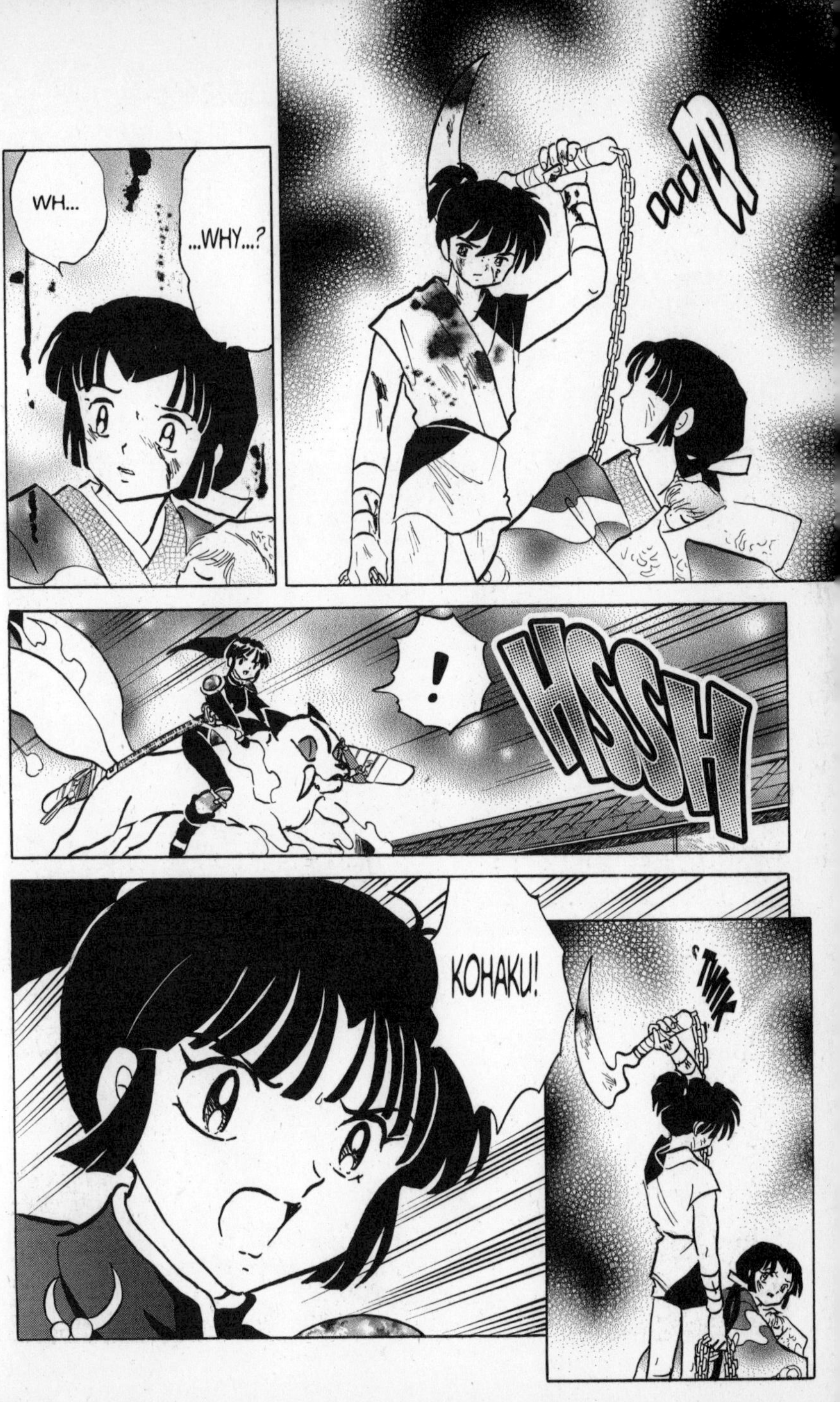
WH...
...WHY...?
!
HSSH
KOHAKU!
TWIK

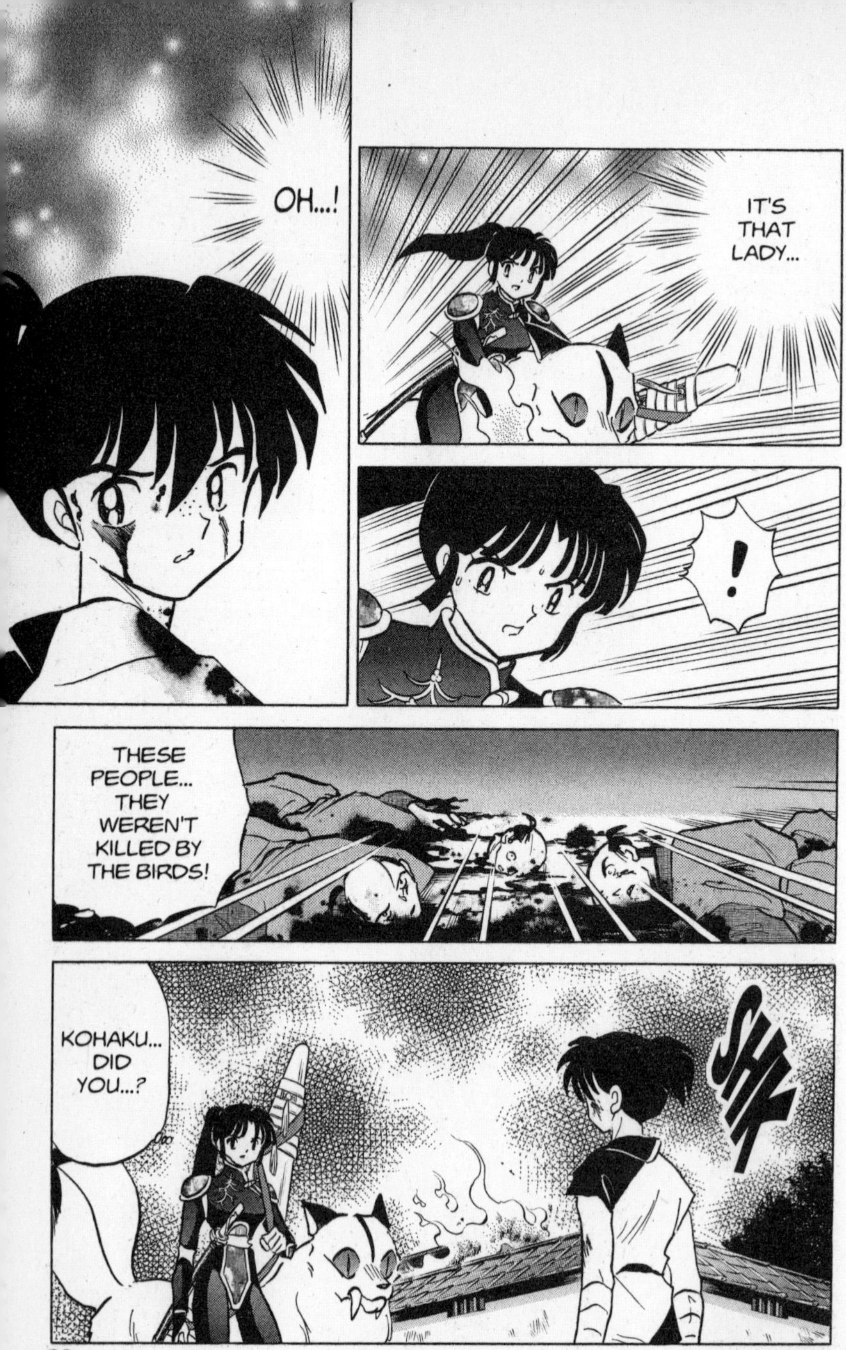
OH...!
IT'S THAT LADY...
!
THESE PEOPLE... THEY WEREN'T KILLED BY THE BIRDS!
KOHAKU... DID YOU...?
SHK

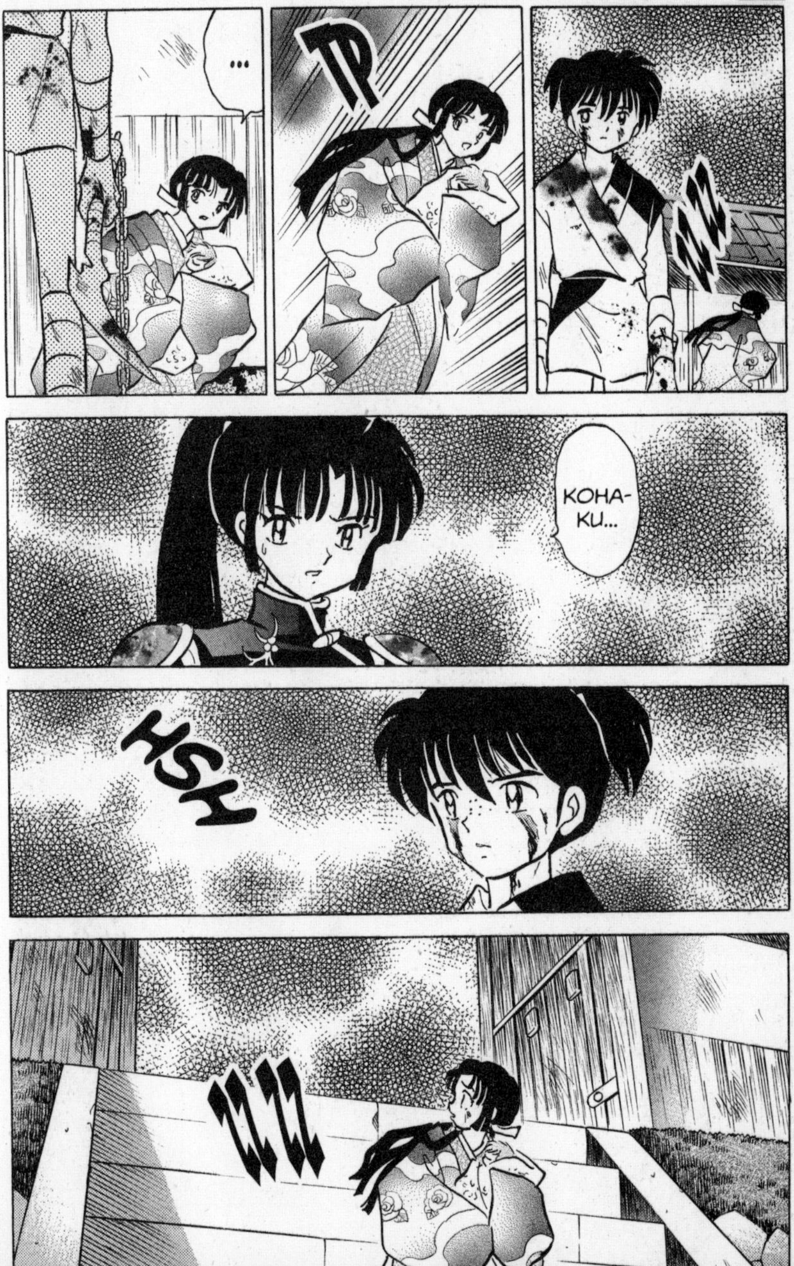
...
TP
KOHA-
KU...
HSH

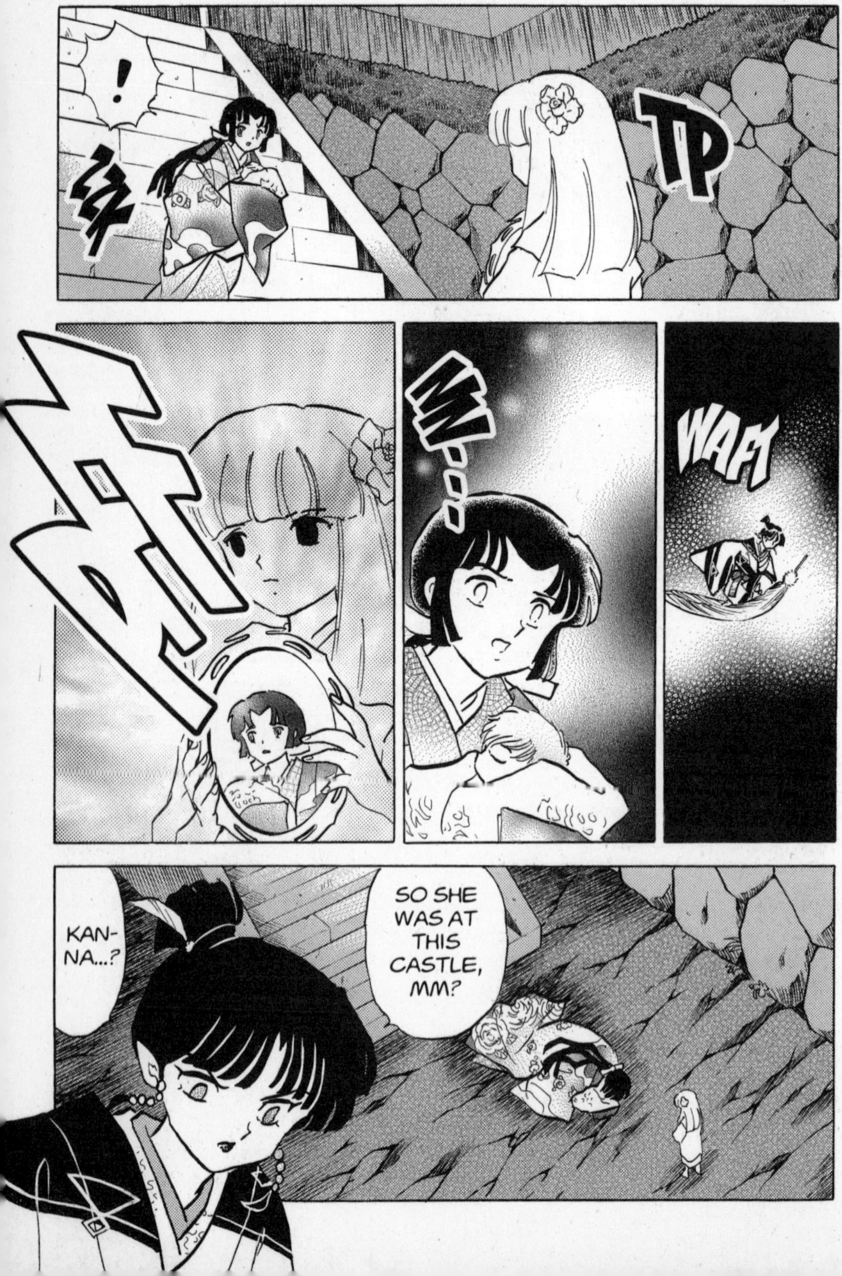
!
TP
MM...
WAFT
KAN-
NA...?
SO SHE
WAS AT
THIS
CASTLE,
MM?

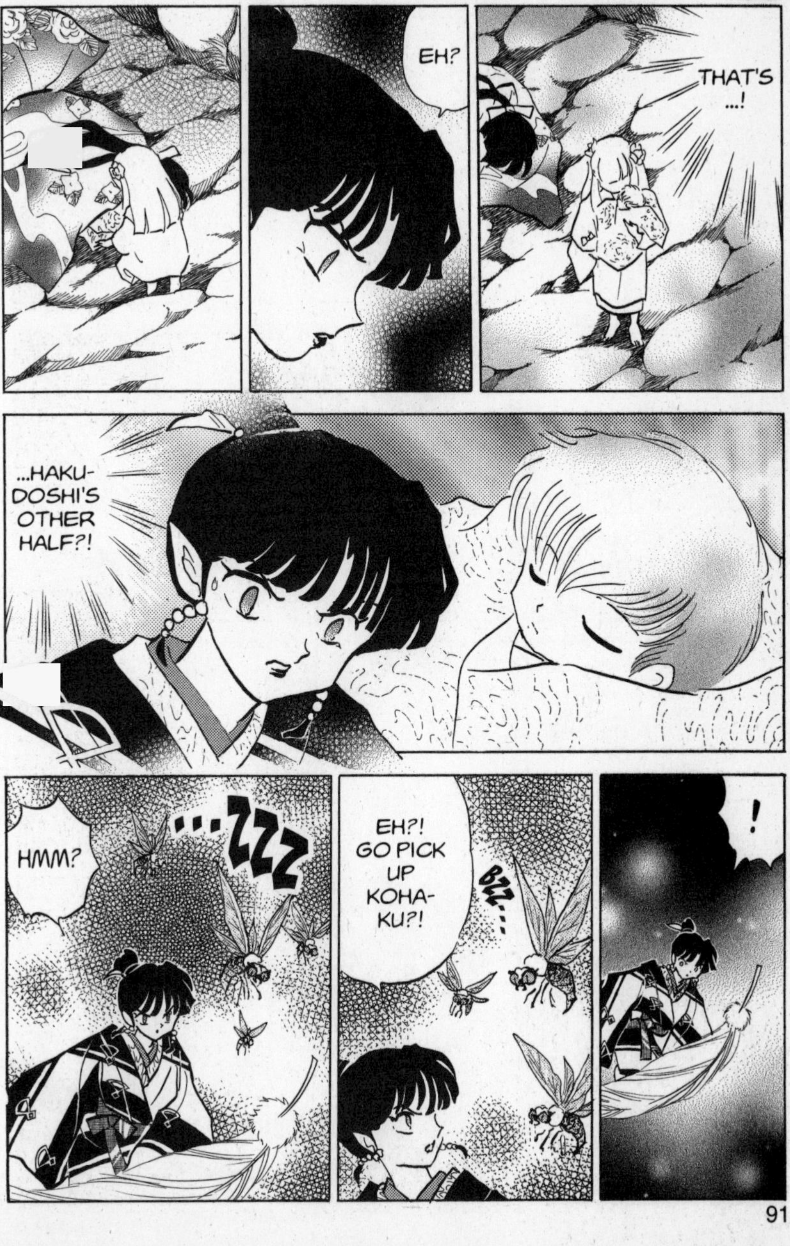
EH?
THAT'S ...!
...HAKU-DOSHI'S OTHER HALF?!
HMM?
...ZZZ
EH?! GO PICK UP KOHA-KU?!
BZZ...
!

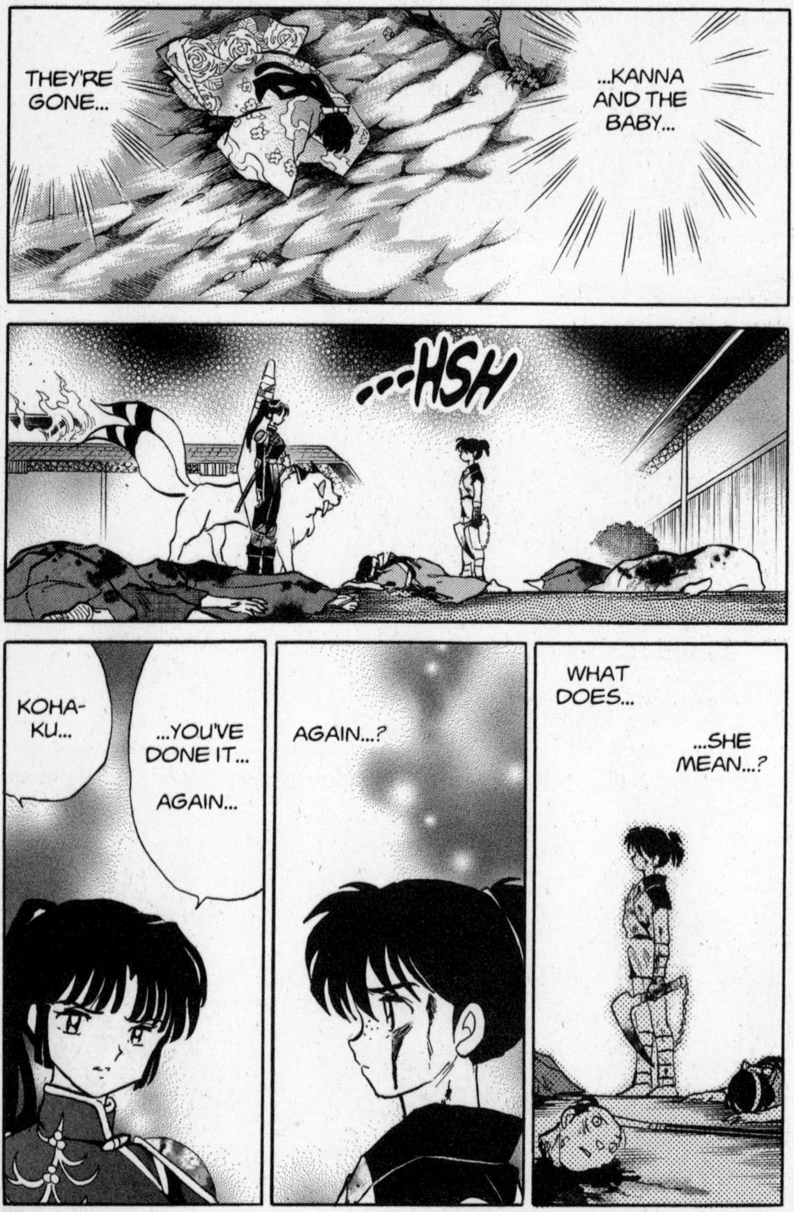
THEY'RE GONE...
...KANNA AND THE BABY...
---HSH
KOHA-KU...
...YOU'VE DONE IT...
AGAIN...
AGAIN...?
WHAT DOES...
...SHE MEAN...?

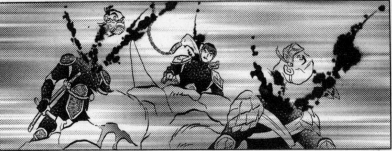

WHAT
...?

WHAT
WAS
THAT
ABOUT
...?!

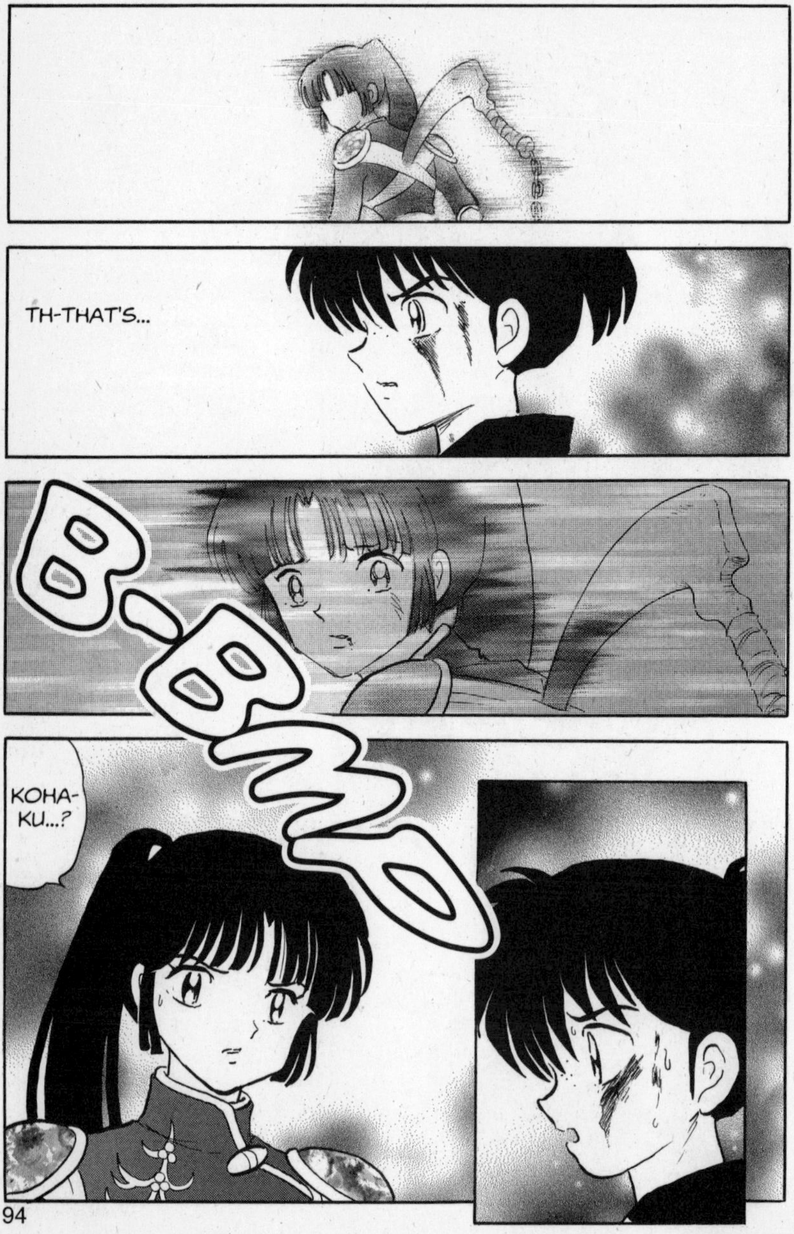
TH-THAT'S...
B-BMP
KOHA-KU...?

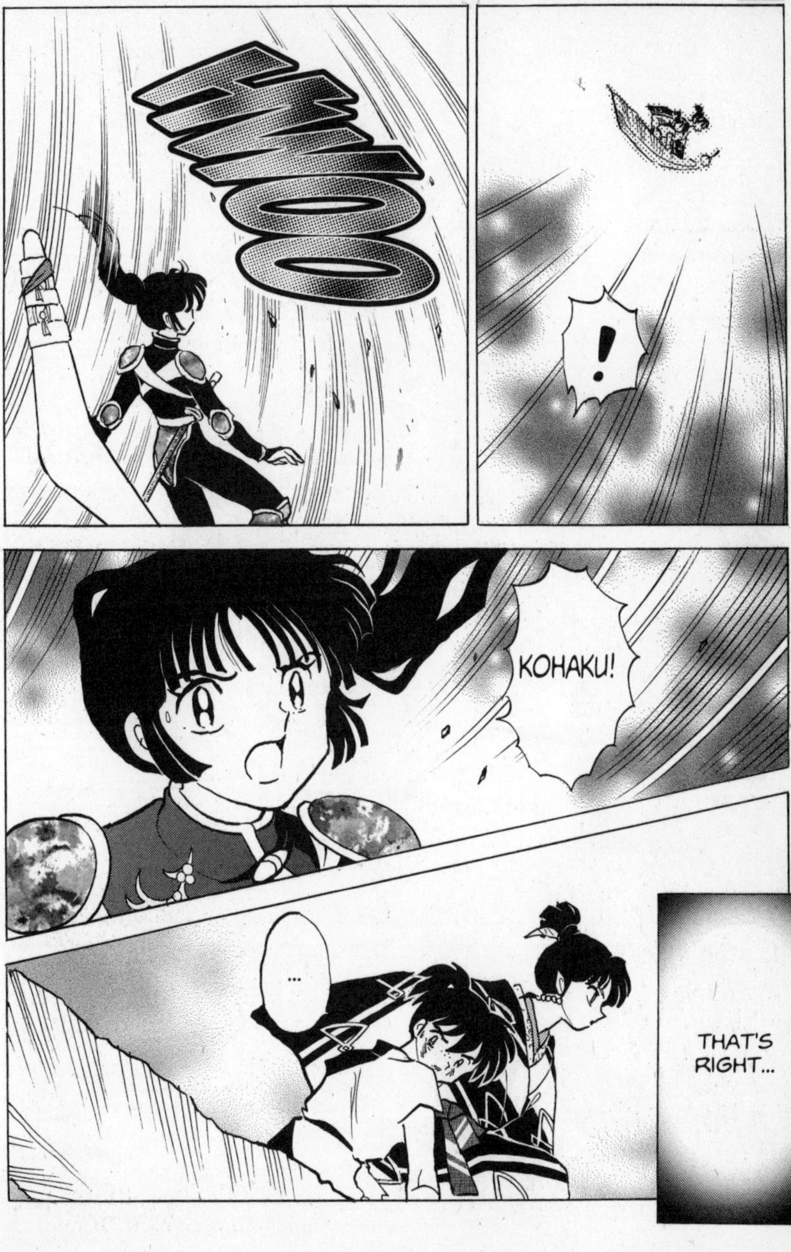
FWOOO
!
KOHAKU!
...
THAT'S RIGHT...

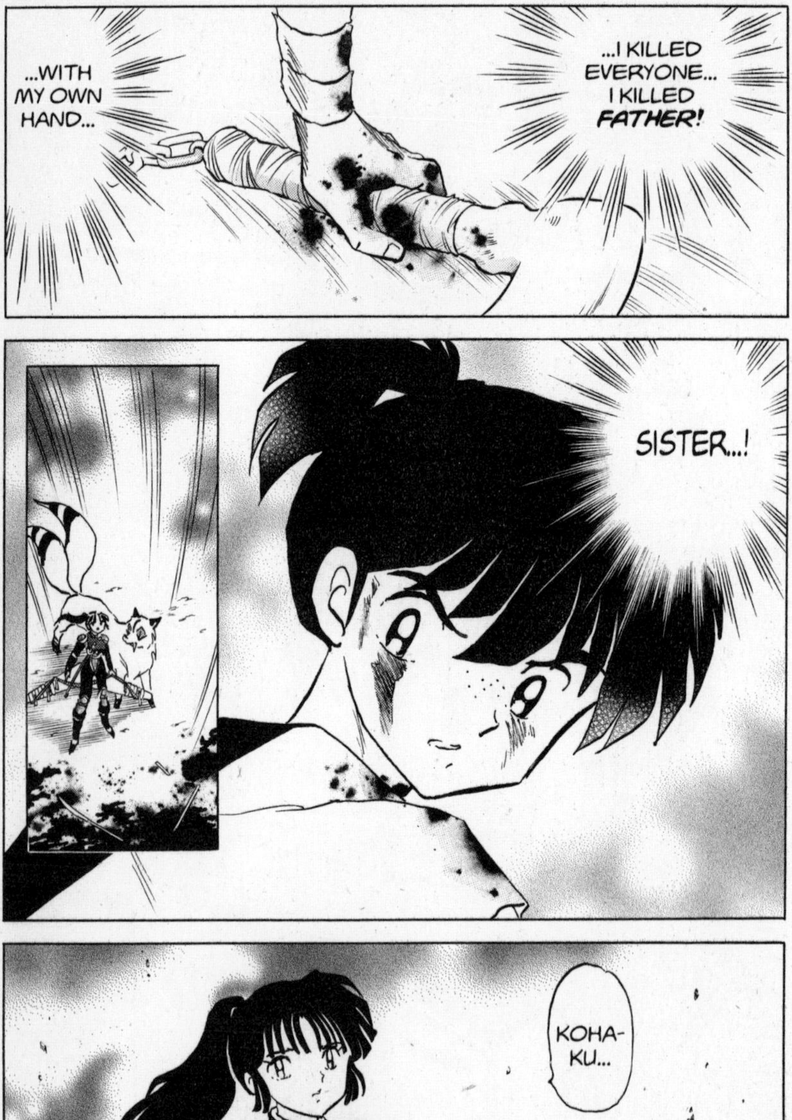
...WITH MY OWN HAND...
...I KILLED EVERYONE... I KILLED **FATHER!**
SISTER...!
KOHA-KU...

SCROLL 6

A BROKEN SPELL

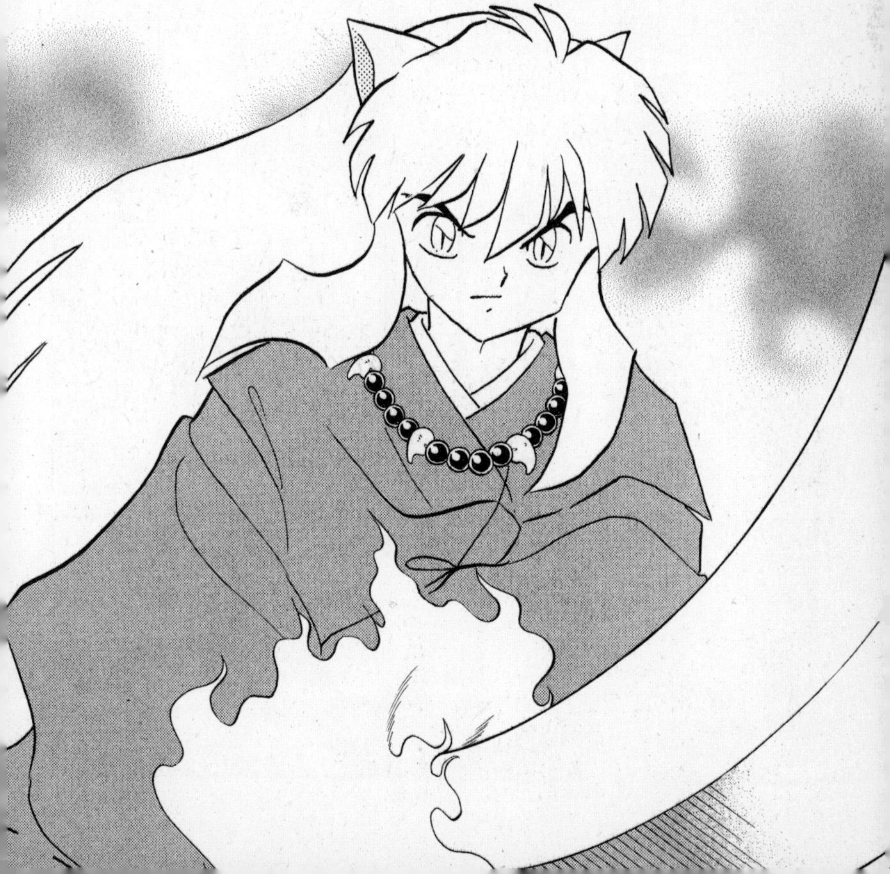

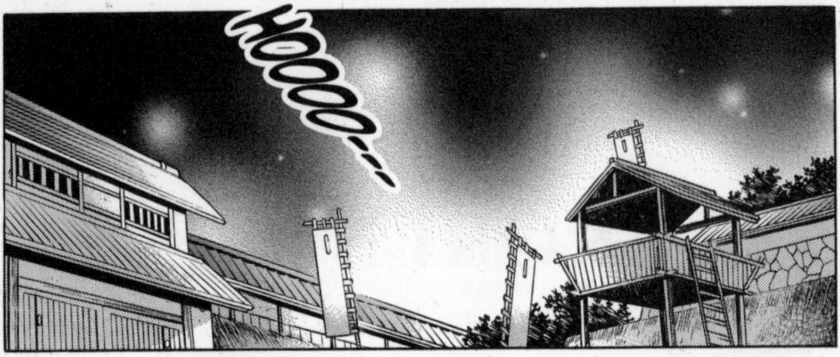
HOOOO---

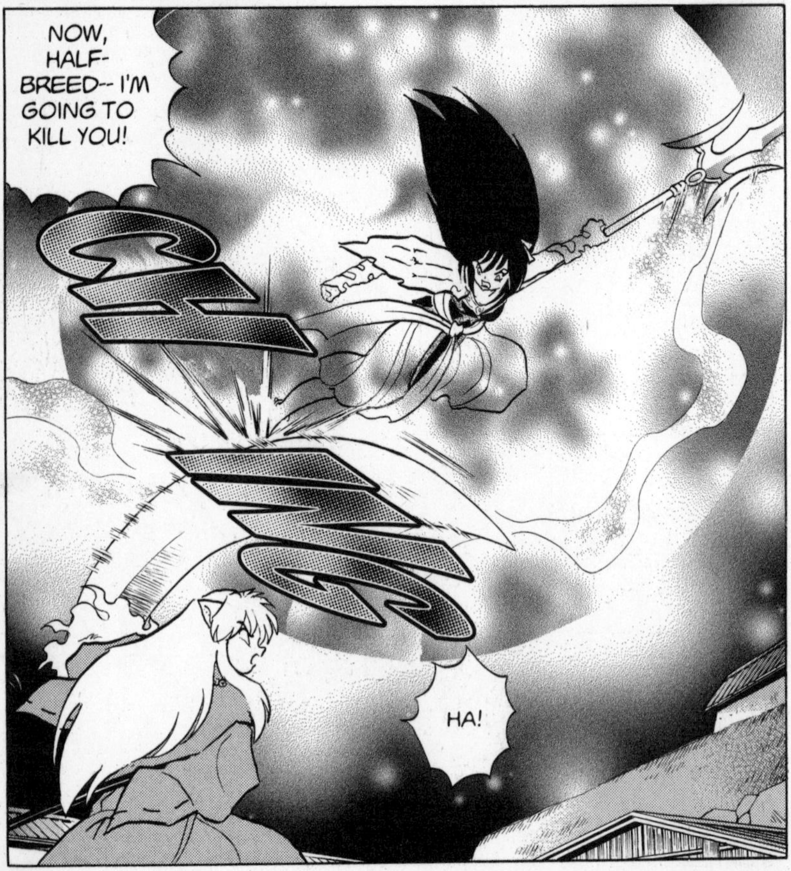
NOW, HALF-BREED-- I'M GOING TO KILL YOU!
CHING
HA!

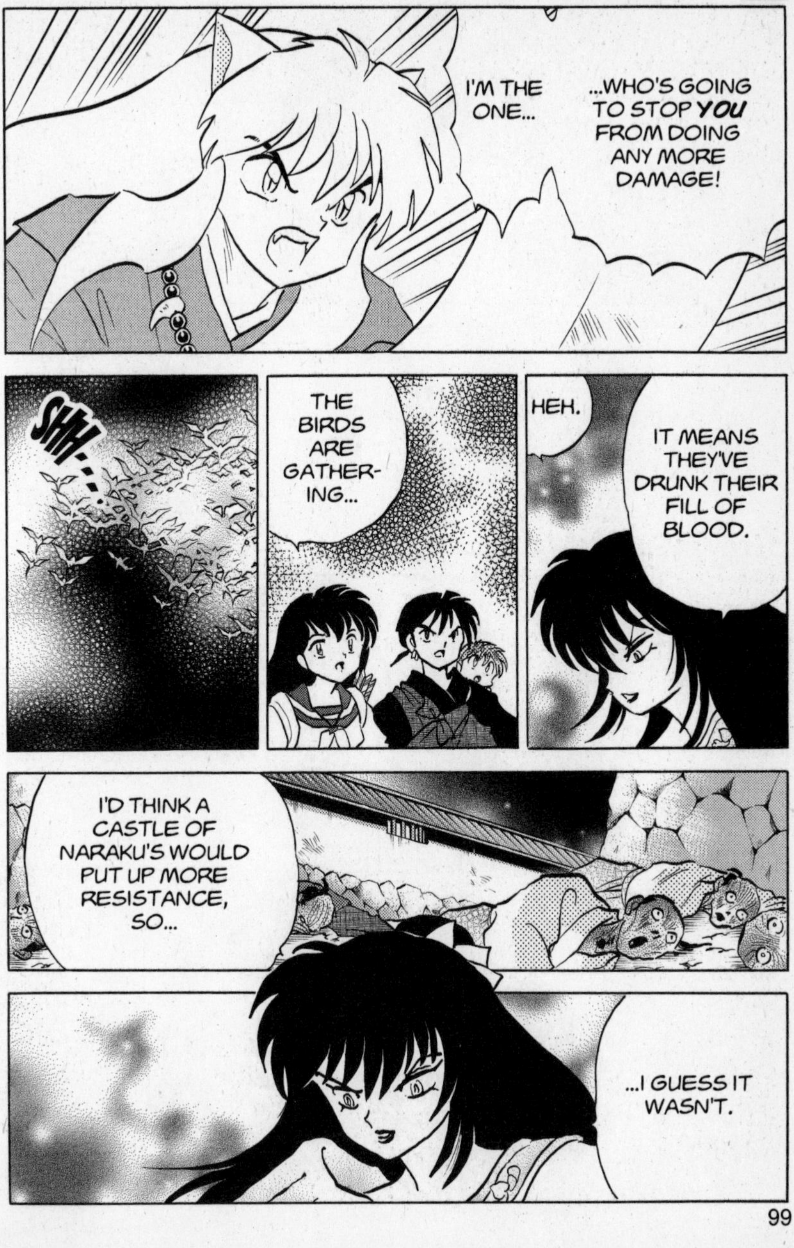
I'M THE ONE...
...WHO'S GOING TO STOP YOU FROM DOING ANY MORE DAMAGE!
SHH...
THE BIRDS ARE GATHERING...
HEH.
IT MEANS THEY'VE DRUNK THEIR FILL OF BLOOD.
I'D THINK A CASTLE OF NARAKU'S WOULD PUT UP MORE RESISTANCE, SO...
...I GUESS IT WASN'T.

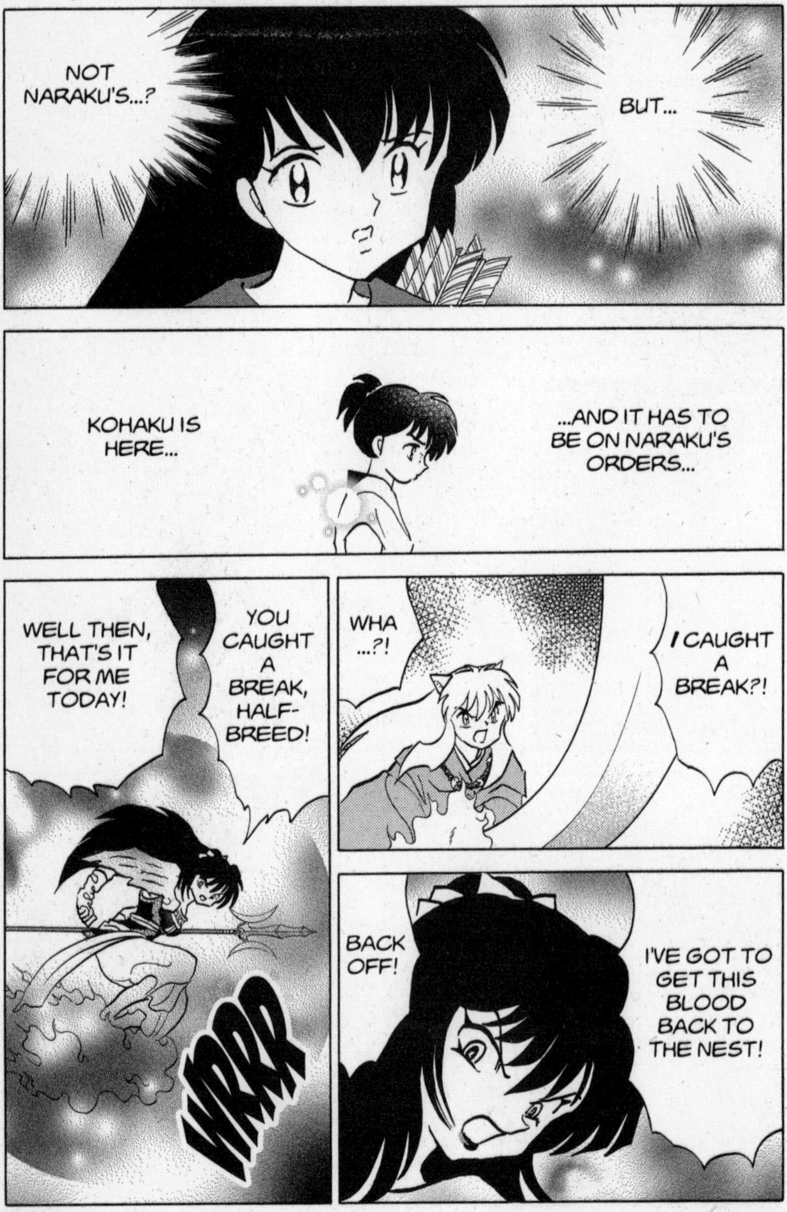
NOT NARAKU'S...?
BUT...
KOHAKU IS HERE...
...AND IT HAS TO BE ON NARAKU'S ORDERS...
WELL THEN, THAT'S IT FOR ME TODAY!
YOU CAUGHT A BREAK, HALF-BREED!
WRRR
WHA ...?!
I CAUGHT A BREAK?!
BACK OFF!
I'VE GOT TO GET THIS BLOOD BACK TO THE NEST!

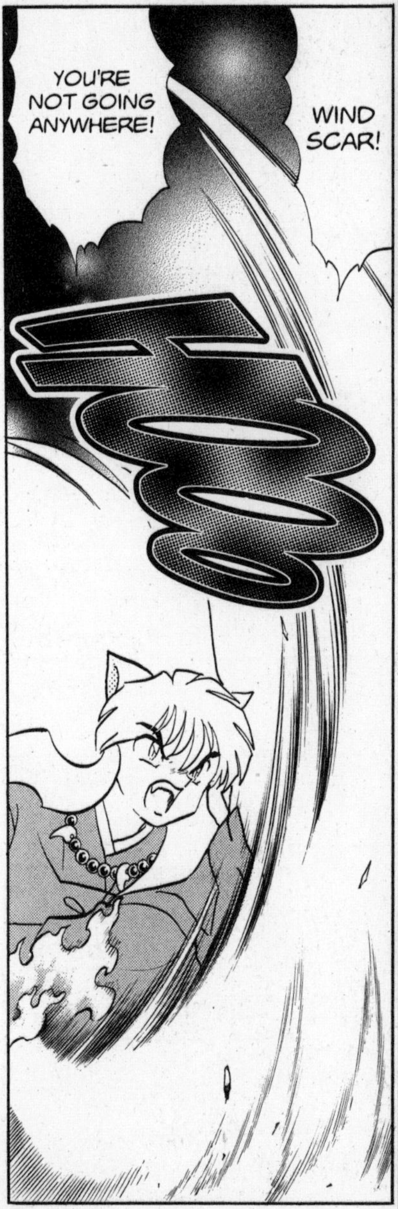
YOU'RE NOT GOING ANYWHERE!
WIND SCAR!
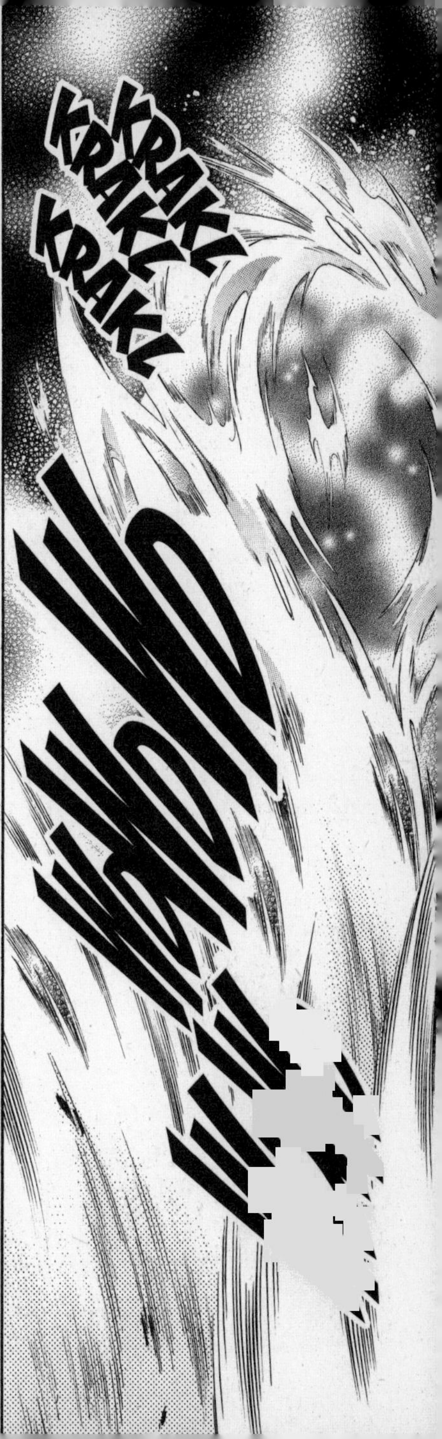
KRAK! KRAK! KRAK!

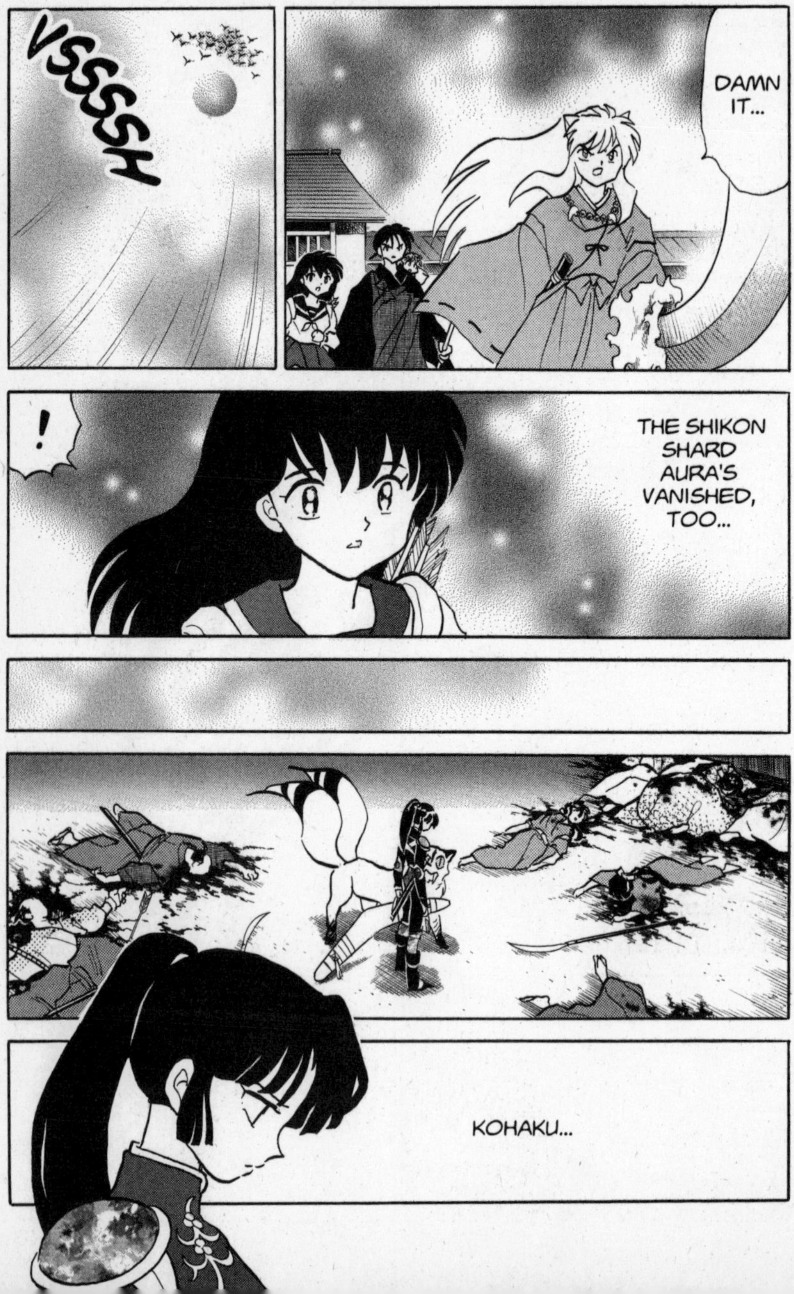
VSSSSH
DAMN IT...
!
THE SHIKON SHARD AURA'S VANISHED, TOO...
KOHAKU...

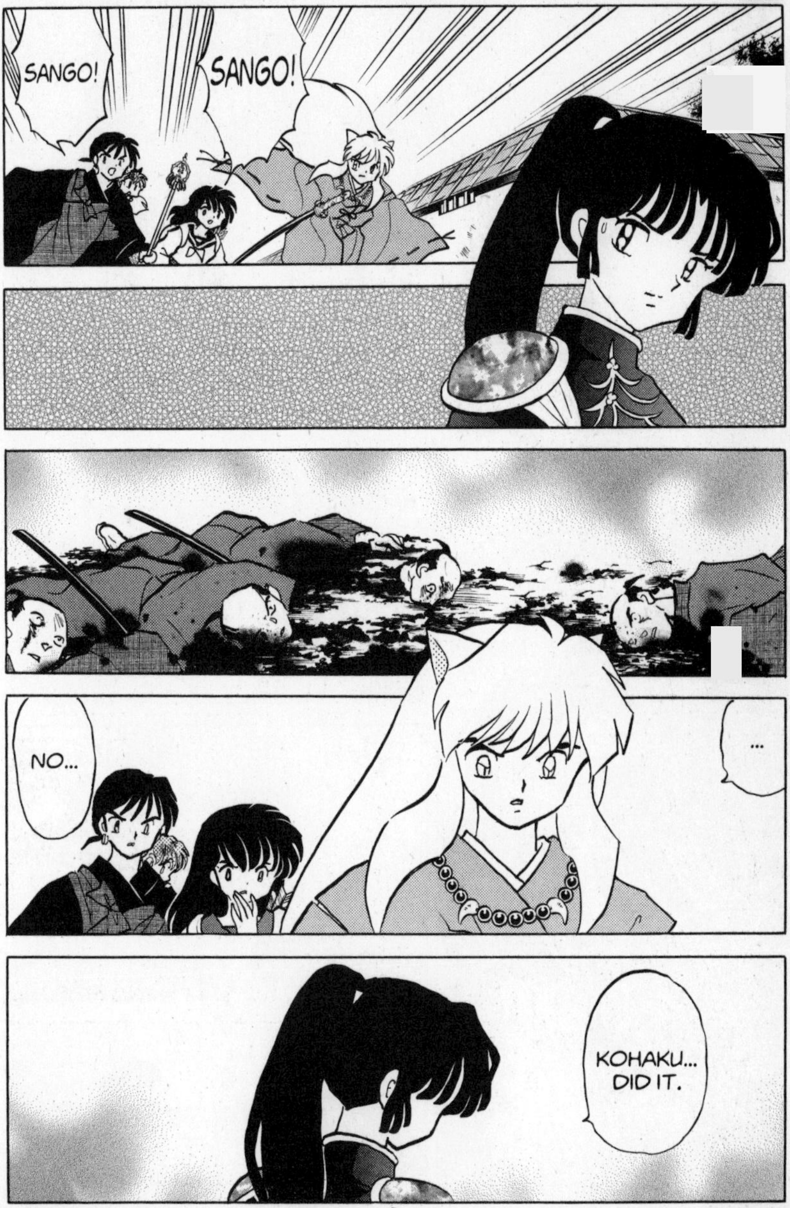
SANGO!
SANGO!
NO...
...
KOHAKU... DID IT.

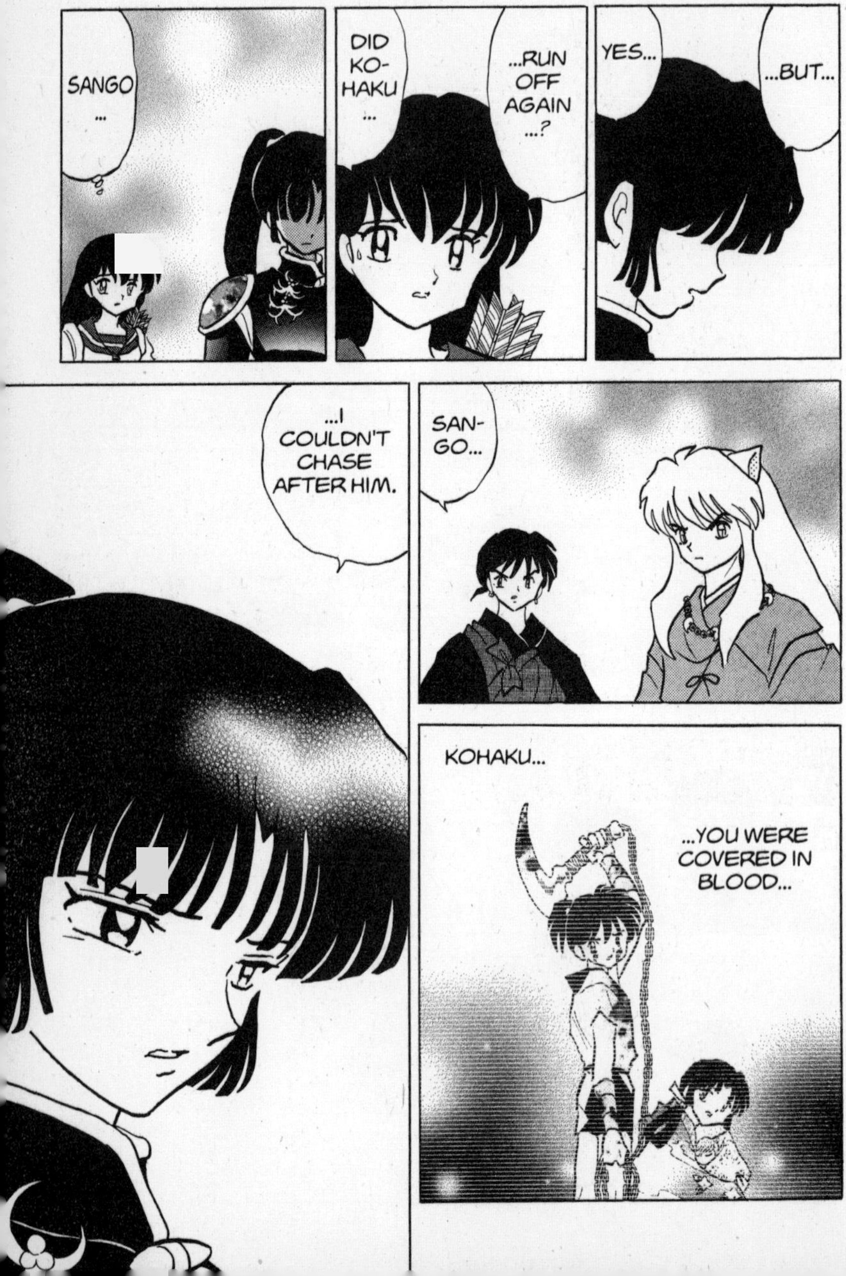
SANGO...
DID KO-HAKU...
...RUN OFF AGAIN...?
YES...
...BUT...
...I COULDN'T CHASE AFTER HIM.
SAN-GO...
KOHAKU...
...YOU WERE COVERED IN BLOOD...

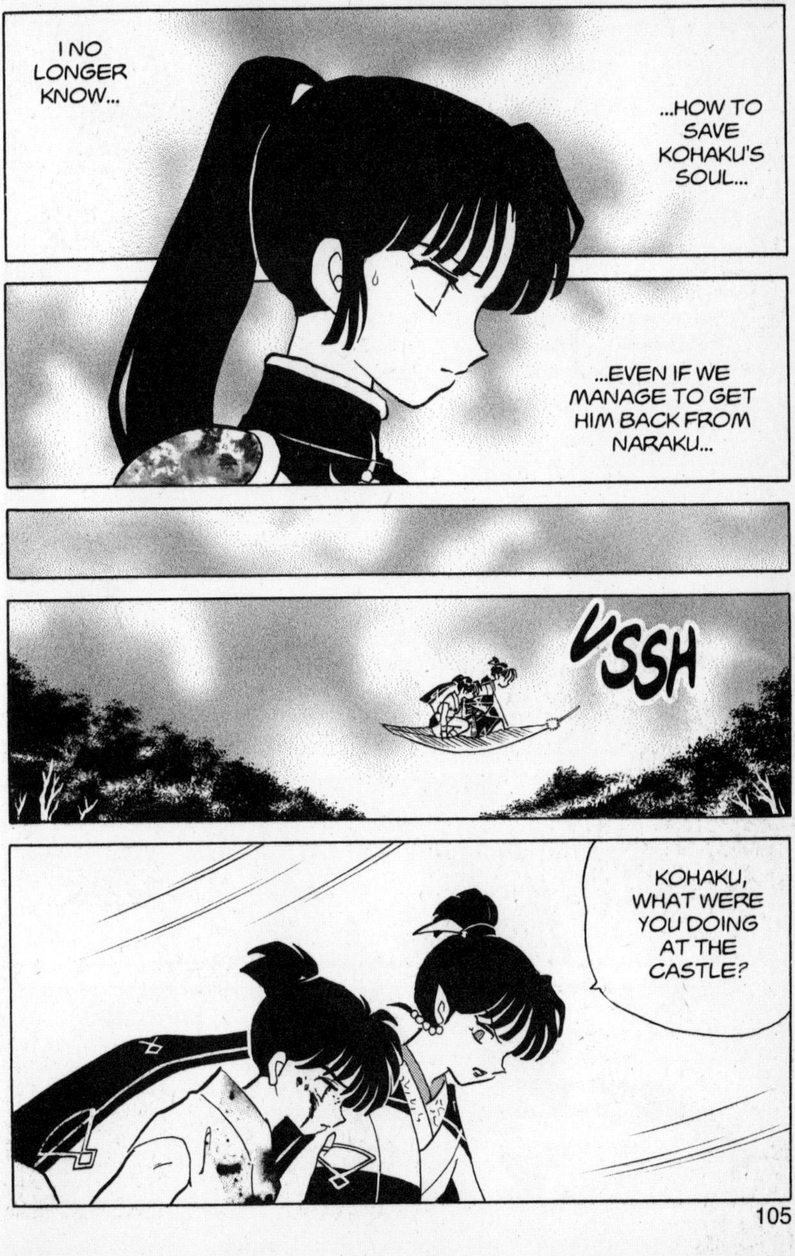
I NO LONGER KNOW...
...HOW TO SAVE KOHAKU'S SOUL...
...EVEN IF WE MANAGE TO GET HIM BACK FROM NARAKU...
VSSH
KOHAKU, WHAT WERE YOU DOING AT THE CASTLE?

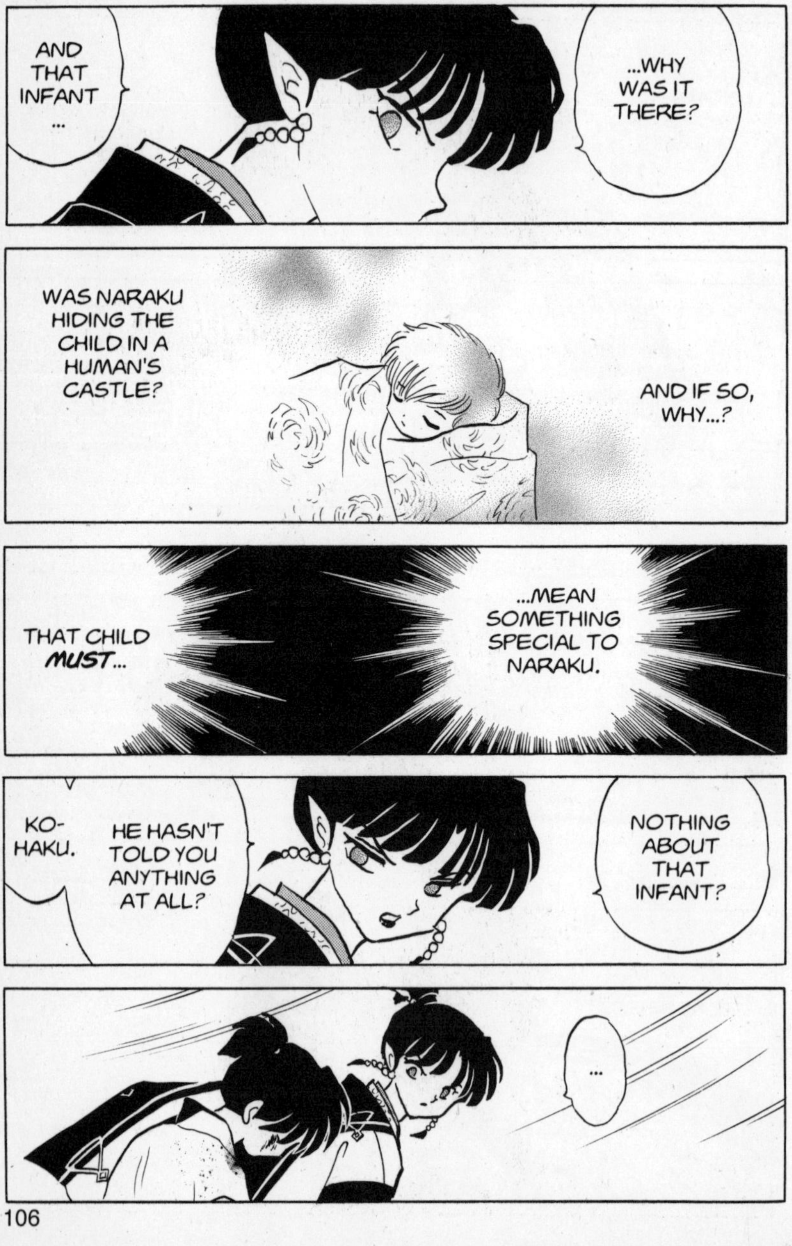

AND THAT INFANT ...
...WHY WAS IT THERE?
WAS NARAKU HIDING THE CHILD IN A HUMAN'S CASTLE?
AND IF SO, WHY...?
THAT CHILD *MUST*...
...MEAN SOMETHING SPECIAL TO NARAKU.
KO-HAKU.
HE HASN'T TOLD YOU ANYTHING AT ALL?
NOTHING ABOUT THAT INFANT?
...

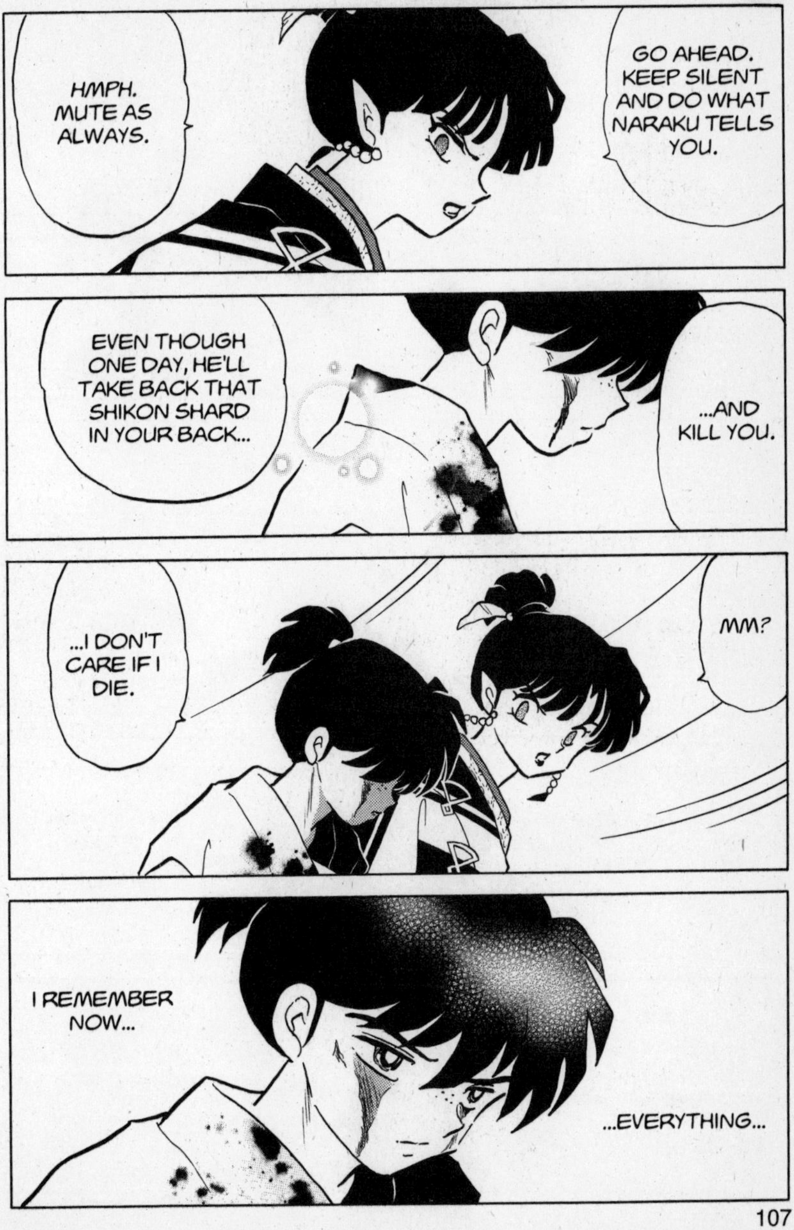
HMPH. MUTE AS ALWAYS.
GO AHEAD. KEEP SILENT AND DO WHAT NARAKU TELLS YOU.
EVEN THOUGH ONE DAY, HE'LL TAKE BACK THAT SHIKON SHARD IN YOUR BACK...
...AND KILL YOU.
...I DON'T CARE IF I DIE.
MM?
I REMEMBER NOW...
...EVERYTHING...

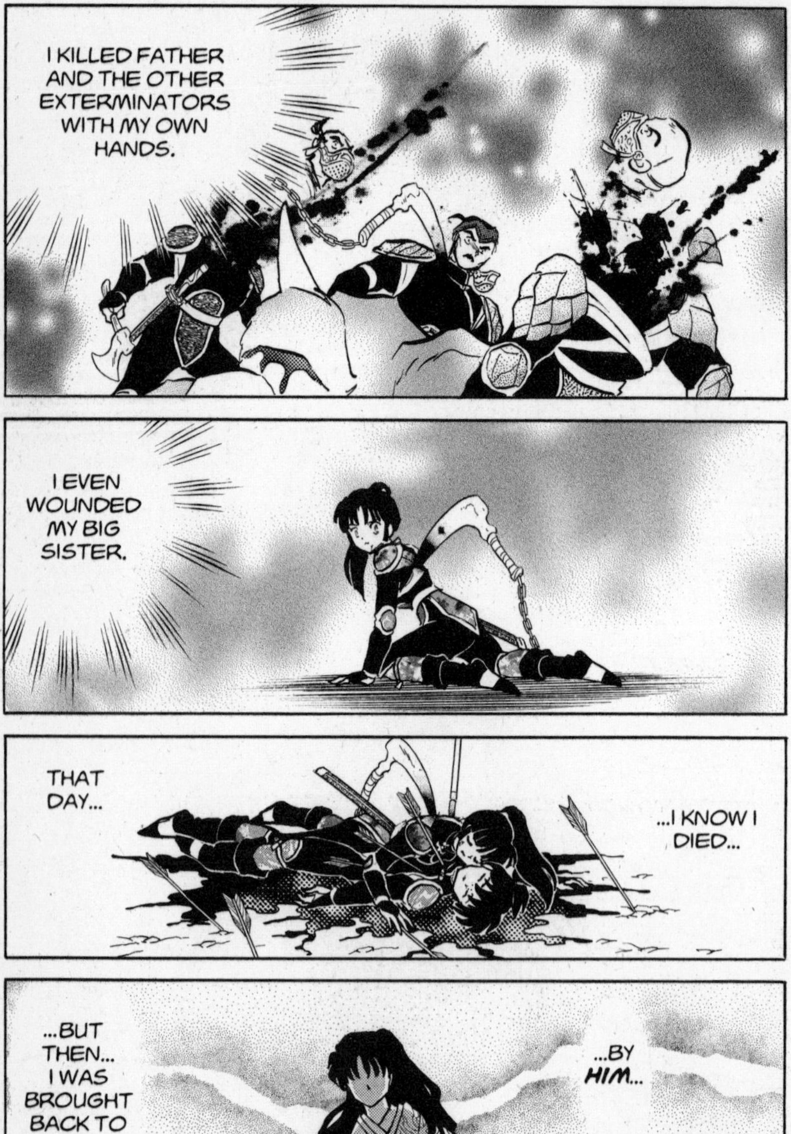
I KILLED FATHER AND THE OTHER EXTERMINATORS WITH MY OWN HANDS.
I EVEN WOUNDED MY BIG SISTER.
THAT DAY...
...I KNOW I DIED...
...BUT THEN... I WAS BROUGHT BACK TO LIFE...
...BY *HIM*...

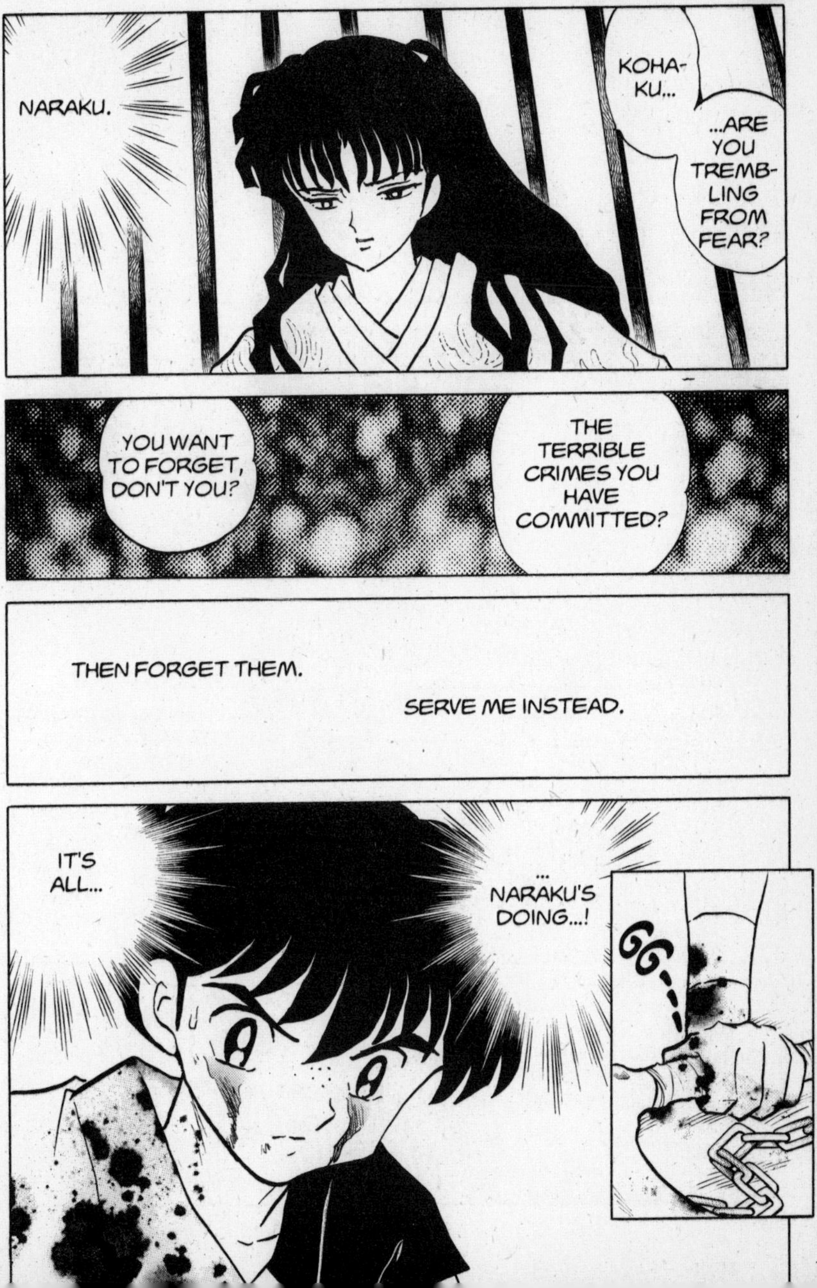
NARAKU.
KOHA-KU...
...ARE YOU TREMB-LING FROM FEAR?
YOU WANT TO FORGET, DON'T YOU?
THE TERRIBLE CRIMES YOU HAVE COMMITTED?
THEN FORGET THEM.
SERVE ME INSTEAD.
IT'S ALL...
...NARAKU'S DOING...!
GG...

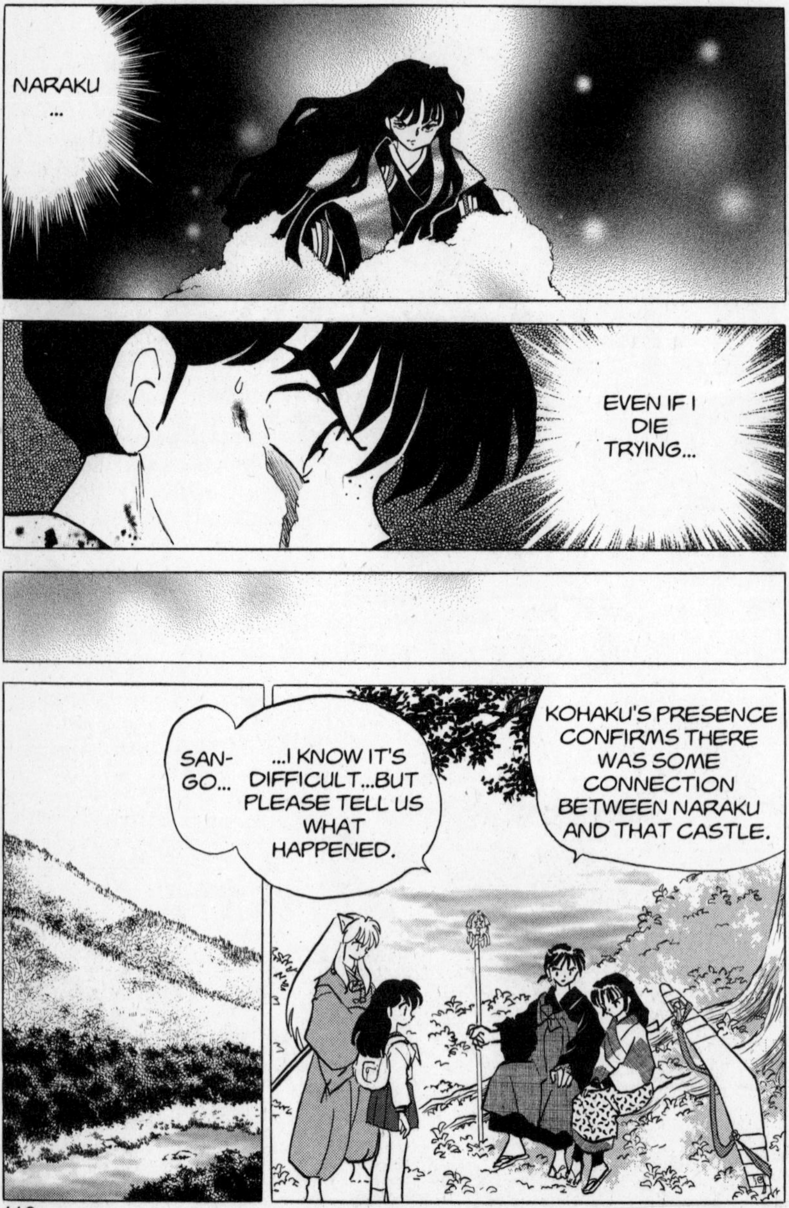
NARAKU ...
EVEN IF I DIE TRYING...
SANGO... ...I KNOW IT'S DIFFICULT...BUT PLEASE TELL US WHAT HAPPENED.
KOHAKU'S PRESENCE CONFIRMS THERE WAS SOME CONNECTION BETWEEN NARAKU AND THAT CASTLE.

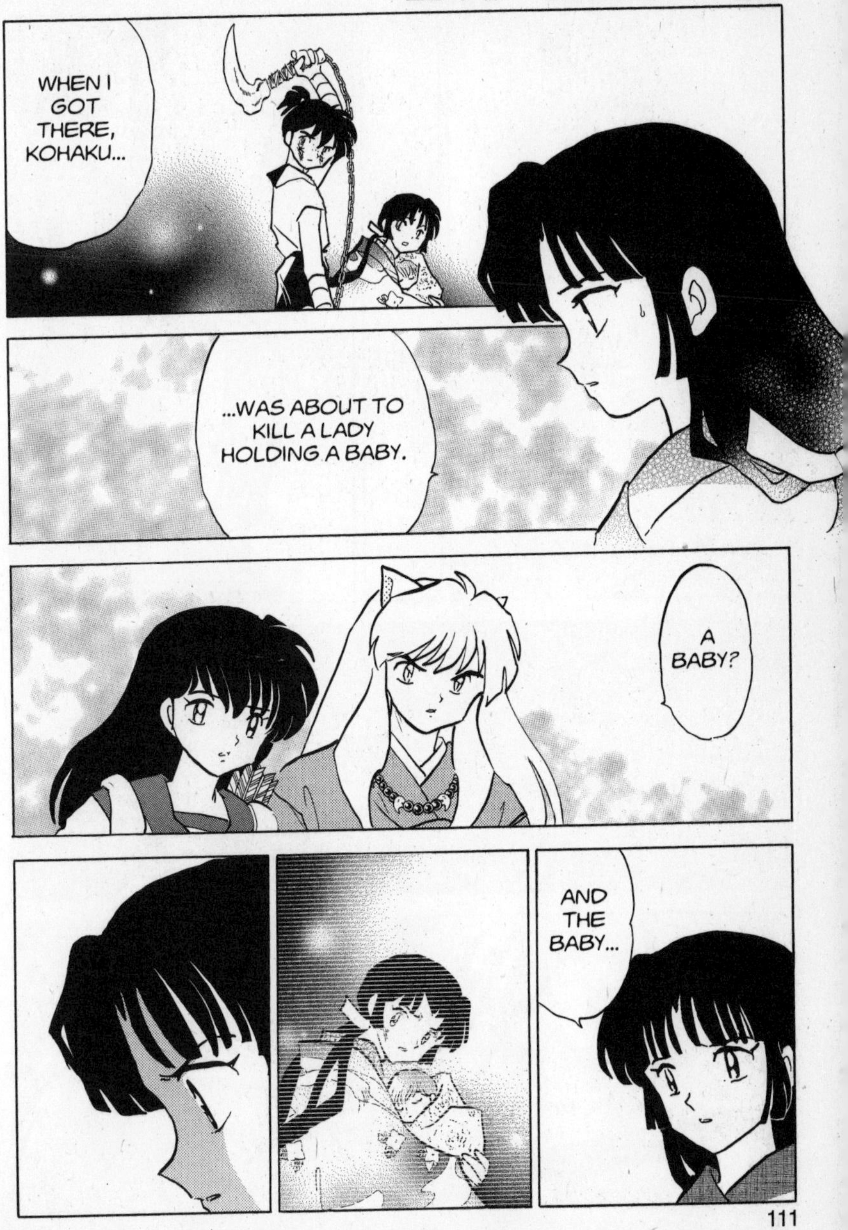
WHEN I GOT THERE, KOHAKU...
...WAS ABOUT TO KILL A LADY HOLDING A BABY.
A BABY?
AND THE BABY...

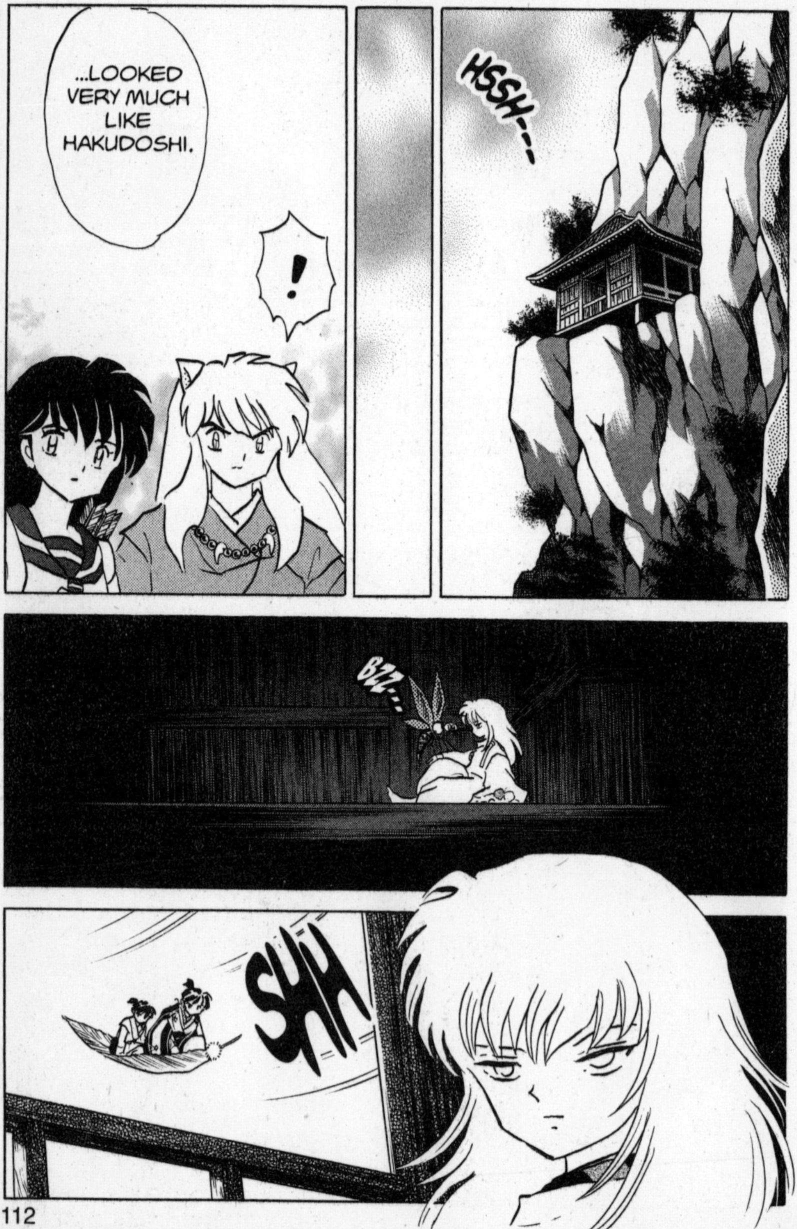

...LOOKED VERY MUCH LIKE HAKUDOSHI.
!
HSSH---
BZZ---
SHH

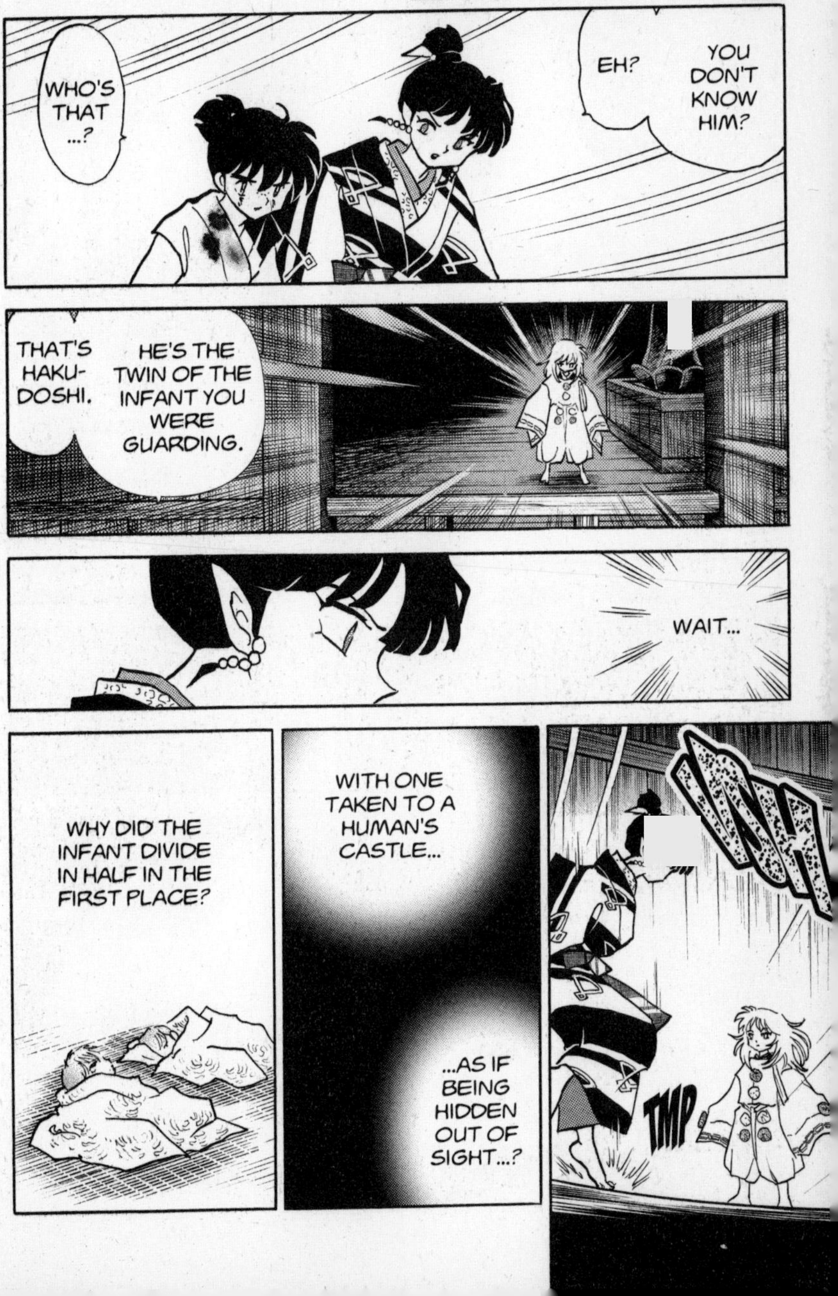
WHO'S THAT ...?
EH?
YOU DON'T KNOW HIM?
THAT'S HAKU-DOSHI.
HE'S THE TWIN OF THE INFANT YOU WERE GUARDING.
WAIT...
WHY DID THE INFANT DIVIDE IN HALF IN THE FIRST PLACE?
WITH ONE TAKEN TO A HUMAN'S CASTLE...
...AS IF BEING HIDDEN OUT OF SIGHT...?
TMP

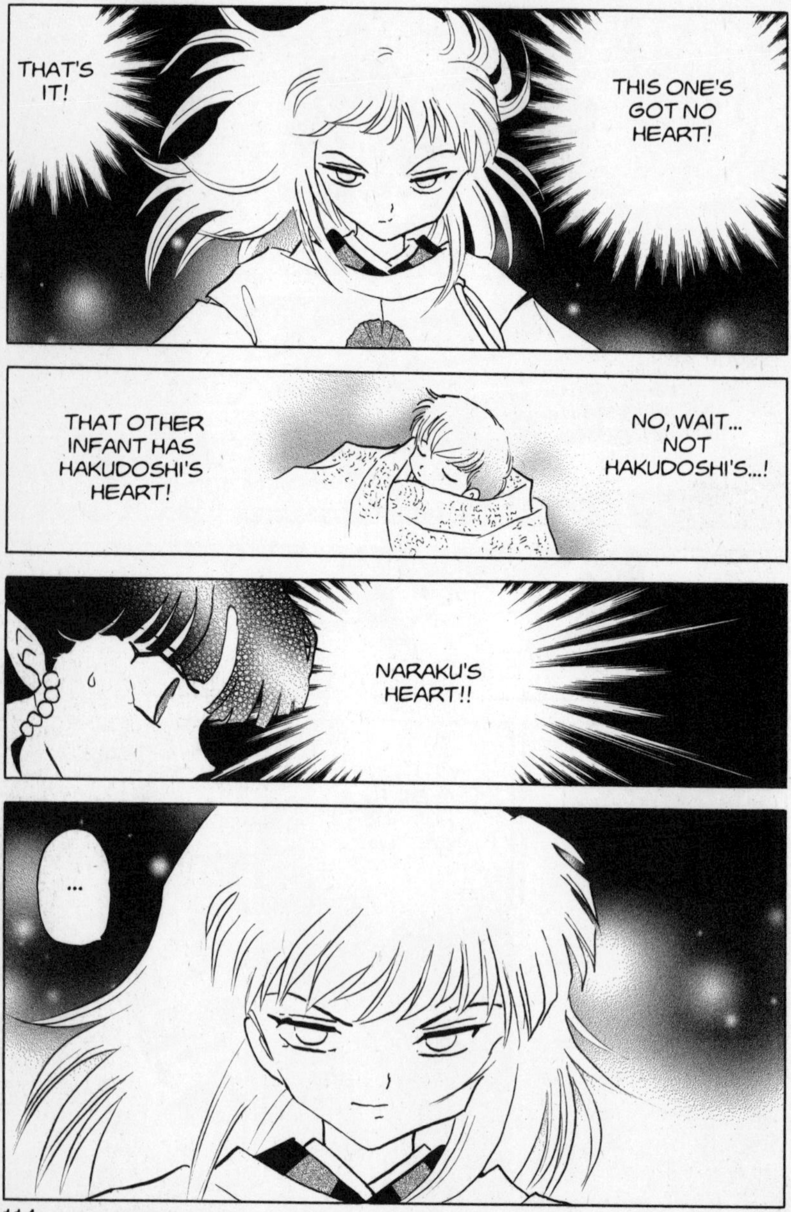
THAT'S IT!
THIS ONE'S GOT NO HEART!
THAT OTHER INFANT HAS HAKUDOSHI'S HEART!
NO, WAIT... NOT HAKUDOSHI'S...!
NARAKU'S HEART!!
...

SCROLL 7

THE SCENT OF THE NEST

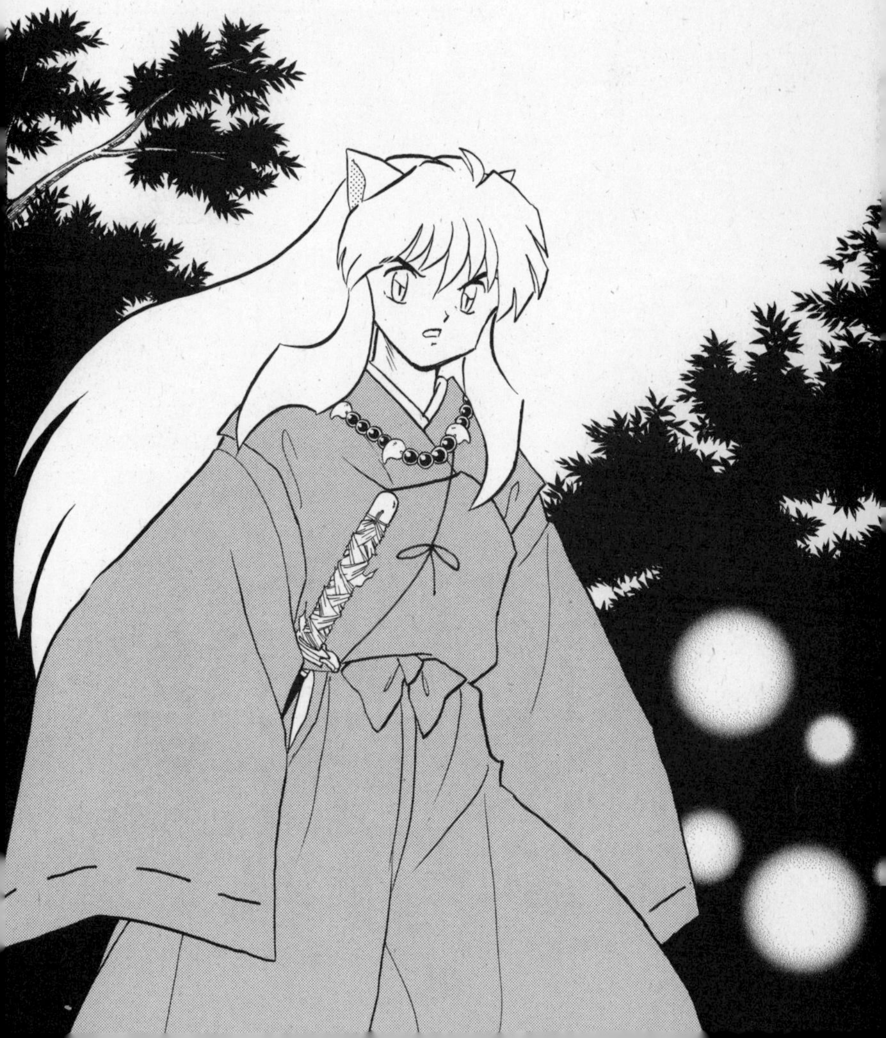

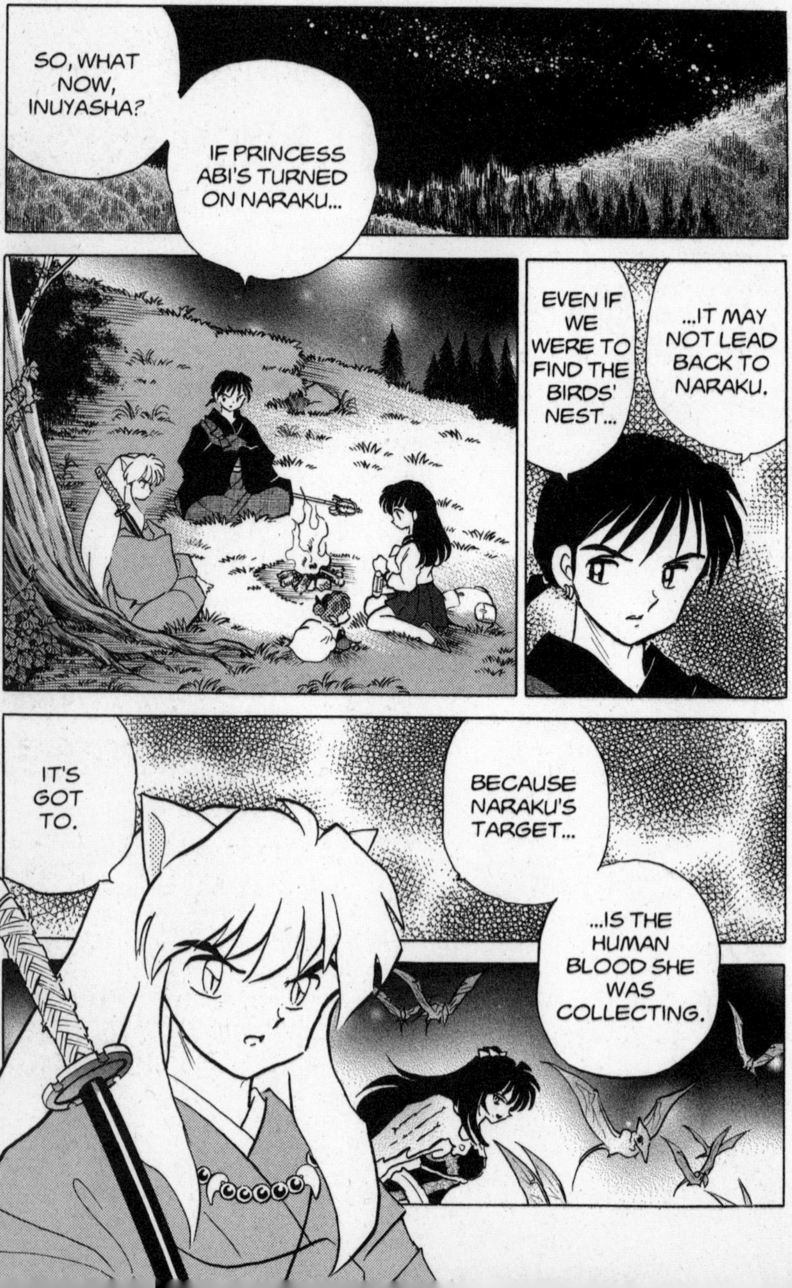
SO, WHAT NOW, INUYASHA?
IF PRINCESS ABI'S TURNED ON NARAKU...
EVEN IF WE WERE TO FIND THE BIRDS' NEST...
...IT MAY NOT LEAD BACK TO NARAKU.
IT'S GOT TO.
BECAUSE NARAKU'S TARGET...
...IS THE HUMAN BLOOD SHE WAS COLLECTING.

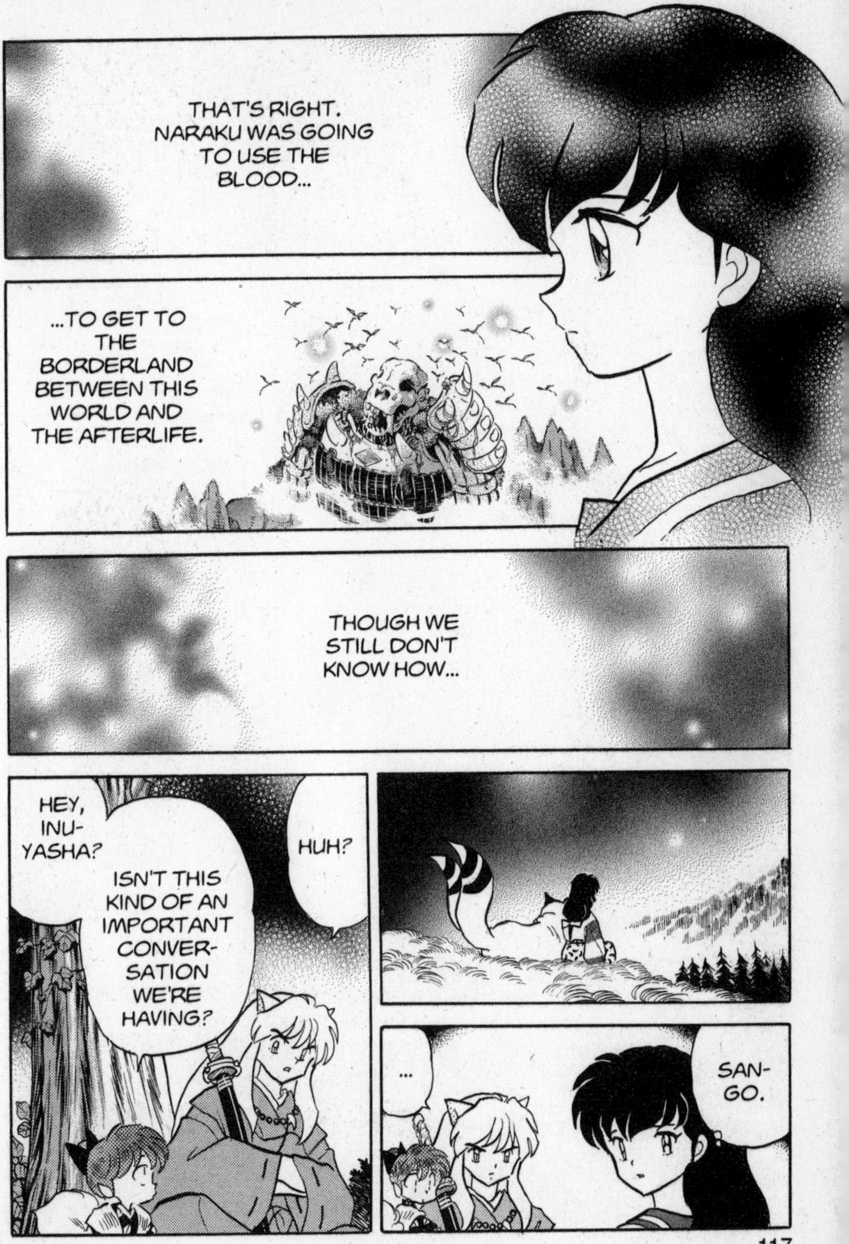
THAT'S RIGHT. NARAKU WAS GOING TO USE THE BLOOD...
...TO GET TO THE BORDERLAND BETWEEN THIS WORLD AND THE AFTERLIFE.
THOUGH WE STILL DON'T KNOW HOW...
HEY, INU-YASHA?
ISN'T THIS KIND OF AN IMPORTANT CONVER-SATION WE'RE HAVING?
HUH?
...
SAN-GO.

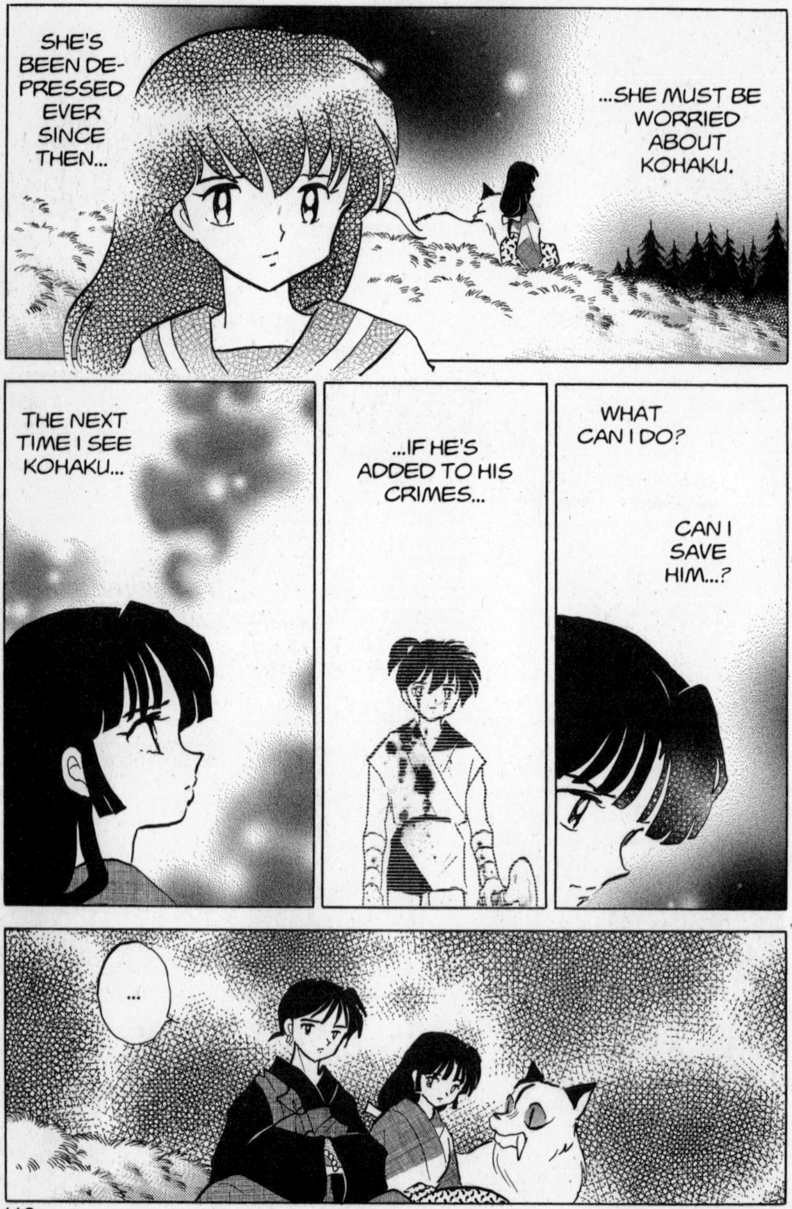
SHE'S BEEN DE-PRESSED EVER SINCE THEN...
...SHE MUST BE WORRIED ABOUT KOHAKU.
THE NEXT TIME I SEE KOHAKU...
...IF HE'S ADDED TO HIS CRIMES...
WHAT CAN I DO?
CAN I SAVE HIM...?
...

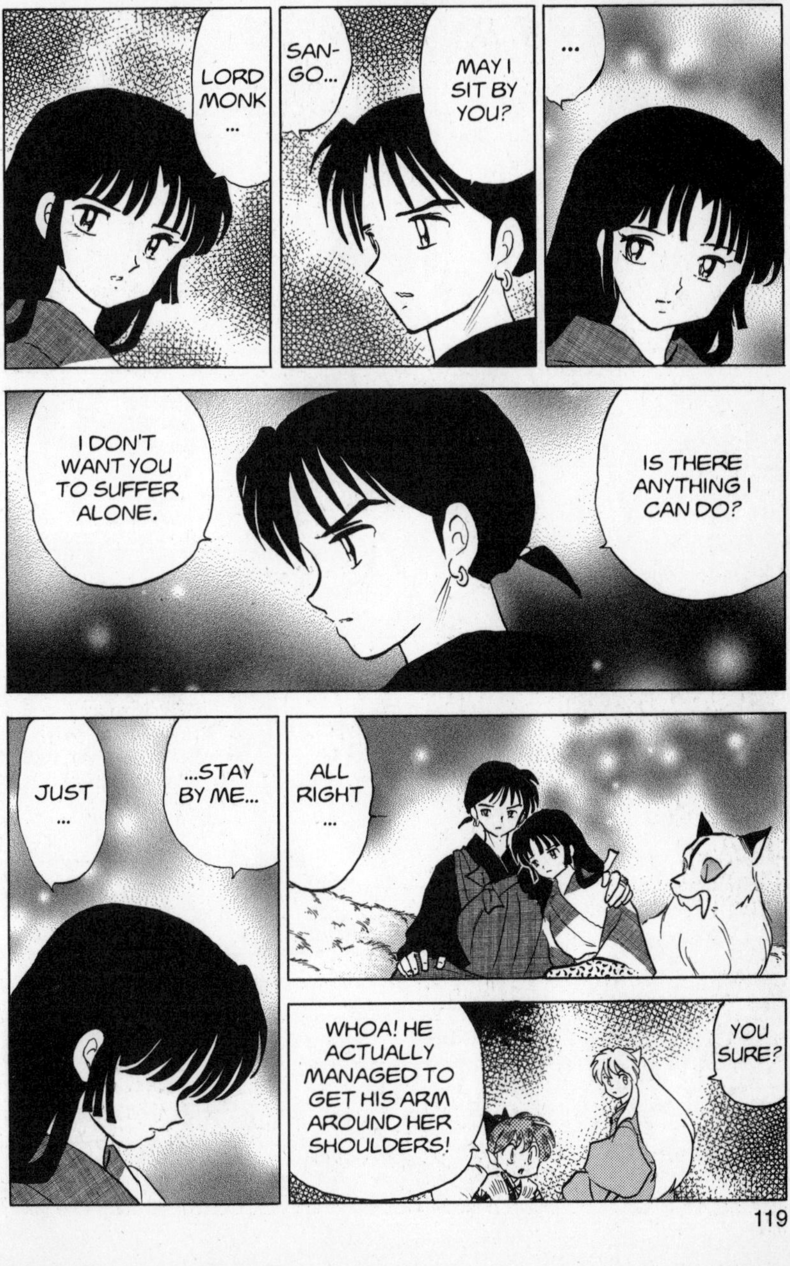
LORD MONK ...
SAN-GO...
MAY I SIT BY YOU?
...
I DON'T WANT YOU TO SUFFER ALONE.
IS THERE ANYTHING I CAN DO?
JUST ...
...STAY BY ME...
ALL RIGHT ...
WHOA! HE ACTUALLY MANAGED TO GET HIS ARM AROUND HER SHOULDERS!
YOU SURE?

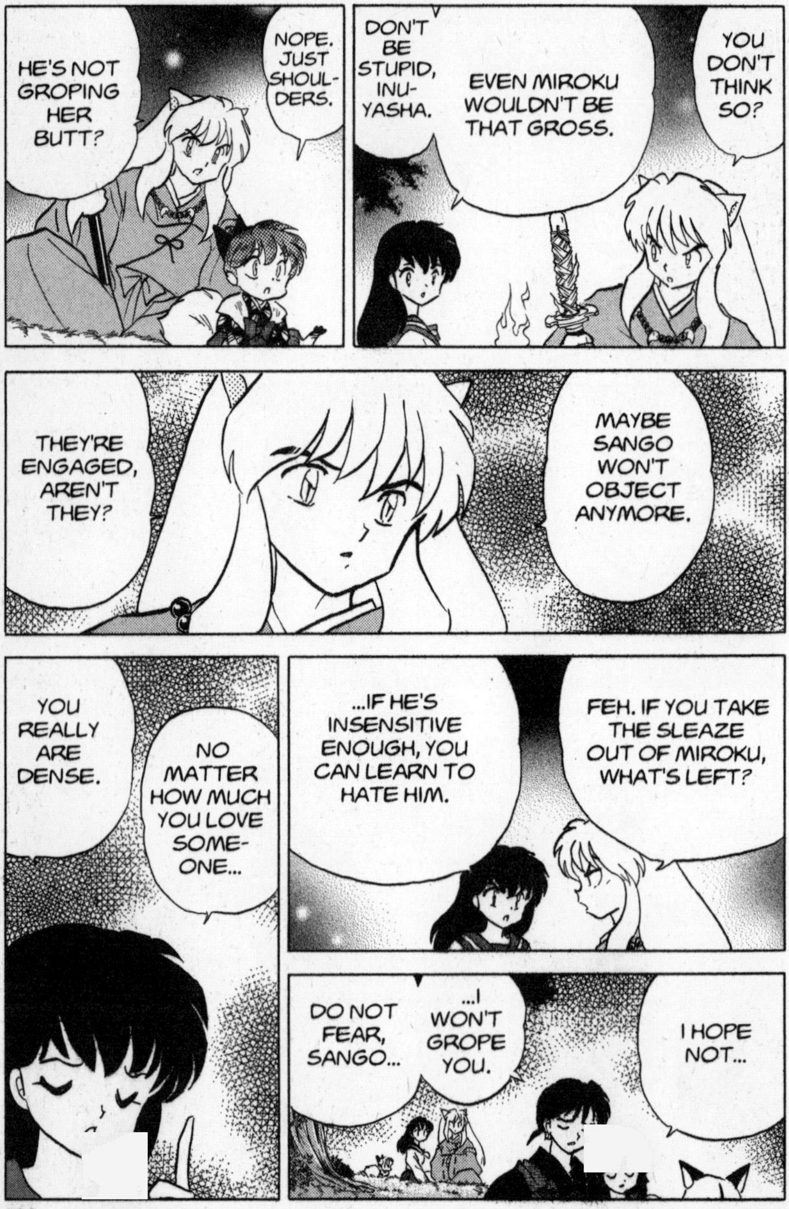
HE'S NOT GROPING HER BUTT?
NOPE. JUST SHOUL-DERS.
DON'T BE STUPID, INU-YASHA.
EVEN MIROKU WOULDN'T BE THAT GROSS.
YOU DON'T THINK SO?
THEY'RE ENGAGED, AREN'T THEY?
MAYBE SANGO WON'T OBJECT ANYMORE.
YOU REALLY ARE DENSE.
NO MATTER HOW MUCH YOU LOVE SOME-ONE...
...IF HE'S INSENSITIVE ENOUGH, YOU CAN LEARN TO HATE HIM.
FEH. IF YOU TAKE THE SLEAZE OUT OF MIROKU, WHAT'S LEFT?
DO NOT FEAR, SANGO...
...I WON'T GROPE YOU.
I HOPE NOT...

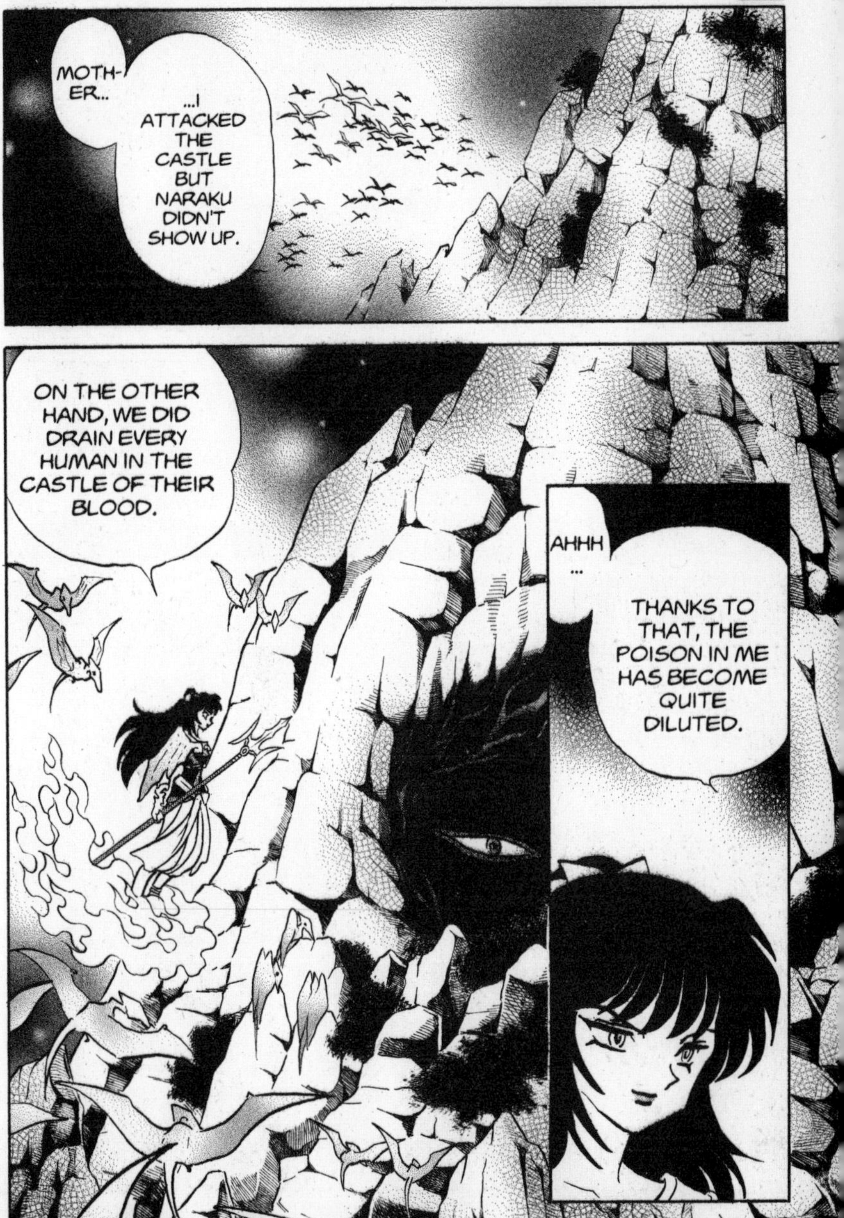
MOTHER...
...I ATTACKED THE CASTLE BUT NARAKU DIDN'T SHOW UP.
ON THE OTHER HAND, WE DID DRAIN EVERY HUMAN IN THE CASTLE OF THEIR BLOOD.
AHHH...
THANKS TO THAT, THE POISON IN ME HAS BECOME QUITE DILUTED.

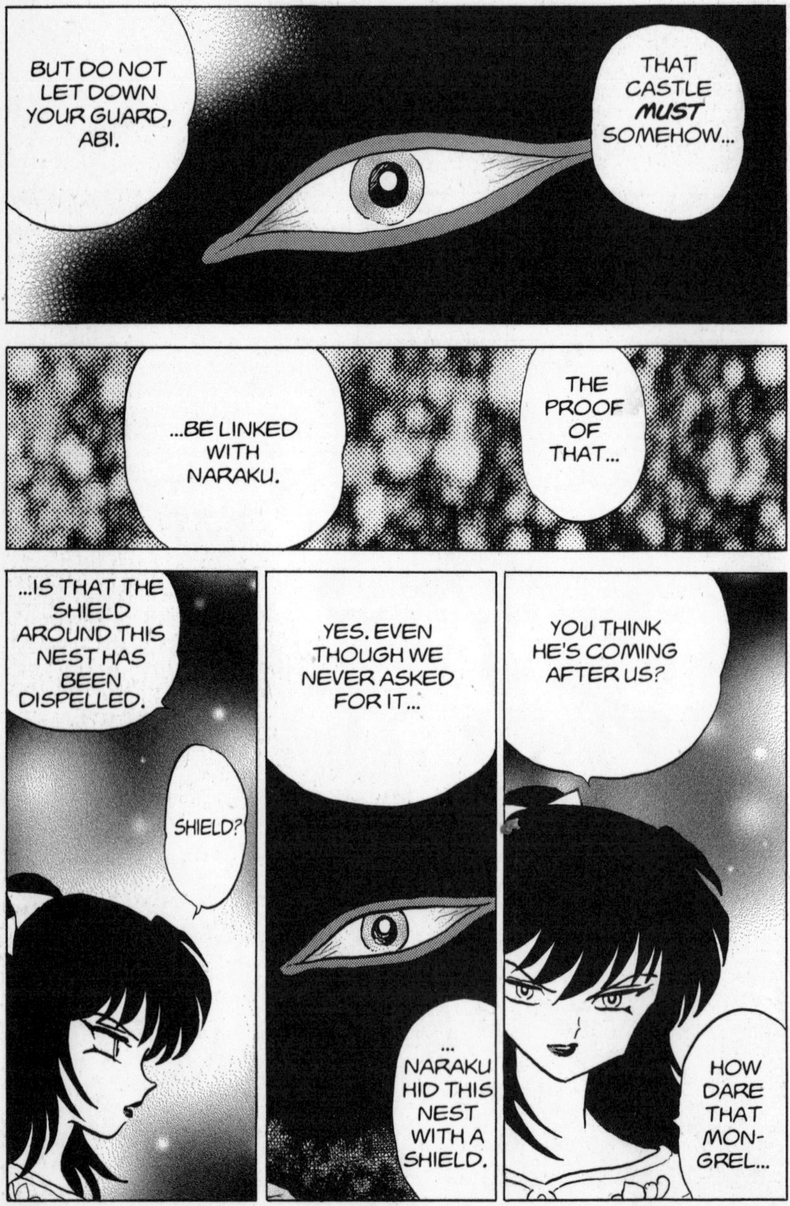
BUT DO NOT LET DOWN YOUR GUARD, ABI.
THAT CASTLE **MUST** SOMEHOW...
...BE LINKED WITH NARAKU.
THE PROOF OF THAT...
...IS THAT THE SHIELD AROUND THIS NEST HAS BEEN DISPELLED.
SHIELD?
YES. EVEN THOUGH WE NEVER ASKED FOR IT...
... NARAKU HID THIS NEST WITH A SHIELD.
YOU THINK HE'S COMING AFTER US?
HOW DARE THAT MON-GREL...

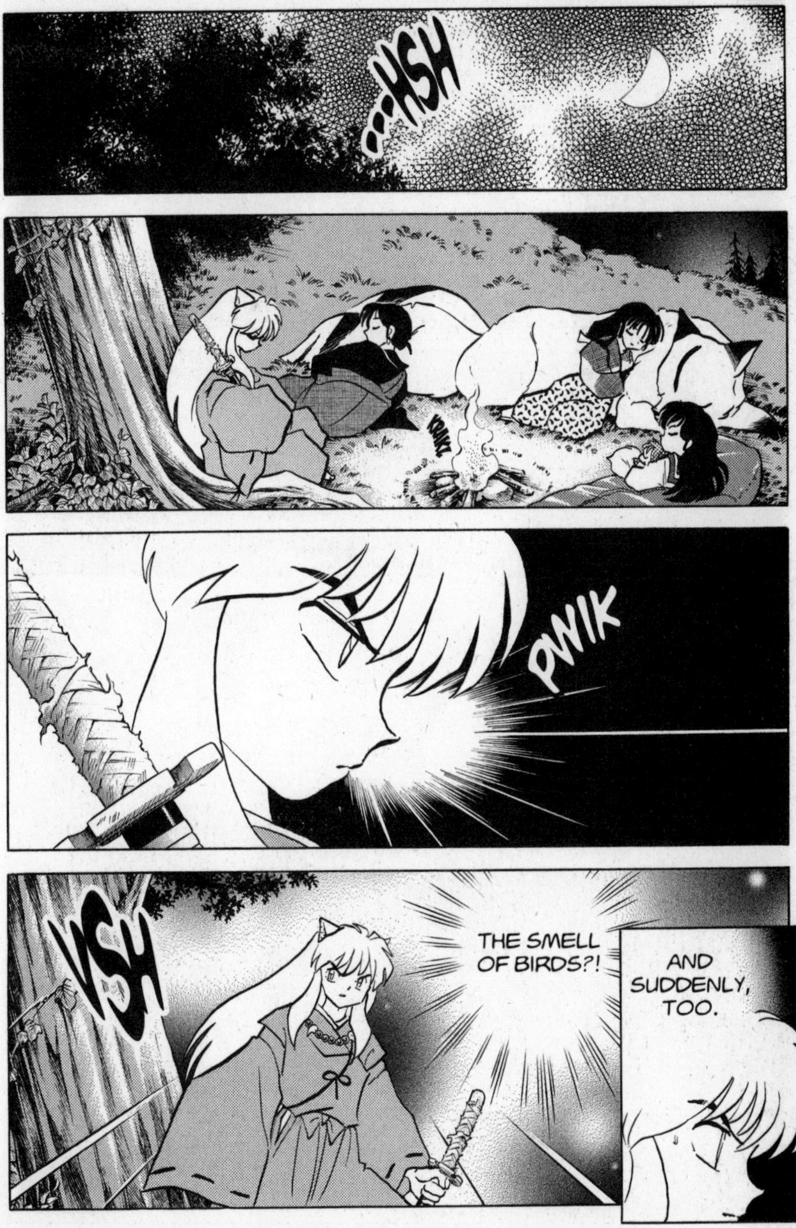
...HSH
PWIK
VSH
THE SMELL OF BIRDS?!
AND SUDDENLY, TOO.

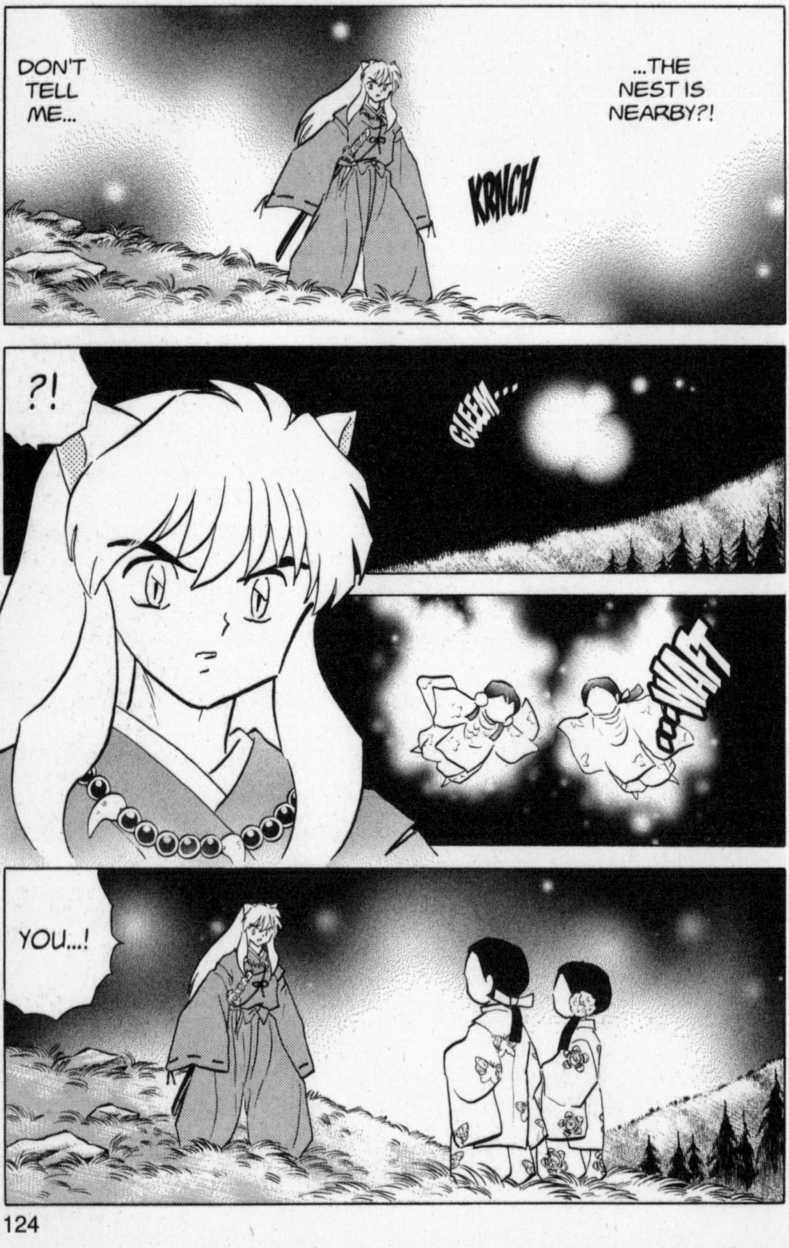
DON'T TELL ME...
...THE NEST IS NEARBY?!
KRNCH
?!
GLEEM...
WAFT
YOU...!

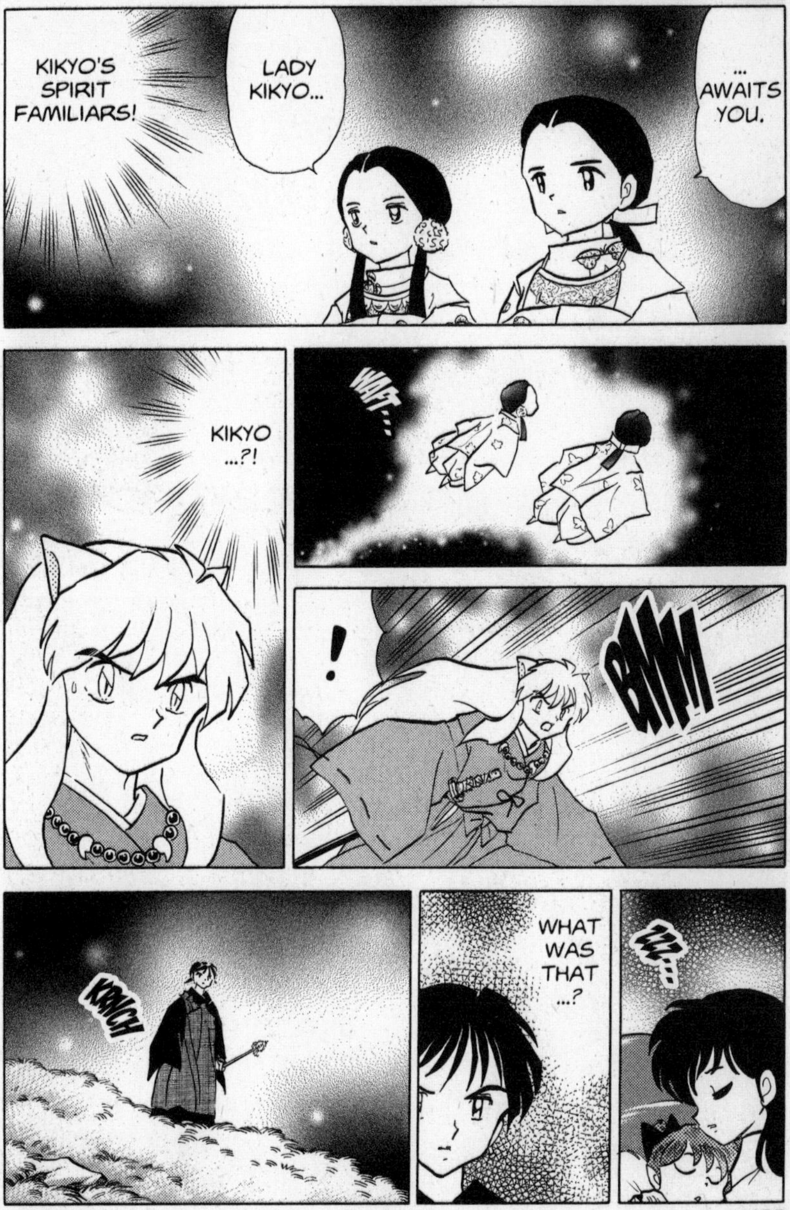
KIKYO'S SPIRIT FAMILIARS!
LADY KIKYO...
... AWAITS YOU.
KIKYO ...?!
WAIT...
!
BMM!
KRNCH
WHAT WAS THAT ...?
ZZZ...

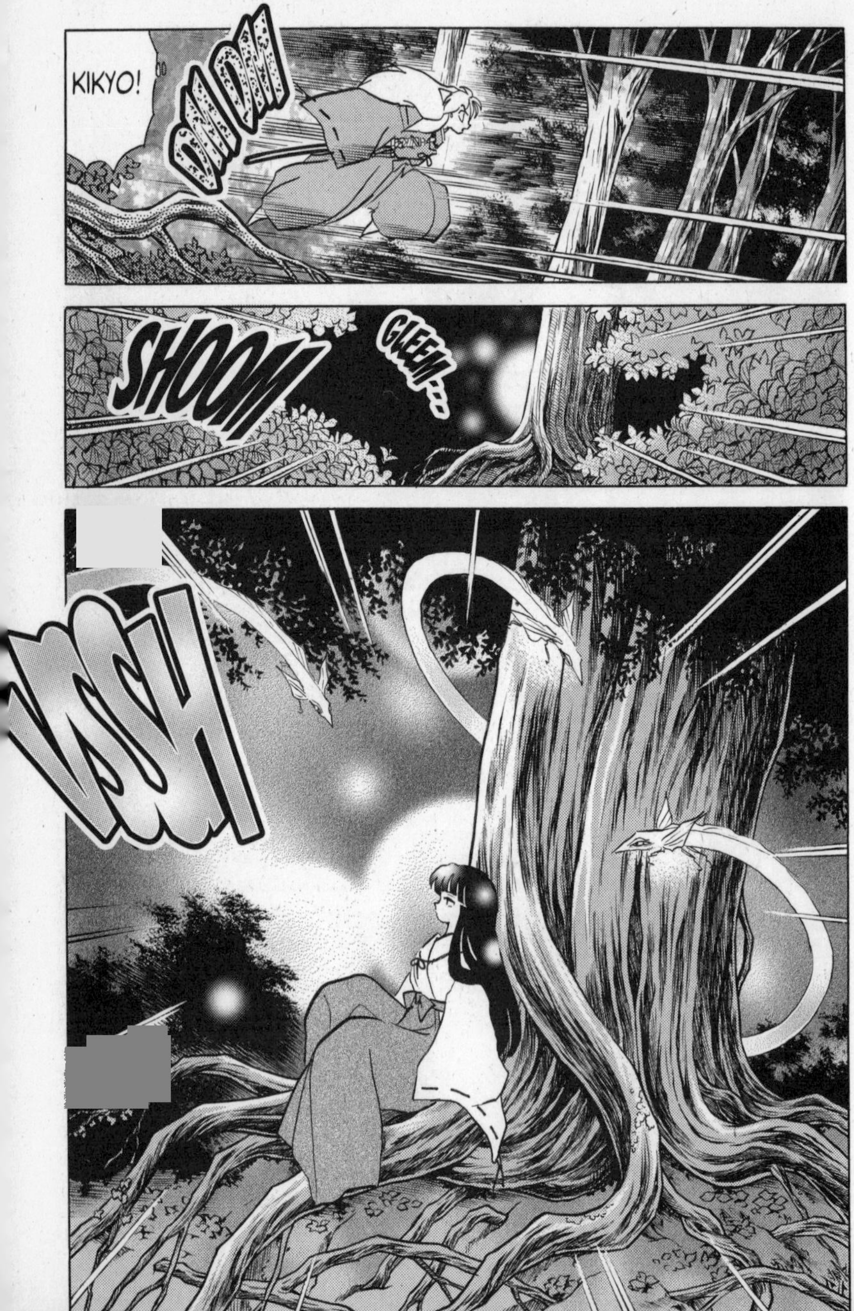
KIKYO!
SHOOM
GLEEM...
VSSH

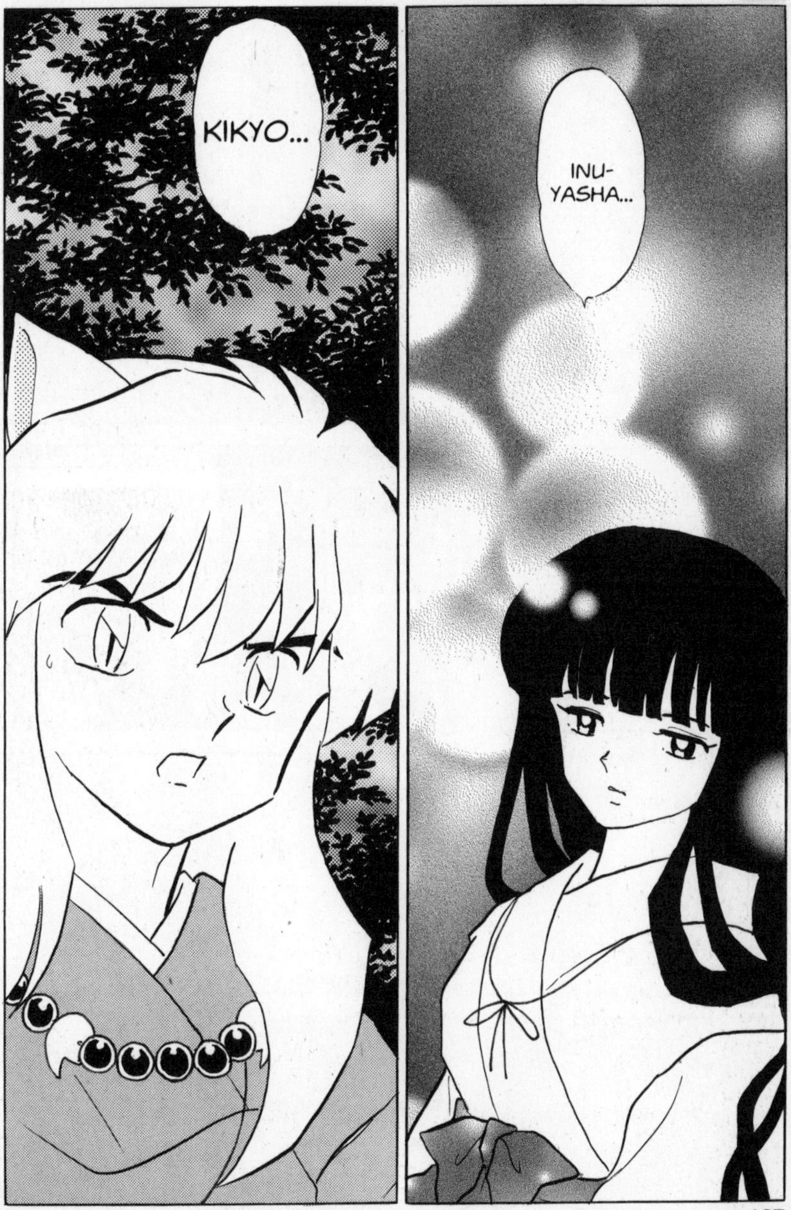
KIKYO...
INU-YASHA...

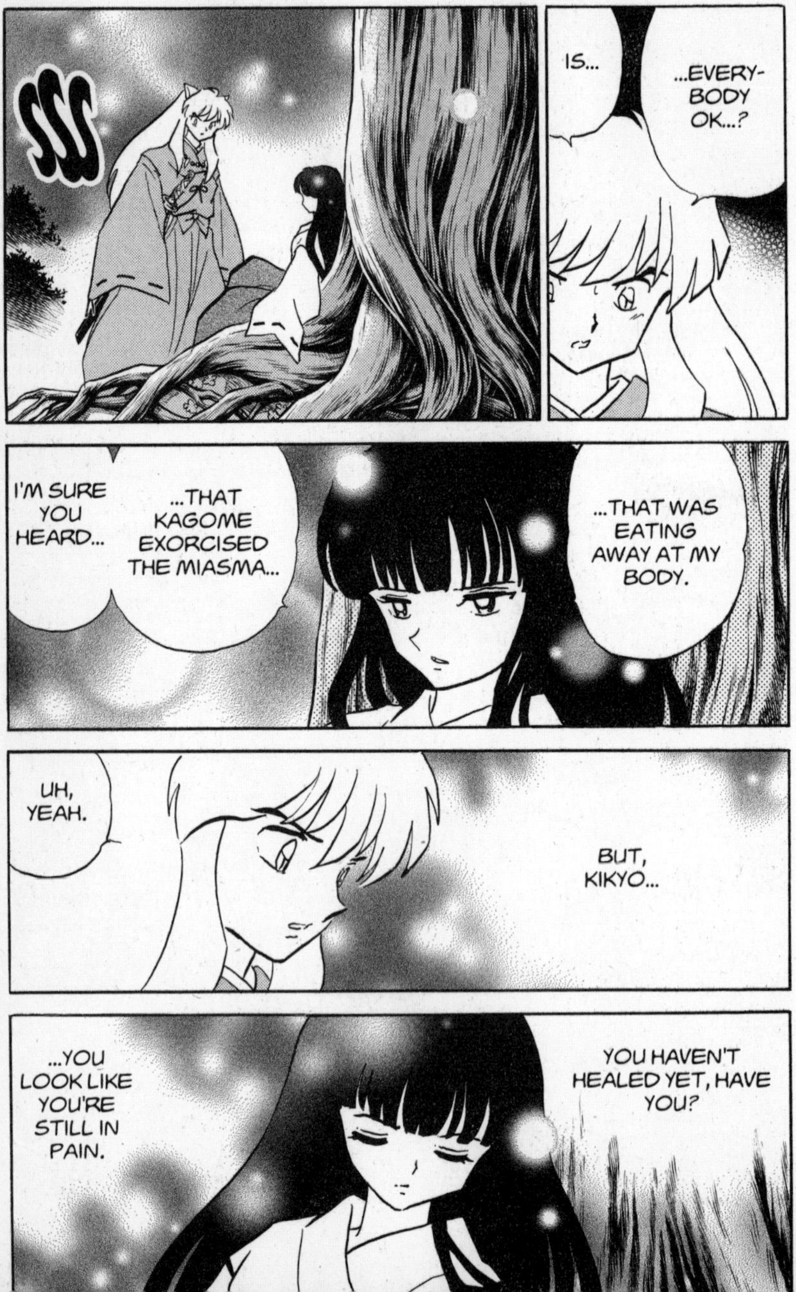
SSS
IS...
...EVERY-BODY OK...?
I'M SURE YOU HEARD...
...THAT KAGOME EXORCISED THE MIASMA...
...THAT WAS EATING AWAY AT MY BODY.
UH, YEAH.
BUT, KIKYO...
...YOU LOOK LIKE YOU'RE STILL IN PAIN.
YOU HAVEN'T HEALED YET, HAVE YOU?

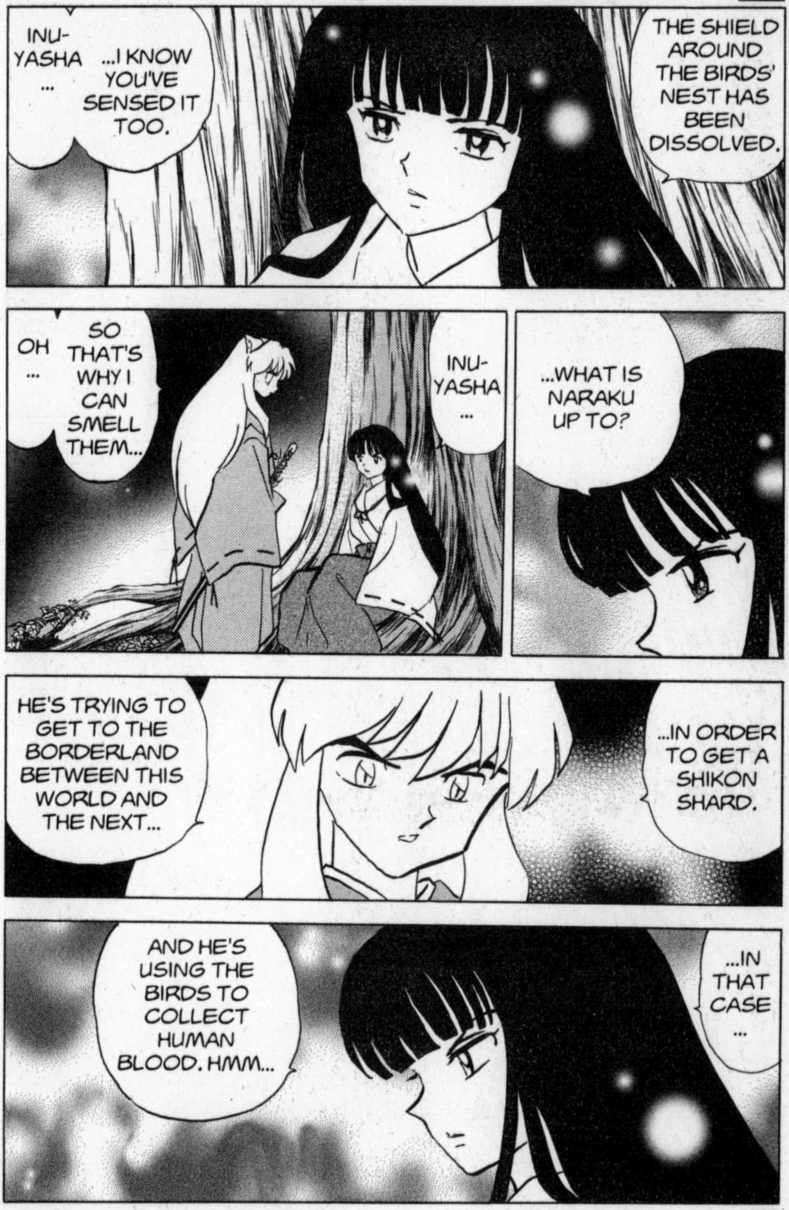
INU-YASHA ...
...I KNOW YOU'VE SENSED IT TOO.
THE SHIELD AROUND THE BIRDS' NEST HAS BEEN DISSOLVED.
OH ...
SO THAT'S WHY I CAN SMELL THEM...
INU-YASHA ...
...WHAT IS NARAKU UP TO?
HE'S TRYING TO GET TO THE BORDERLAND BETWEEN THIS WORLD AND THE NEXT...
...IN ORDER TO GET A SHIKON SHARD.
AND HE'S USING THE BIRDS TO COLLECT HUMAN BLOOD. HMM...
...IN THAT CASE ...

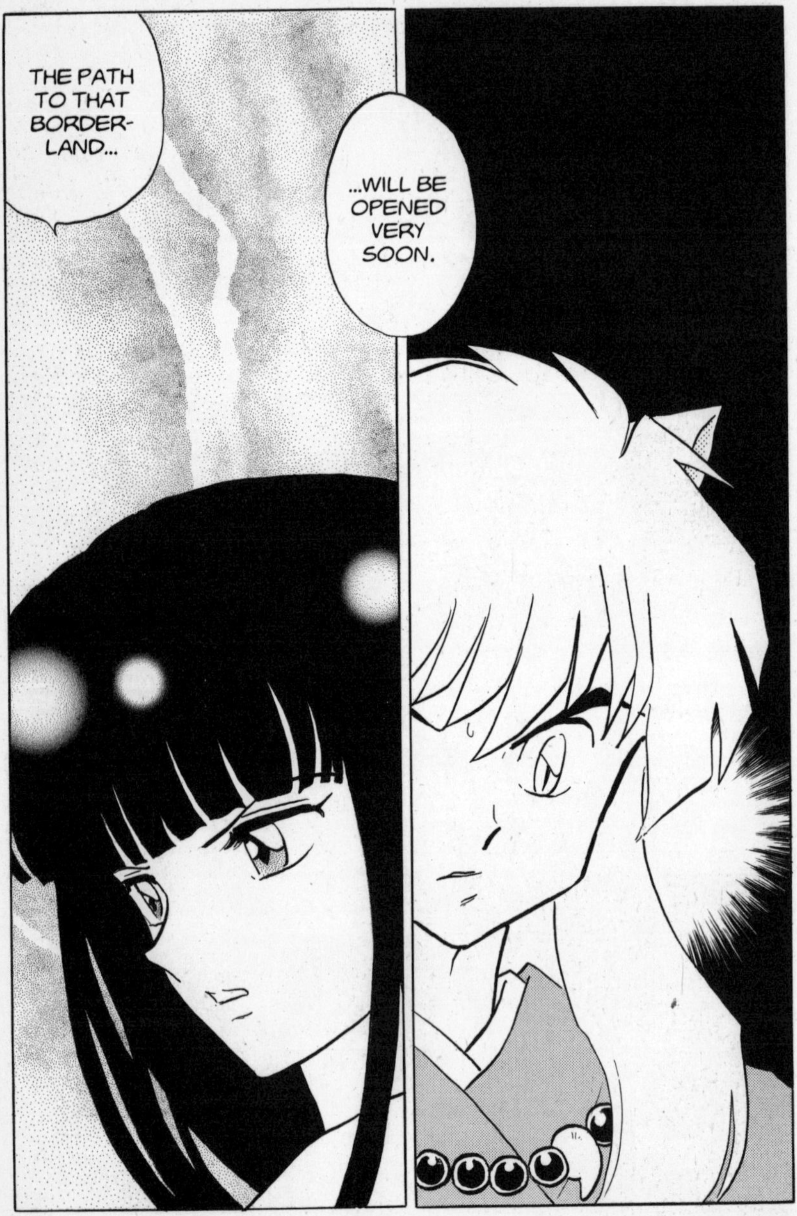
THE PATH TO THAT BORDER-LAND...
...WILL BE OPENED VERY SOON.

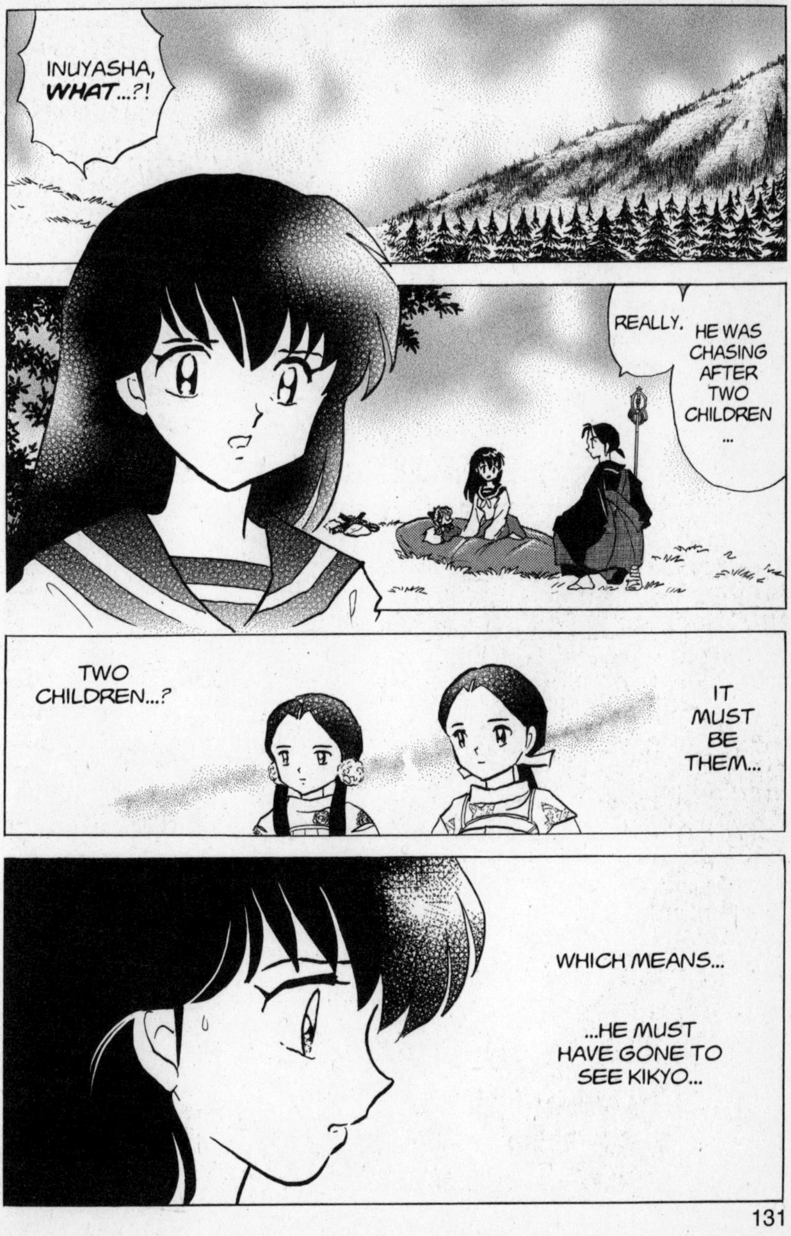
INUYASHA, **WHAT**...?!
REALLY.
HE WAS CHASING AFTER TWO CHILDREN...
TWO CHILDREN...?
IT MUST BE THEM...
WHICH MEANS...
...HE MUST HAVE GONE TO SEE KIKYO...

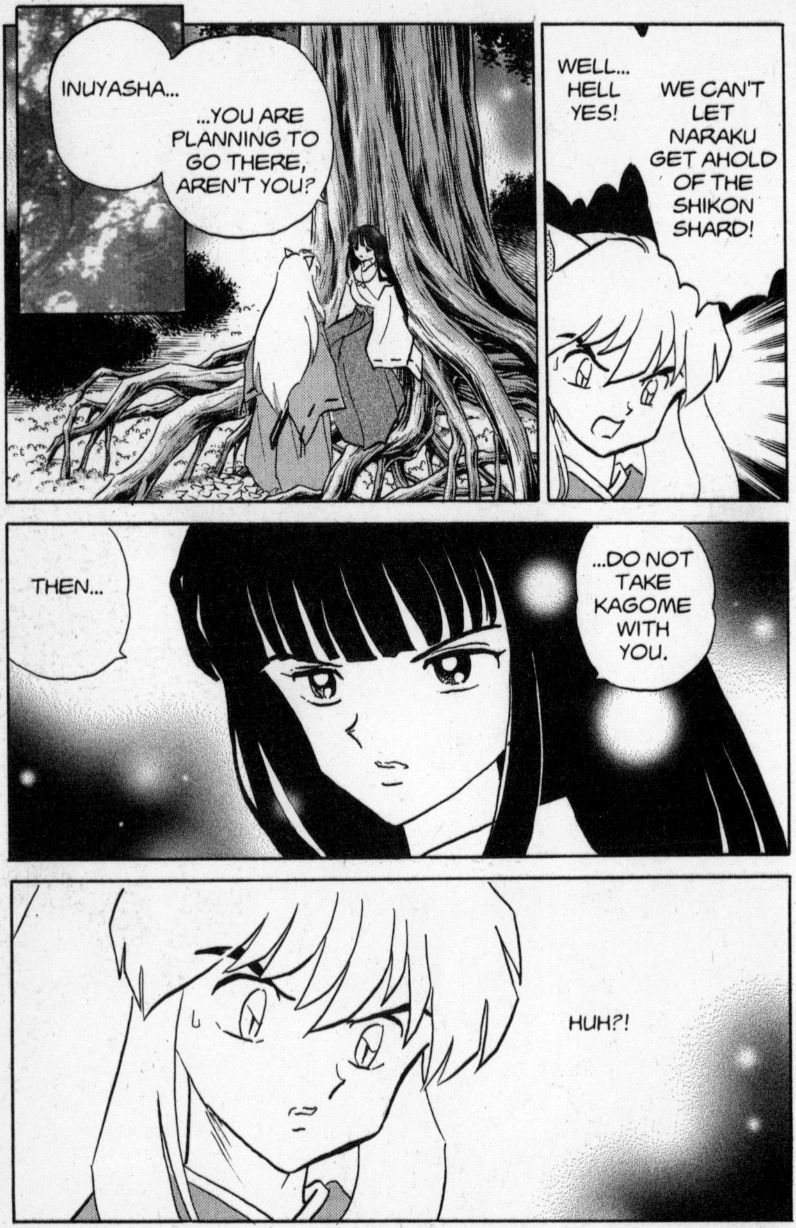
INUYASHA...
...YOU ARE PLANNING TO GO THERE, AREN'T YOU?
WELL... HELL YES!
WE CAN'T LET NARAKU GET AHOLD OF THE SHIKON SHARD!
THEN...
...DO NOT TAKE KAGOME WITH YOU.
HUH?!

SCROLL 8
THE ARROW PASSES ON

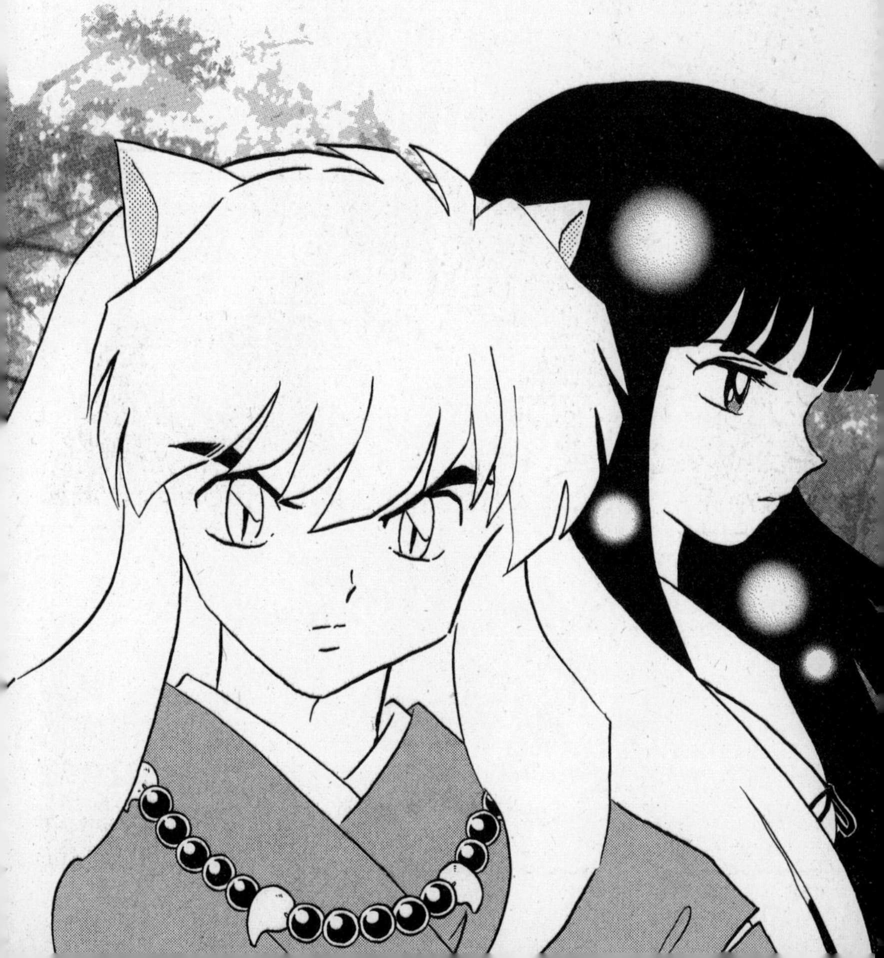

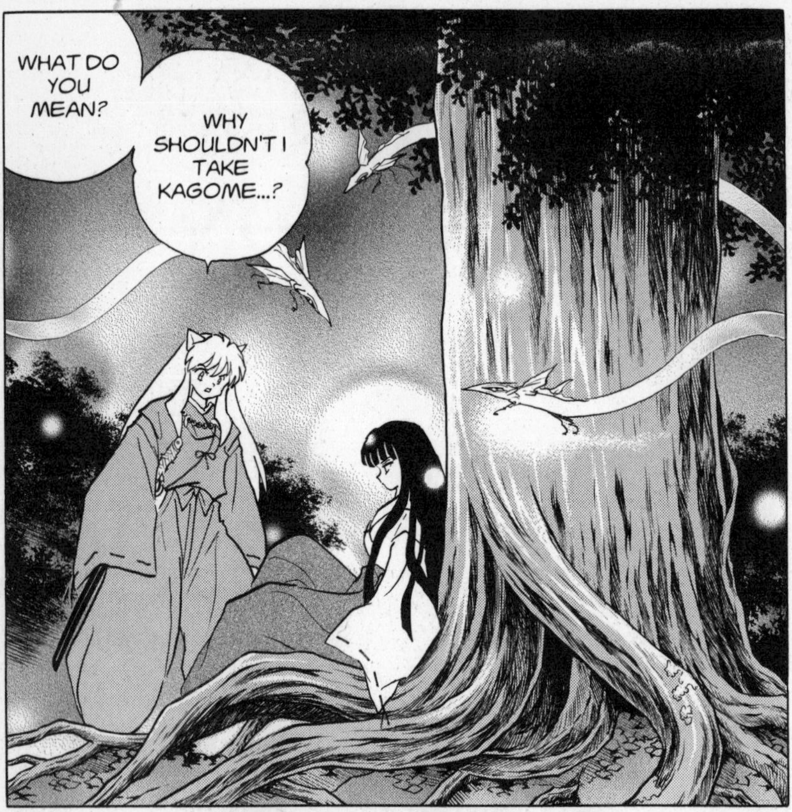
WHAT DO YOU MEAN?
WHY SHOULDN'T I TAKE KAGOME...?

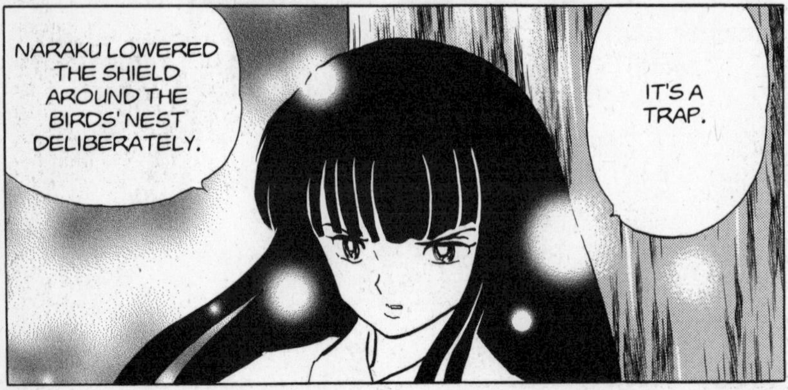
NARAKU LOWERED THE SHIELD AROUND THE BIRDS' NEST DELIBERATELY.
IT'S A TRAP.

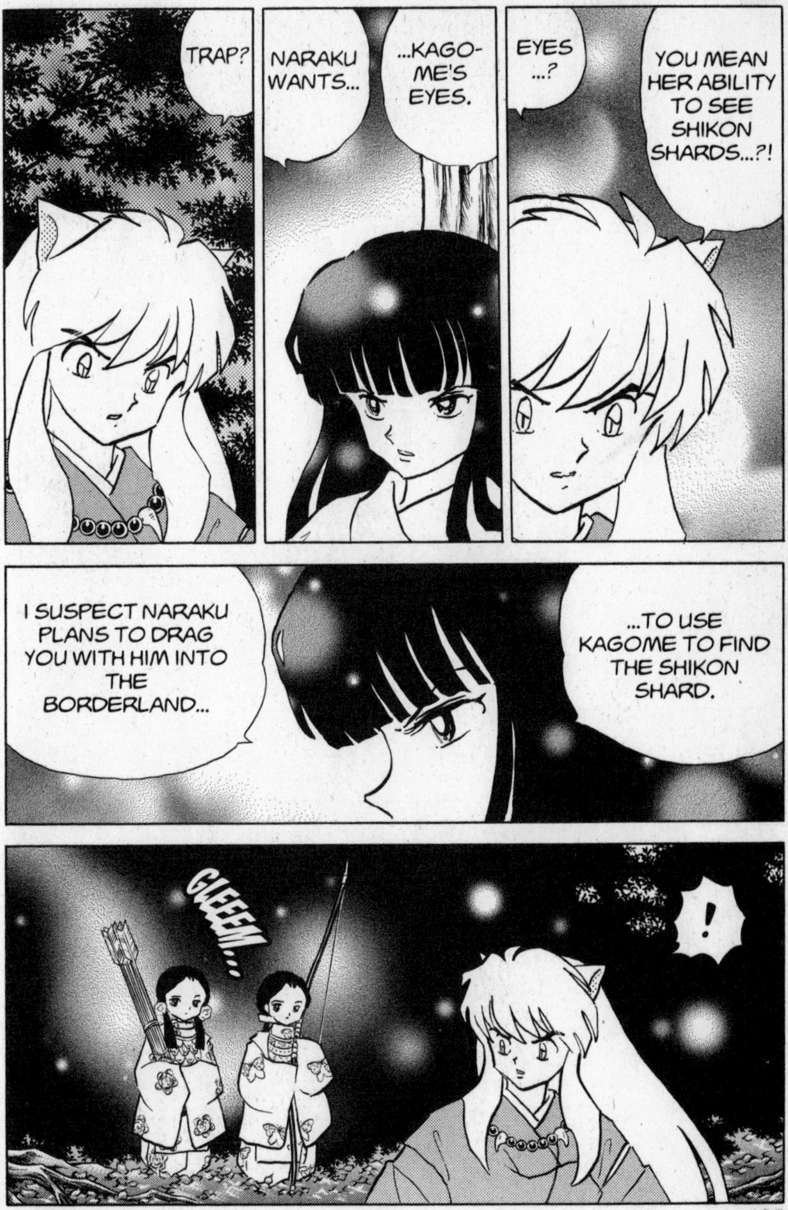
TRAP?
NARAKU WANTS...
...KAGO-ME'S EYES.
EYES ...?
YOU MEAN HER ABILITY TO SEE SHIKON SHARDS...?!
I SUSPECT NARAKU PLANS TO DRAG YOU WITH HIM INTO THE BORDERLAND...
...TO USE KAGOME TO FIND THE SHIKON SHARD.
GLEEEM...
!

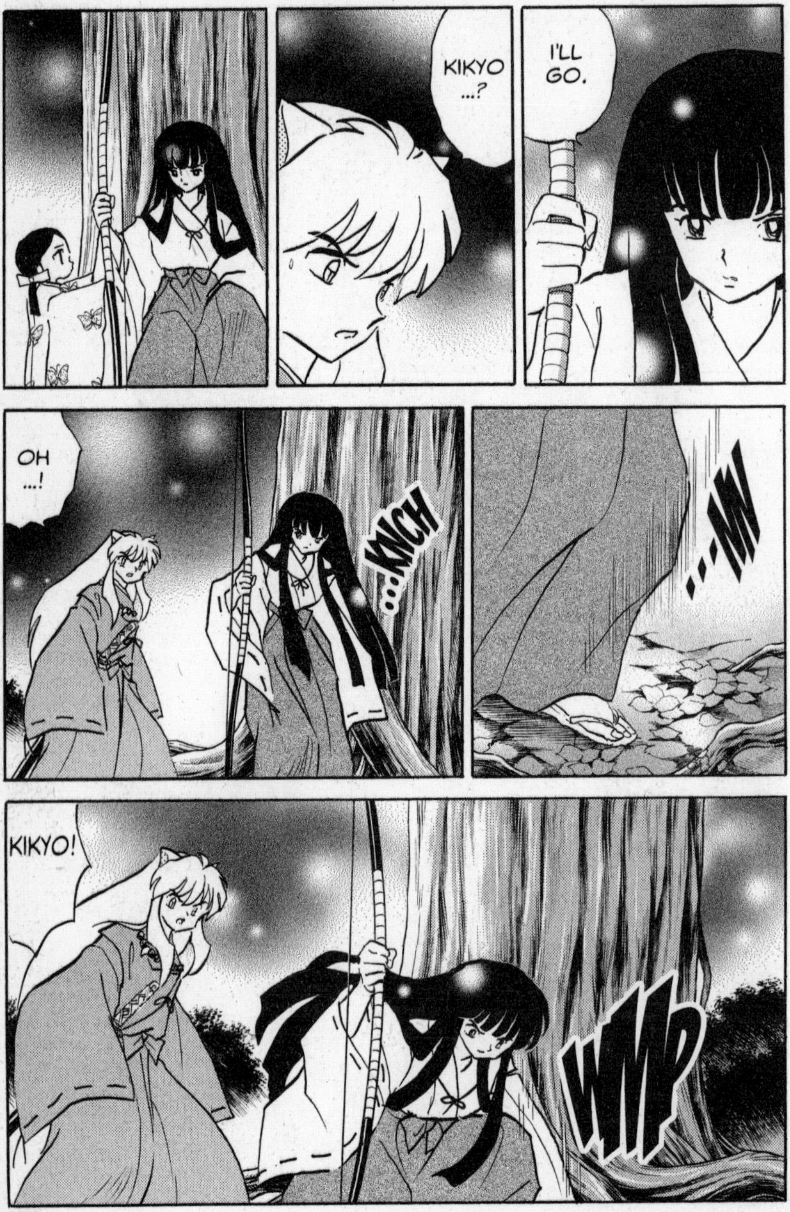
KIKYO ...?
I'LL GO.
OH ...!
...KNCH
...NN
KIKYO!
WMP

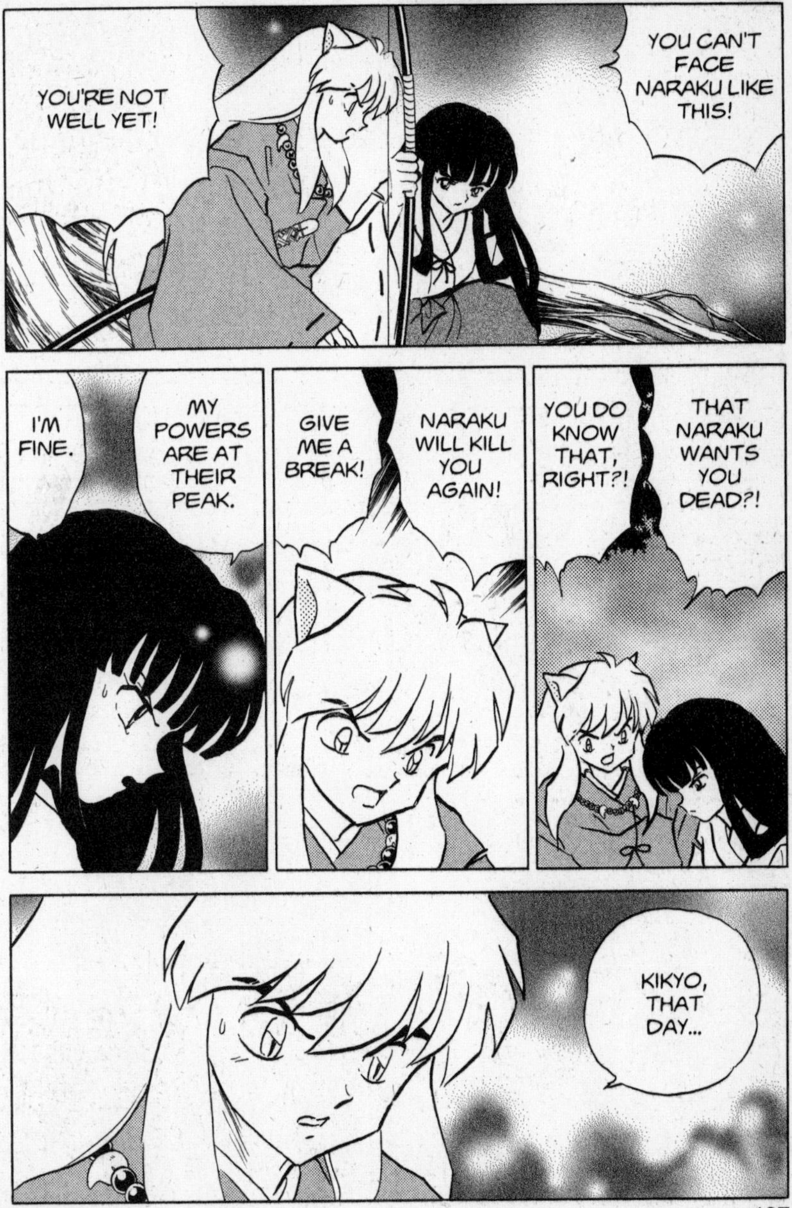
YOU'RE NOT WELL YET!
YOU CAN'T FACE NARAKU LIKE THIS!
I'M FINE.
MY POWERS ARE AT THEIR PEAK.
GIVE ME A BREAK!
NARAKU WILL KILL YOU AGAIN!
YOU DO KNOW THAT, RIGHT?!
THAT NARAKU WANTS YOU DEAD?!
KIKYO, THAT DAY...

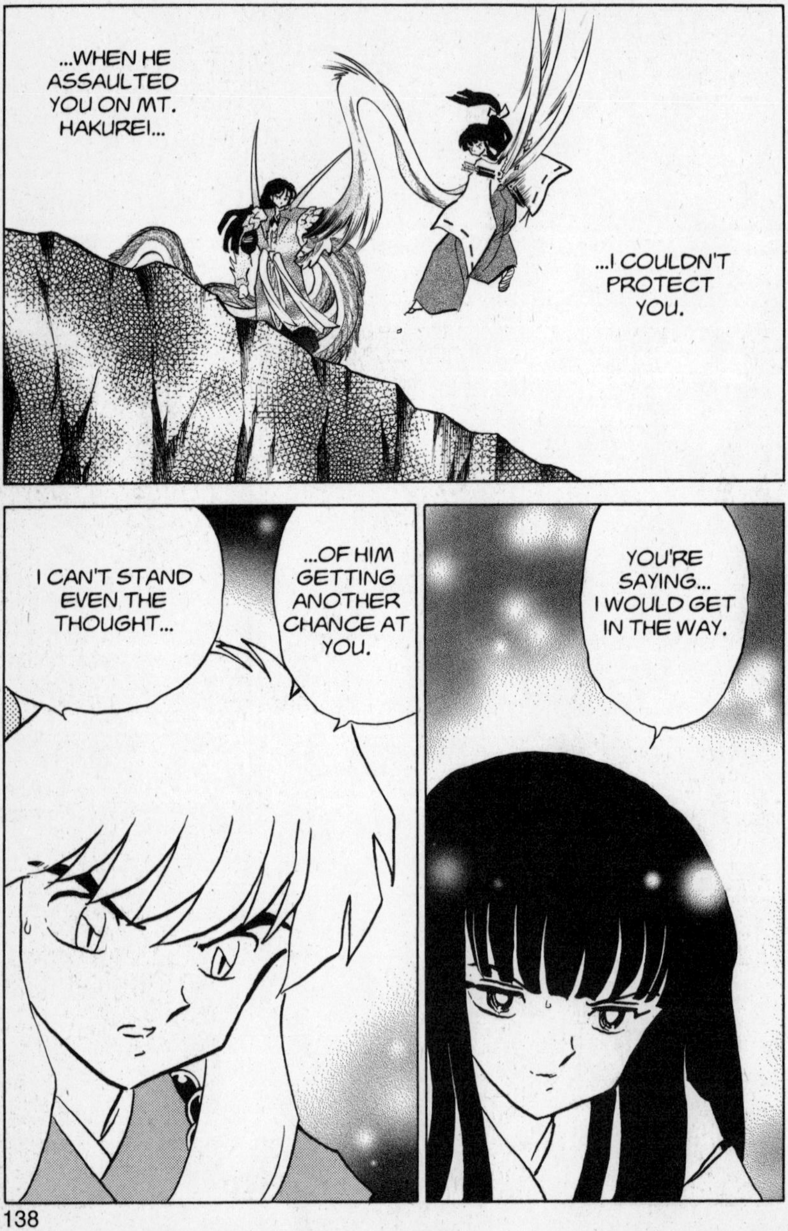
...WHEN HE ASSAULTED YOU ON MT. HAKUREI...
...I COULDN'T PROTECT YOU.
I CAN'T STAND EVEN THE THOUGHT...
...OF HIM GETTING ANOTHER CHANCE AT YOU.
YOU'RE SAYING... I WOULD GET IN THE WAY.

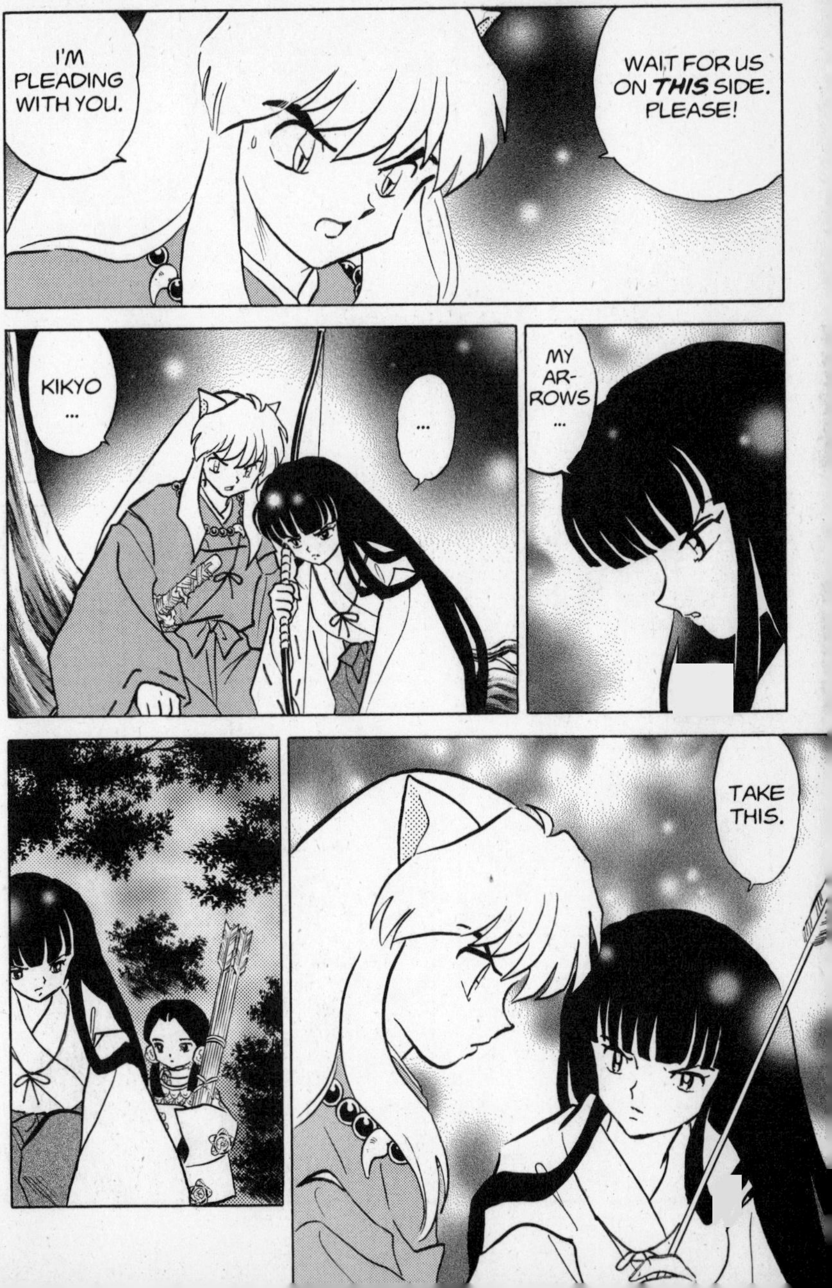
I'M PLEADING WITH YOU.
WAIT FOR US ON **THIS** SIDE. PLEASE!
KIKYO ...
...
MY AR-ROWS ...
TAKE THIS.

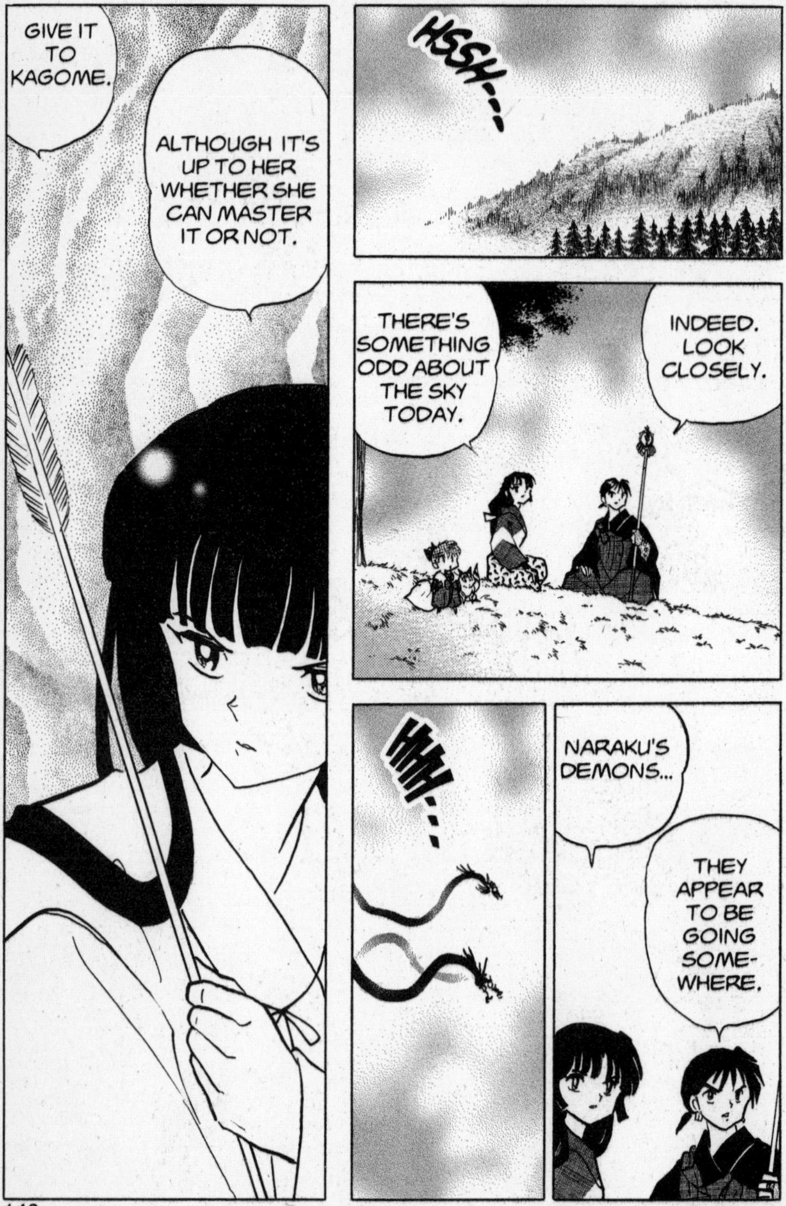
GIVE IT TO KAGOME.
ALTHOUGH IT'S UP TO HER WHETHER SHE CAN MASTER IT OR NOT.
HSSH...
THERE'S SOMETHING ODD ABOUT THE SKY TODAY.
INDEED. LOOK CLOSELY.
HHH...
NARAKU'S DEMONS...
THEY APPEAR TO BE GOING SOME-WHERE.

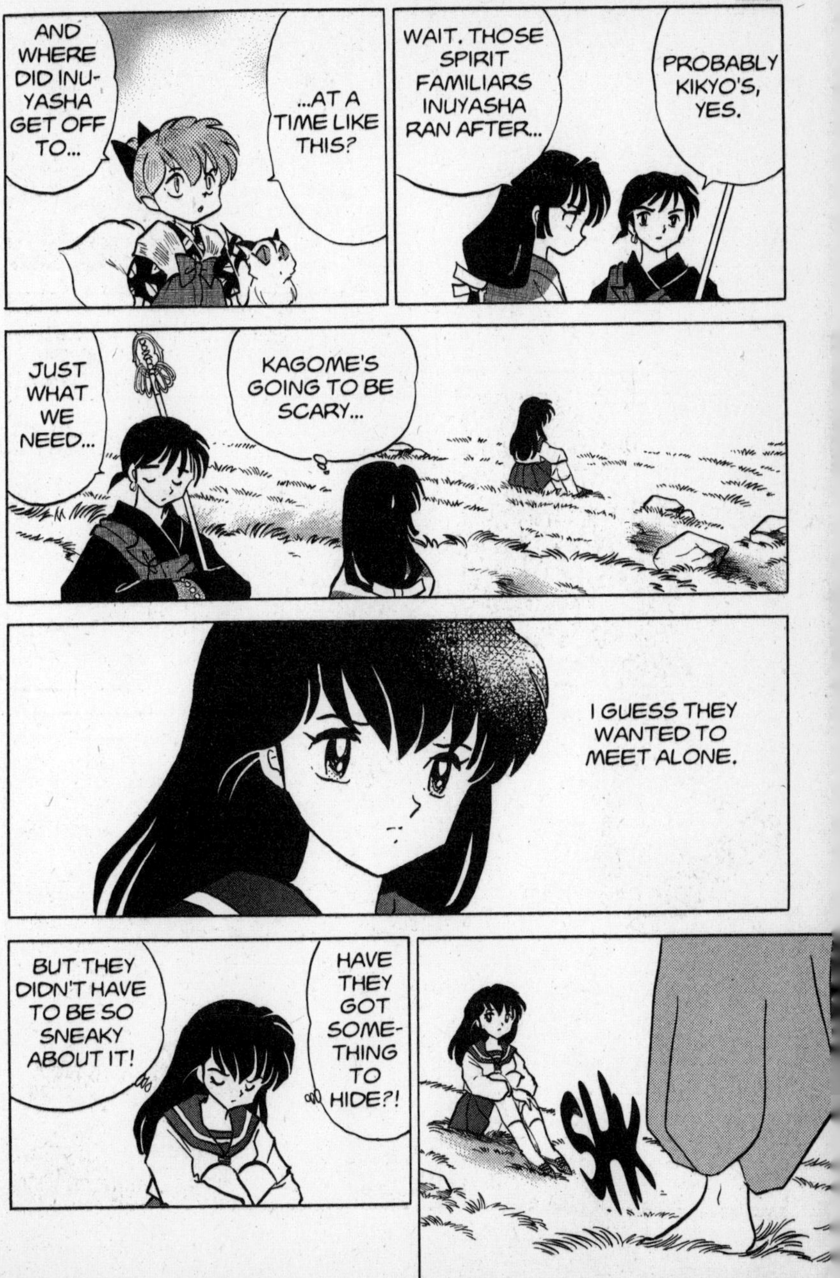
AND WHERE DID INU-YASHA GET OFF TO...
...AT A TIME LIKE THIS?
WAIT. THOSE SPIRIT FAMILIARS INUYASHA RAN AFTER...
PROBABLY KIKYO'S, YES.
JUST WHAT WE NEED...
KAGOME'S GOING TO BE SCARY...
I GUESS THEY WANTED TO MEET ALONE.
BUT THEY DIDN'T HAVE TO BE SO SNEAKY ABOUT IT!
HAVE THEY GOT SOMETHING TO HIDE?!
SHK

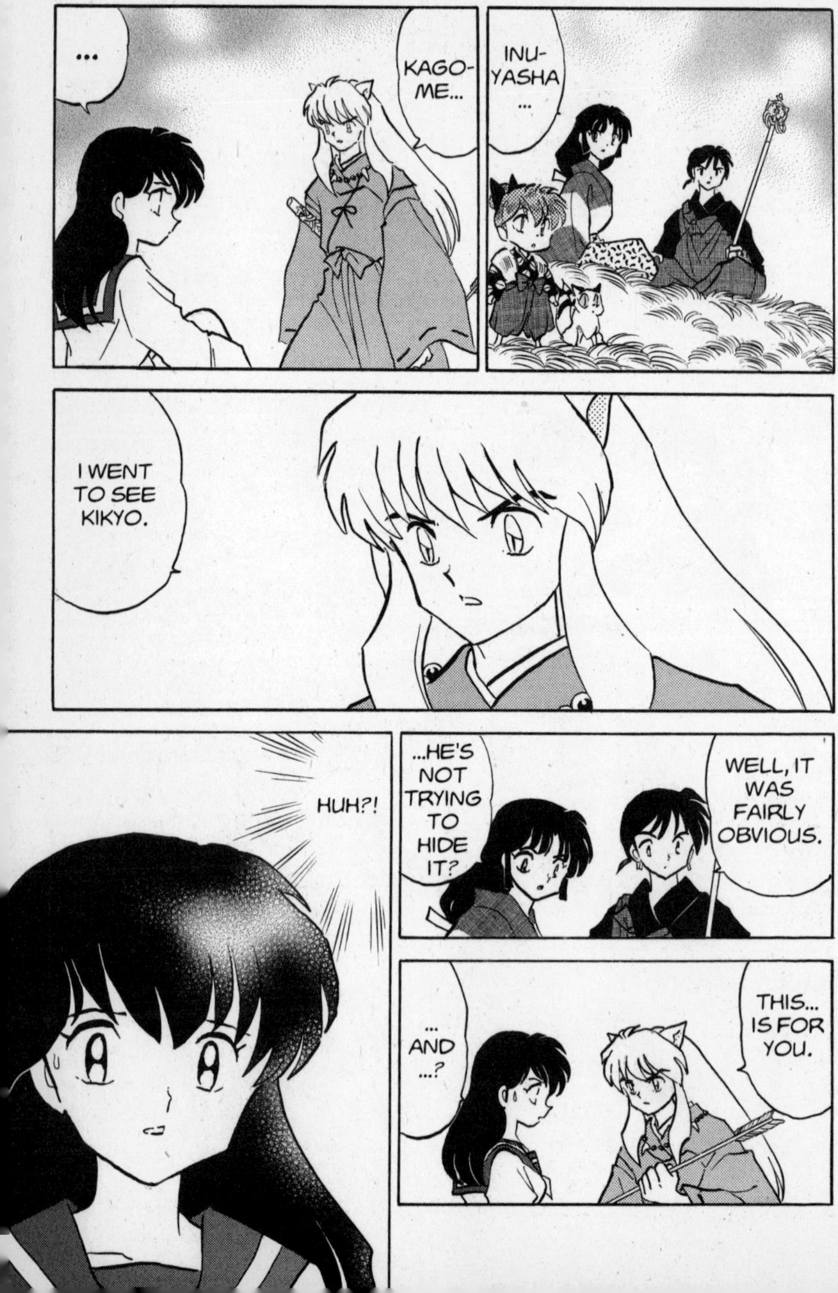
...
KAGO-ME...
INU-YASHA ...
I WENT TO SEE KIKYO.
HUH?!
...HE'S NOT TRYING TO HIDE IT?
WELL, IT WAS FAIRLY OBVIOUS.
... AND ...?
THIS... IS FOR YOU.

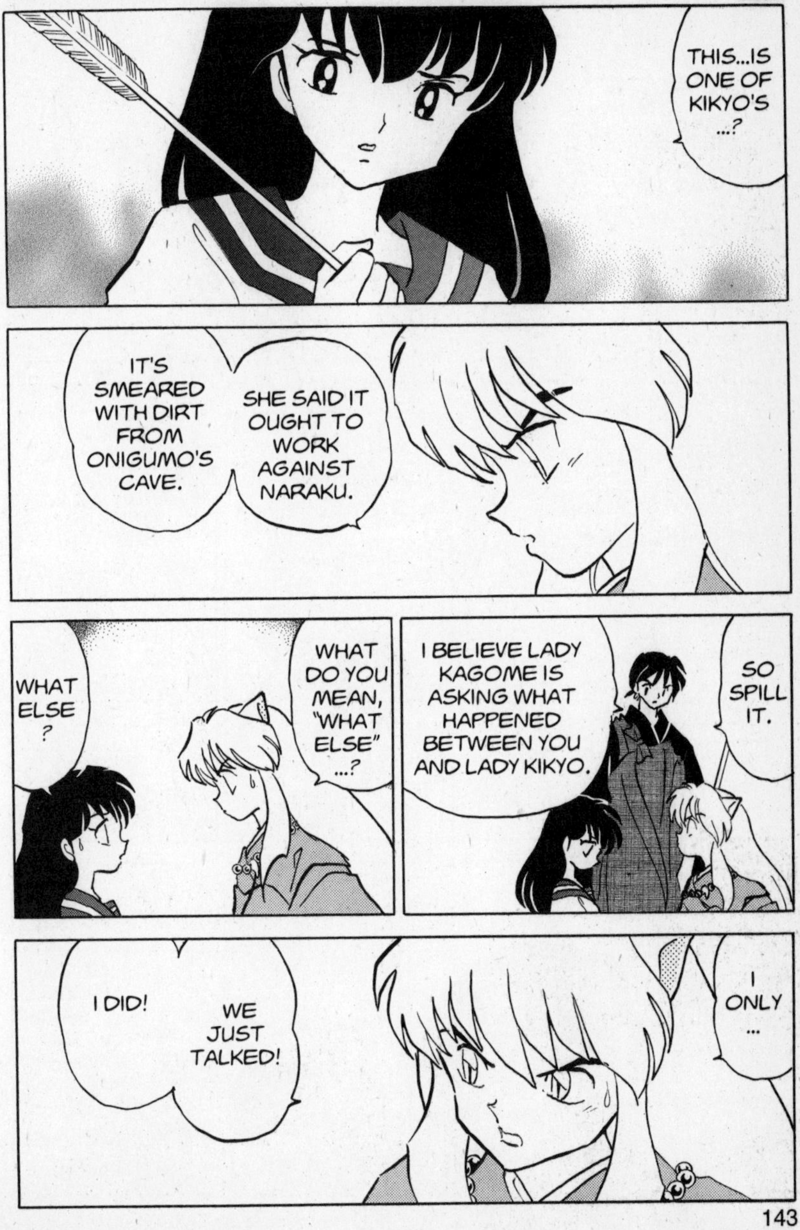
THIS...IS ONE OF KIKYO'S ...?
IT'S SMEARED WITH DIRT FROM ONIGUMO'S CAVE.
SHE SAID IT OUGHT TO WORK AGAINST NARAKU.
WHAT ELSE ?
WHAT DO YOU MEAN, "WHAT ELSE" ...?
I BELIEVE LADY KAGOME IS ASKING WHAT HAPPENED BETWEEN YOU AND LADY KIKYO.
SO SPILL IT.
I DID!
WE JUST TALKED!
I ONLY ...

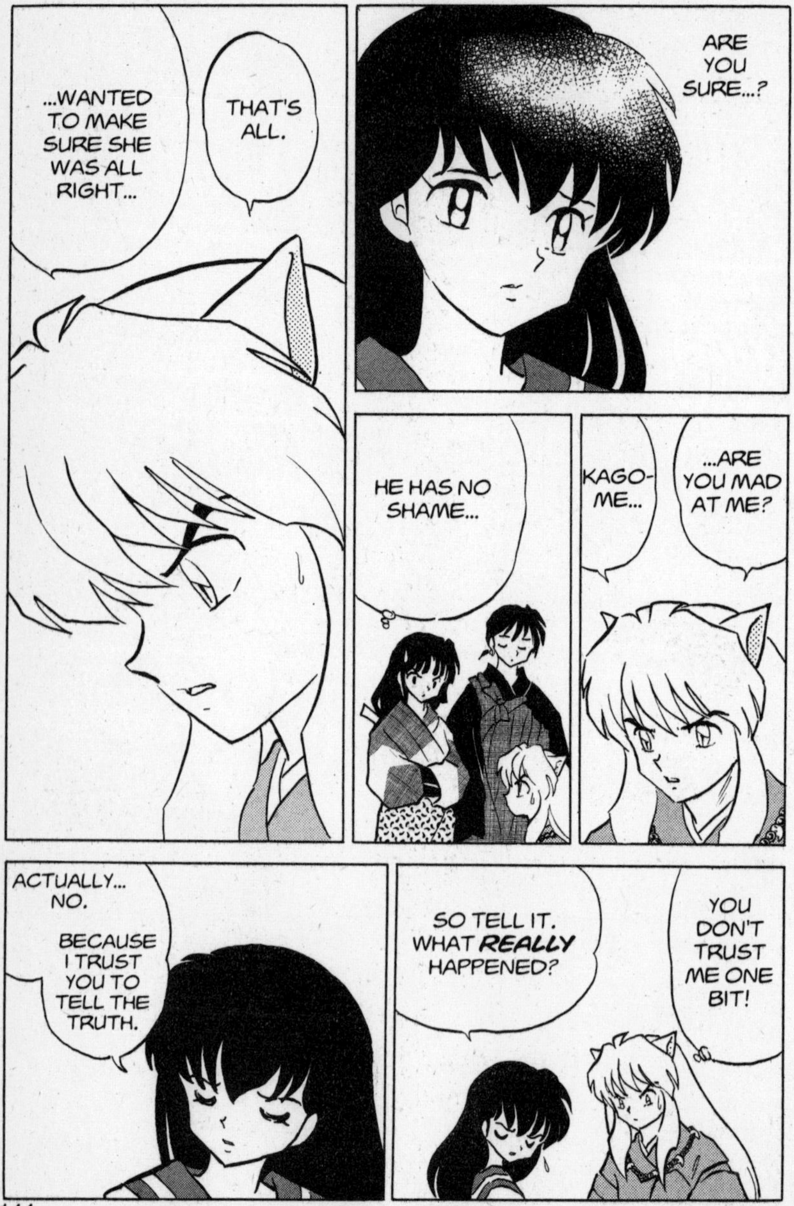
...WANTED TO MAKE SURE SHE WAS ALL RIGHT...
THAT'S ALL.
ARE YOU SURE...?
HE HAS NO SHAME...
KAGO-ME...
...ARE YOU MAD AT ME?
ACTUALLY... NO.
BECAUSE I TRUST YOU TO TELL THE TRUTH.
SO TELL IT. WHAT **REALLY** HAPPENED?
YOU DON'T TRUST ME ONE BIT!

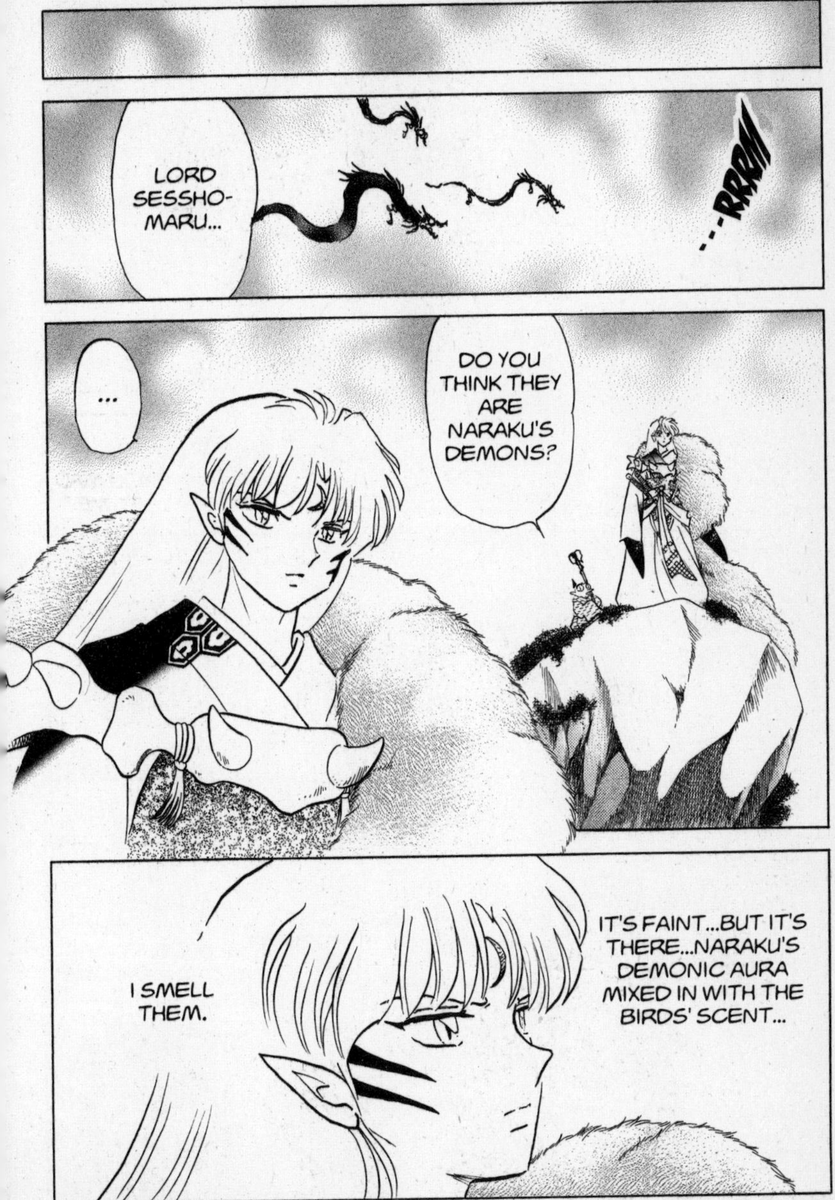
LORD SESSHO-MARU...
...RRRM
...
DO YOU THINK THEY ARE NARAKU'S DEMONS?
I SMELL THEM.
IT'S FAINT...BUT IT'S THERE...NARAKU'S DEMONIC AURA MIXED IN WITH THE BIRDS' SCENT...

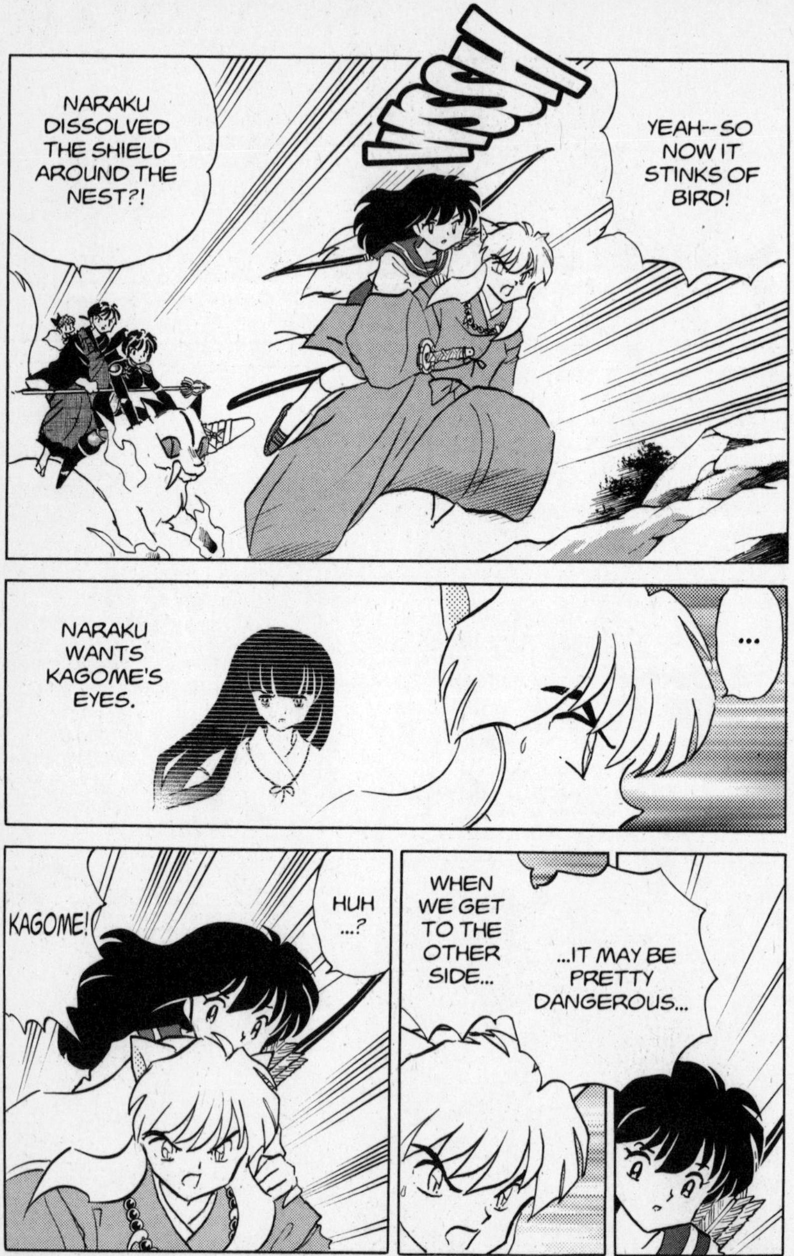
NARAKU DISSOLVED THE SHIELD AROUND THE NEST?!
WOOSH
YEAH--SO NOW IT STINKS OF BIRD!
NARAKU WANTS KAGOME'S EYES.
...
KAGOME!
HUH ...?
WHEN WE GET TO THE OTHER SIDE...
...IT MAY BE PRETTY DANGEROUS...

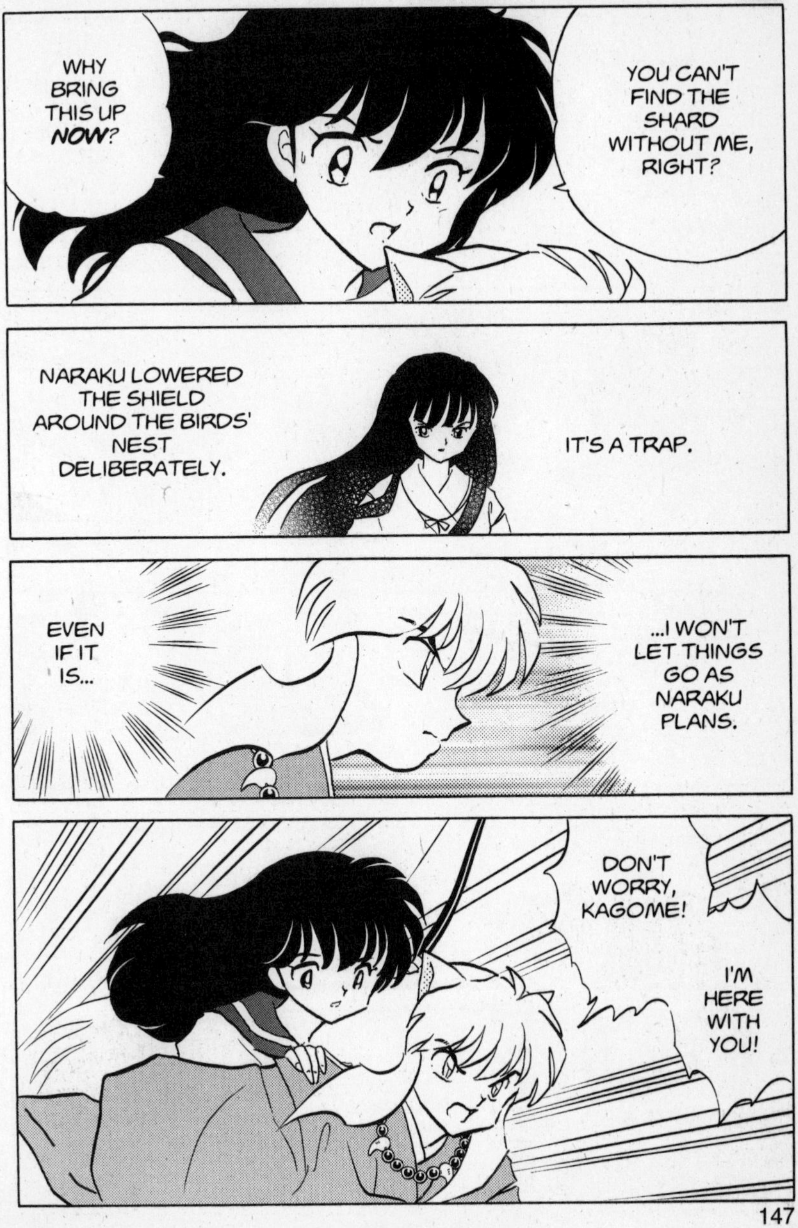
WHY BRING THIS UP *NOW*?
YOU CAN'T FIND THE SHARD WITHOUT ME, RIGHT?
NARAKU LOWERED THE SHIELD AROUND THE BIRDS' NEST DELIBERATELY.
IT'S A TRAP.
EVEN IF IT IS...
...I WON'T LET THINGS GO AS NARAKU PLANS.
DON'T WORRY, KAGOME!
I'M HERE WITH YOU!

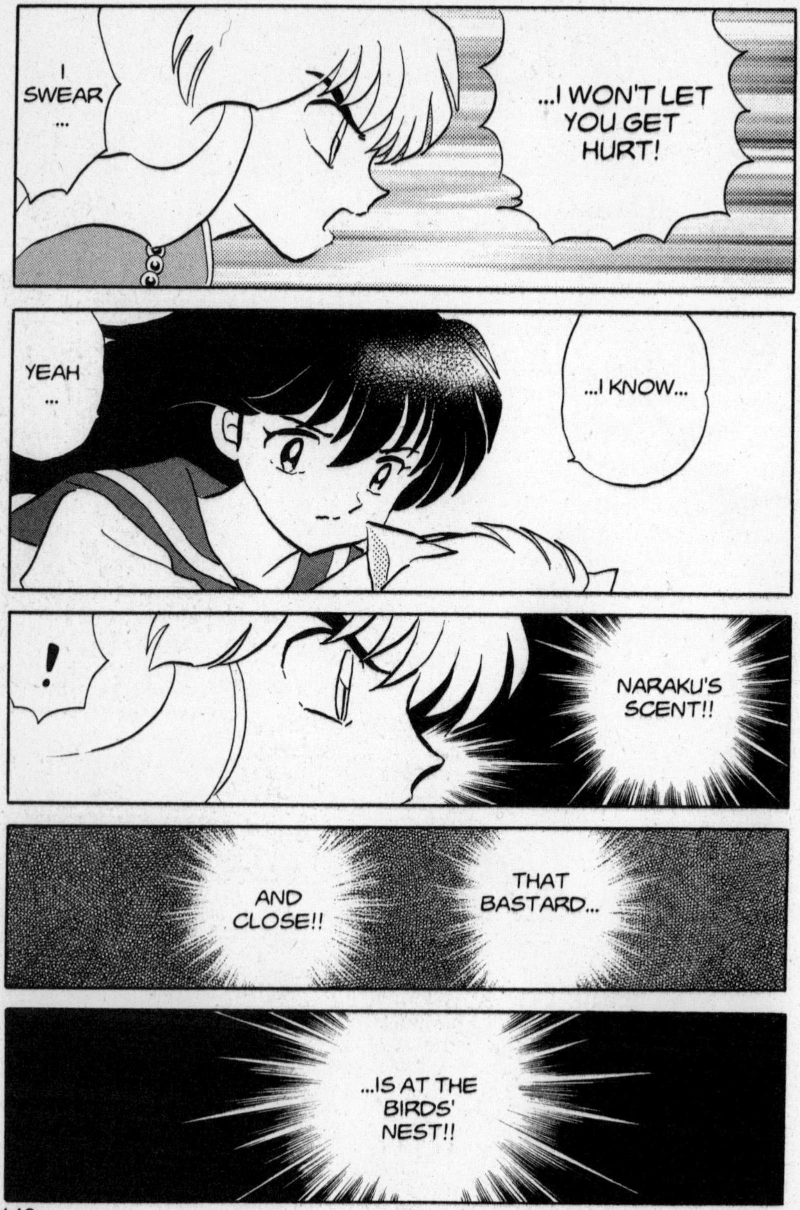
I SWEAR ...
...I WON'T LET YOU GET HURT!
YEAH ...
...I KNOW...
!
NARAKU'S SCENT!!
AND CLOSE!!
THAT BASTARD...
...IS AT THE BIRDS' NEST!!

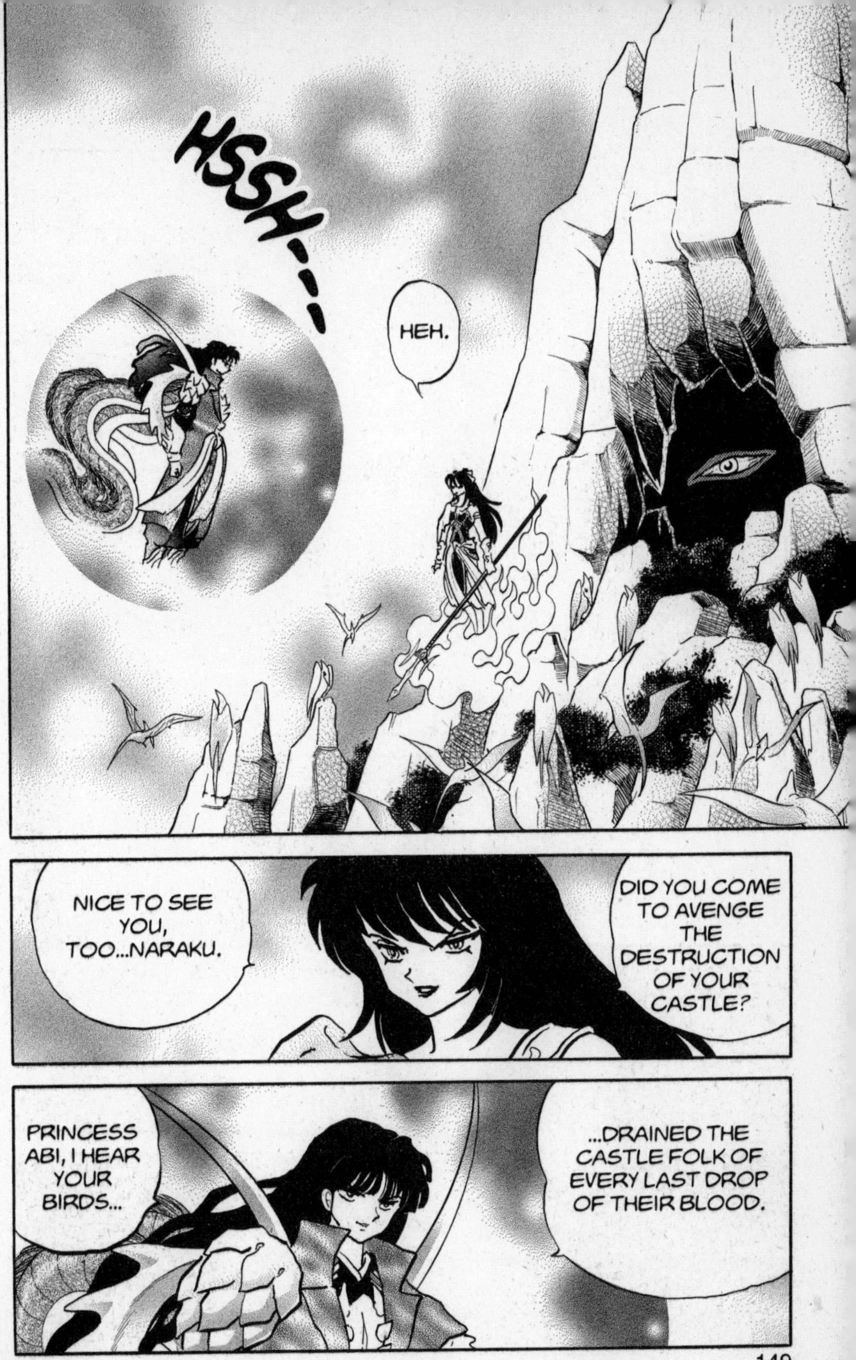
HSSH...
HEH.
NICE TO SEE YOU, TOO...NARAKU.
DID YOU COME TO AVENGE THE DESTRUCTION OF YOUR CASTLE?
PRINCESS ABI, I HEAR YOUR BIRDS...
...DRAINED THE CASTLE FOLK OF EVERY LAST DROP OF THEIR BLOOD.

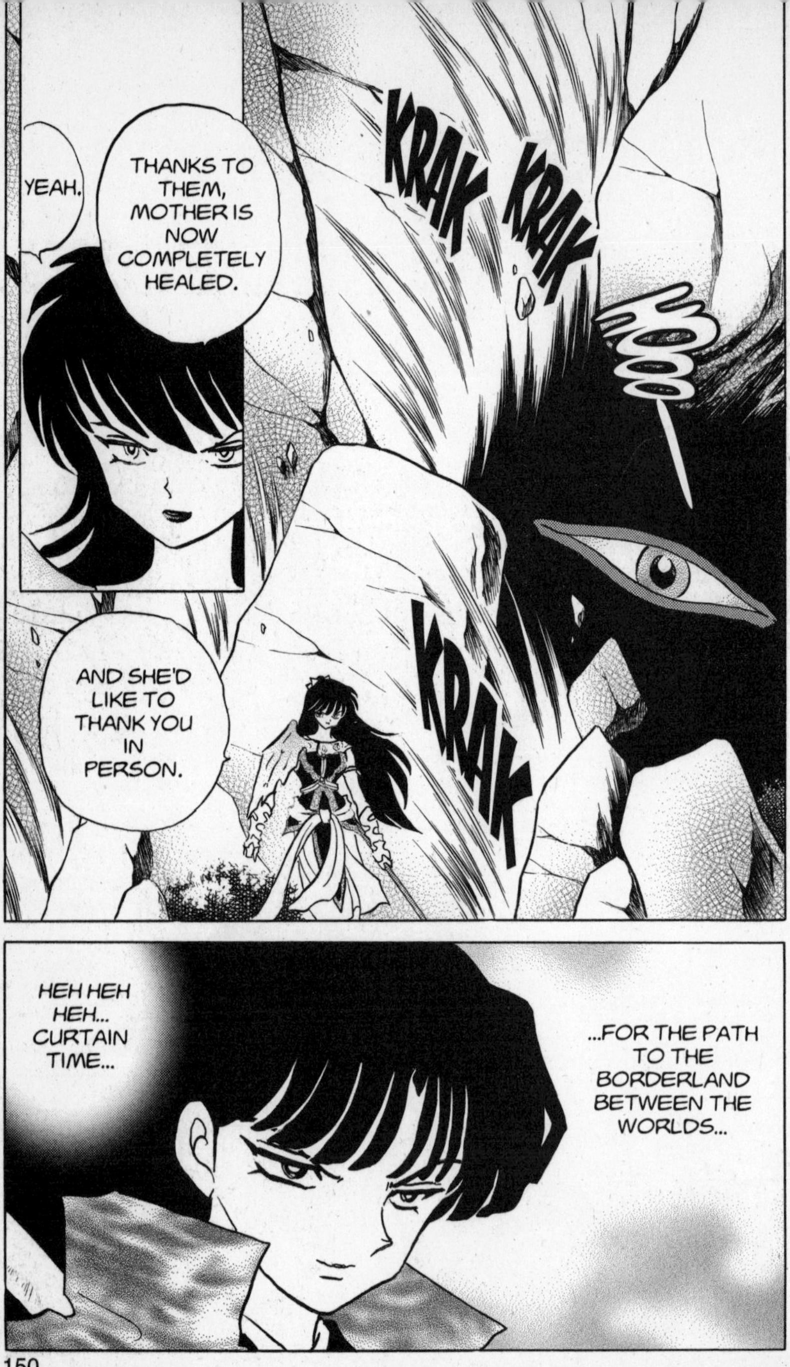
YEAH.
THANKS TO THEM, MOTHER IS NOW COMPLETELY HEALED.
KRAK KRAK
WHOOO
AND SHE'D LIKE TO THANK YOU IN PERSON.
KRAK
HEH HEH HEH... CURTAIN TIME...
...FOR THE PATH TO THE BORDERLAND BETWEEN THE WORLDS...

SCROLL 9

THE STEEL FOWL

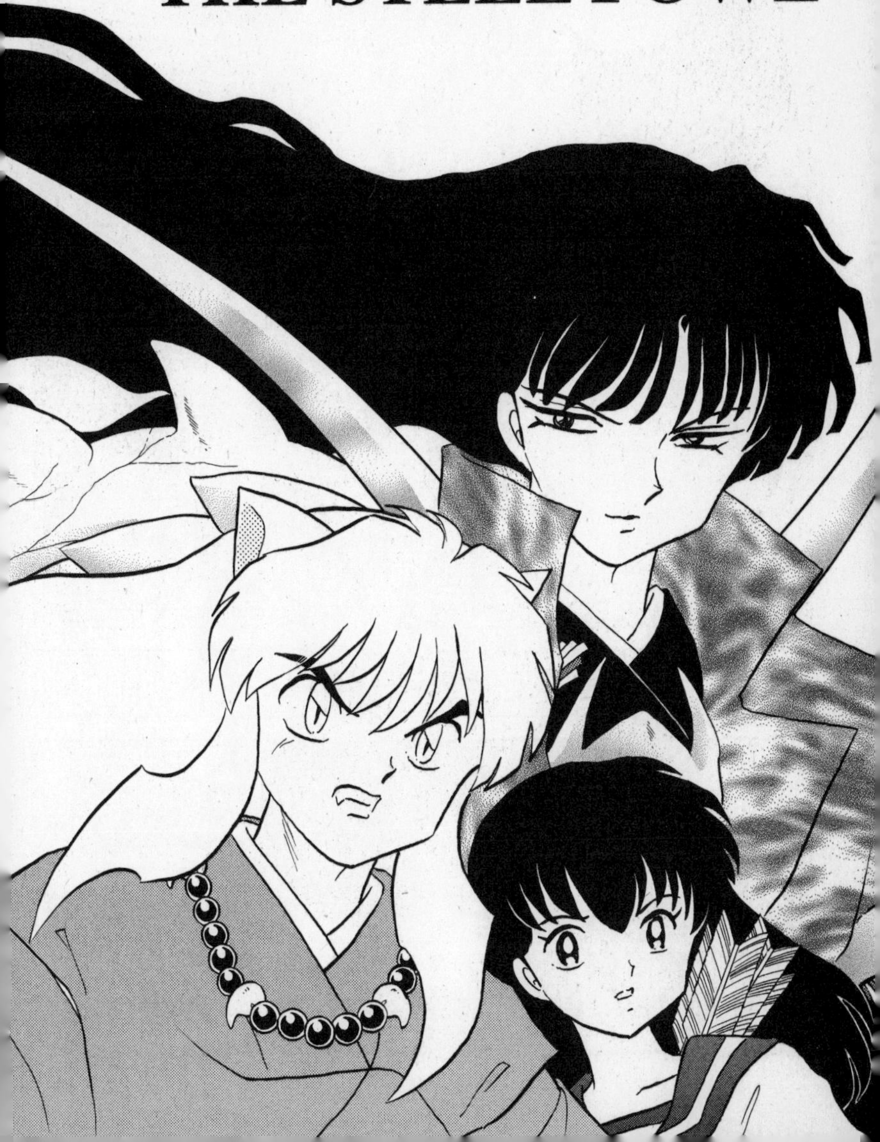

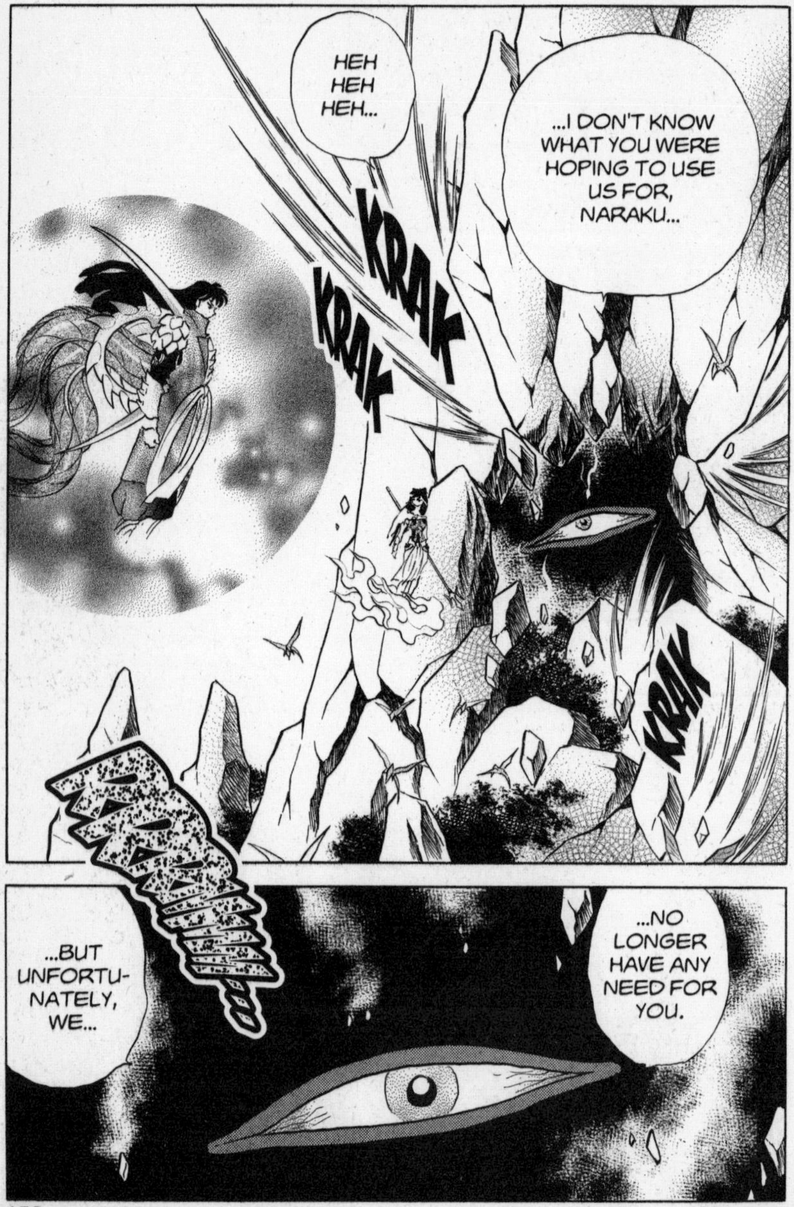
HEH HEH HEH...
...I DON'T KNOW WHAT YOU WERE HOPING TO USE US FOR, NARAKU...
KRAK
KRAK
KRAK
...BUT UNFORTU-NATELY, WE...
...NO LONGER HAVE ANY NEED FOR YOU.

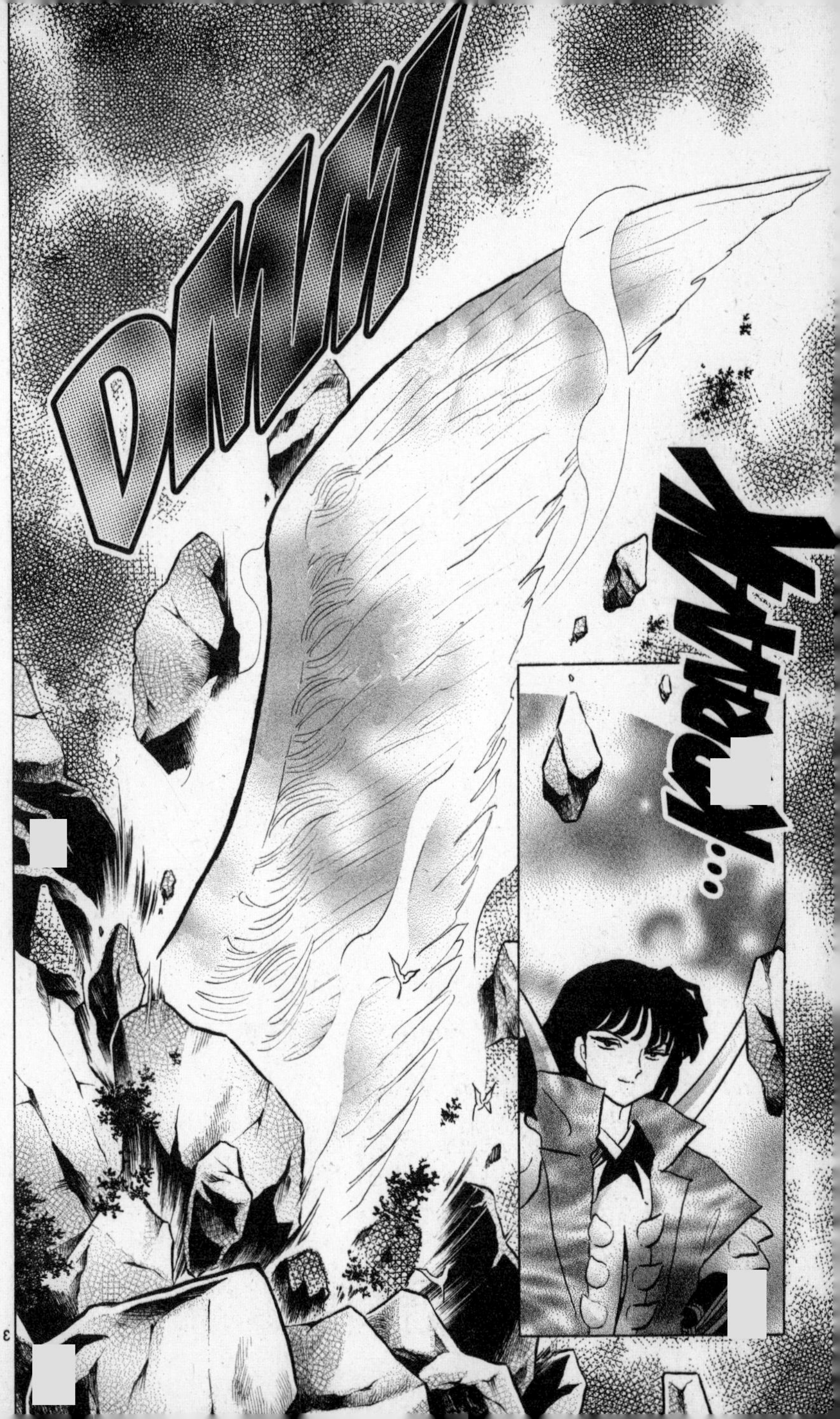
DMM
...KRAAK

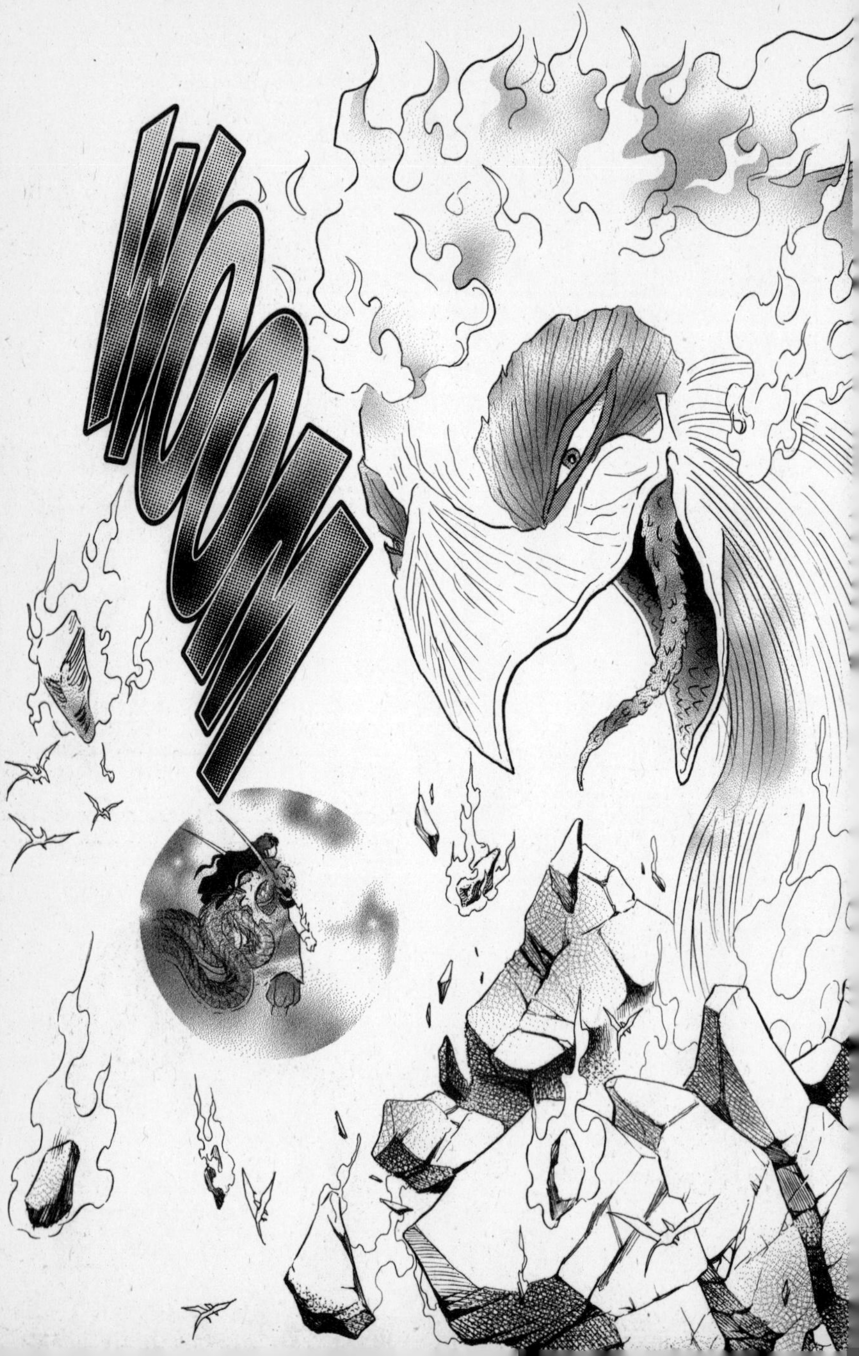

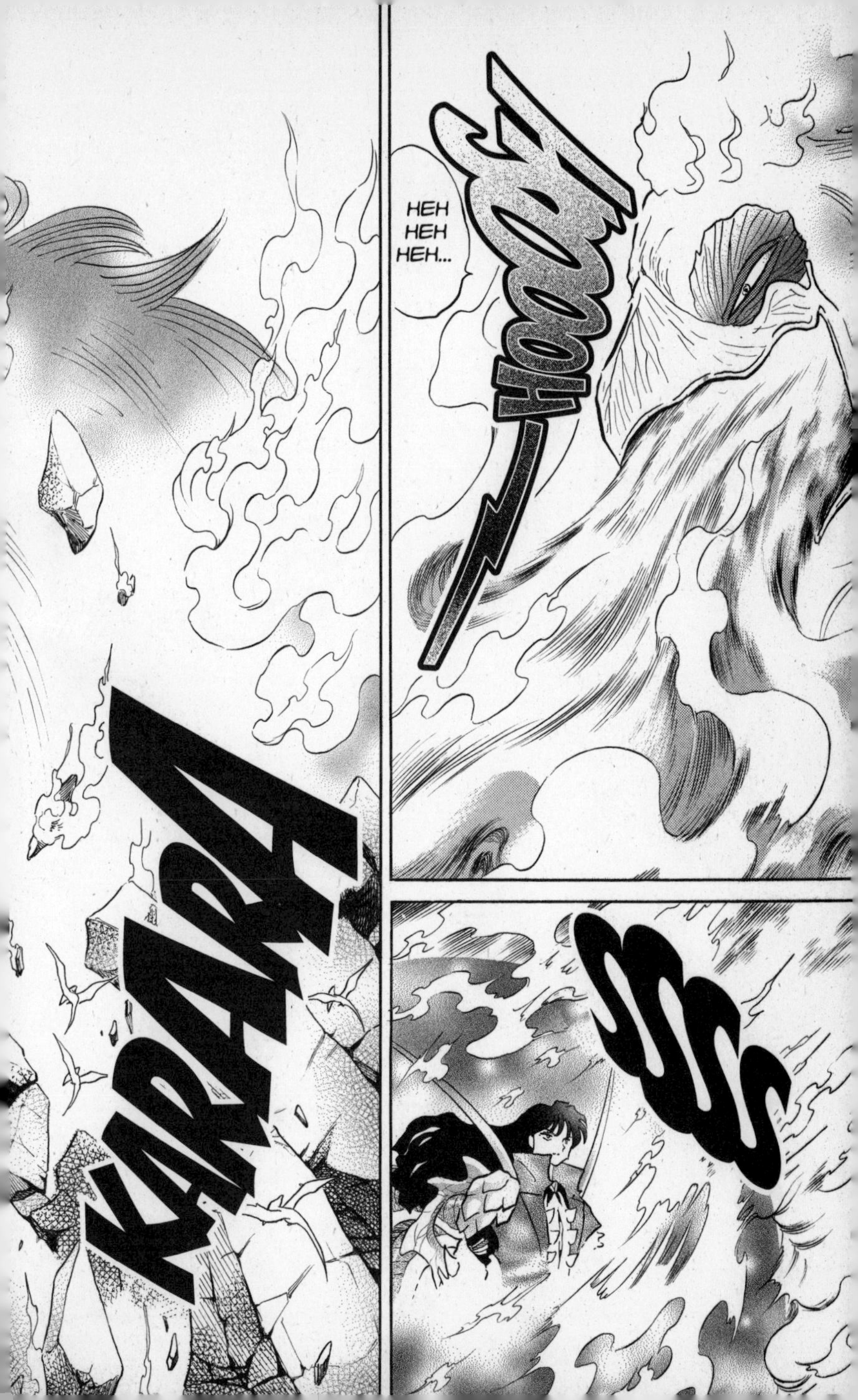
KRAKA
HEH HEH HEH...

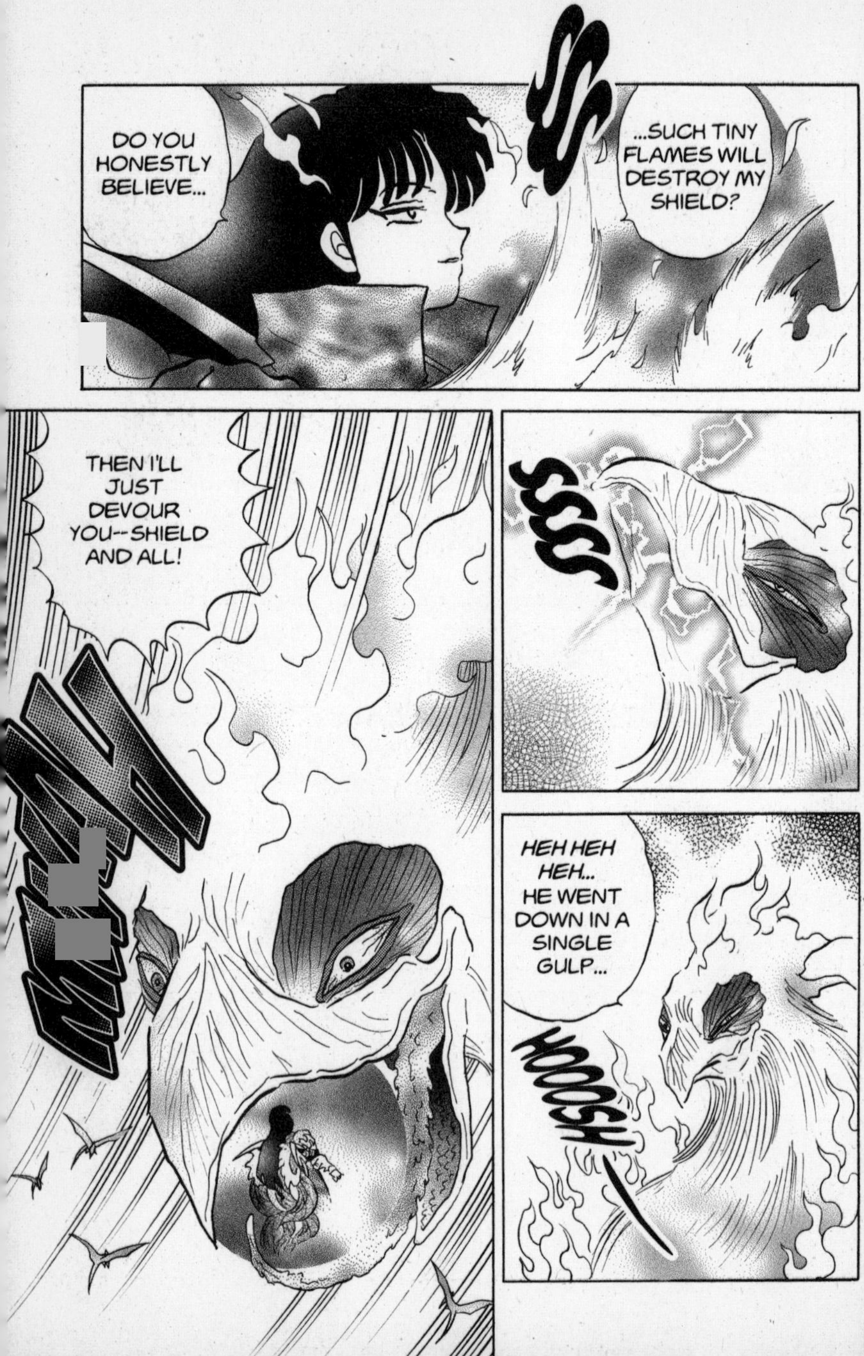
DO YOU HONESTLY BELIEVE...
SSS
...SUCH TINY FLAMES WILL DESTROY MY SHIELD?
THEN I'LL JUST DEVOUR YOU--SHIELD AND ALL!
SSSS
HEH HEH HEH... HE WENT DOWN IN A SINGLE GULP...
HOOOSH

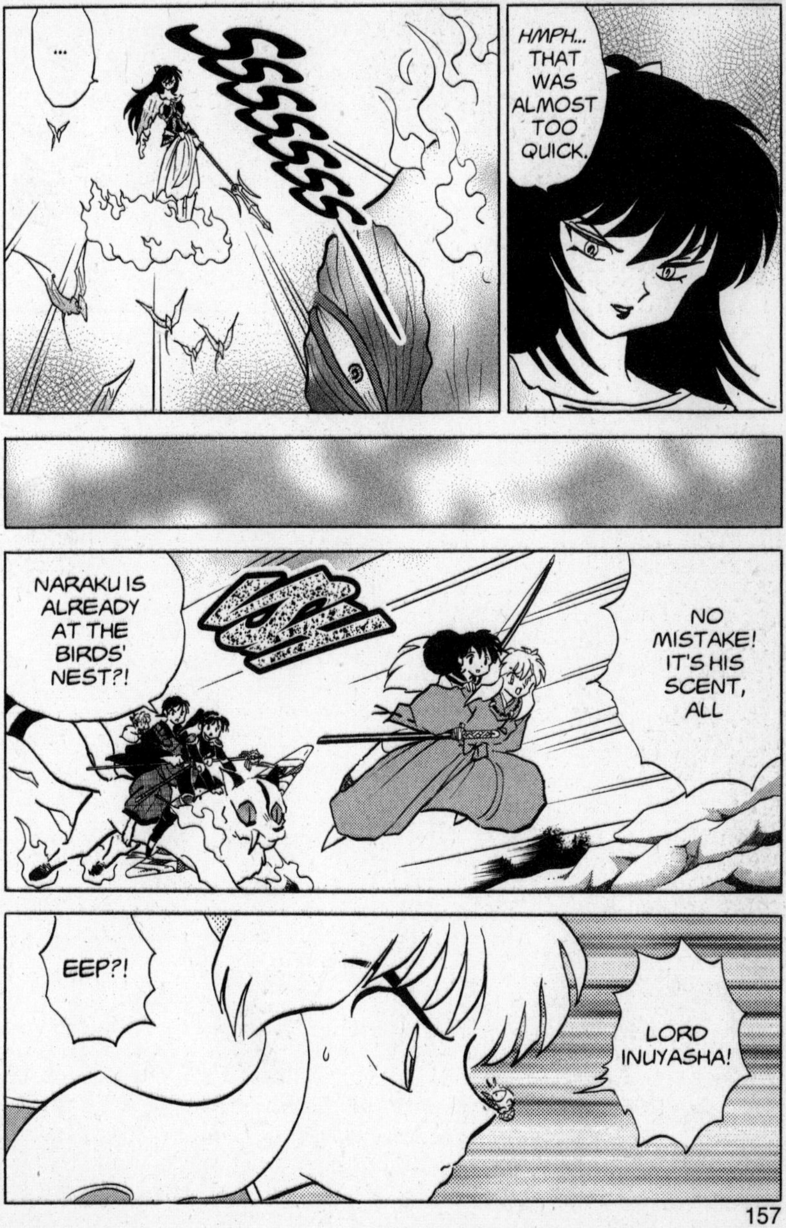
...
HMPH... THAT WAS ALMOST TOO QUICK.
NARAKU IS ALREADY AT THE BIRDS' NEST?!
NO MISTAKE! IT'S HIS SCENT, ALL
EEP?!
LORD INUYASHA!

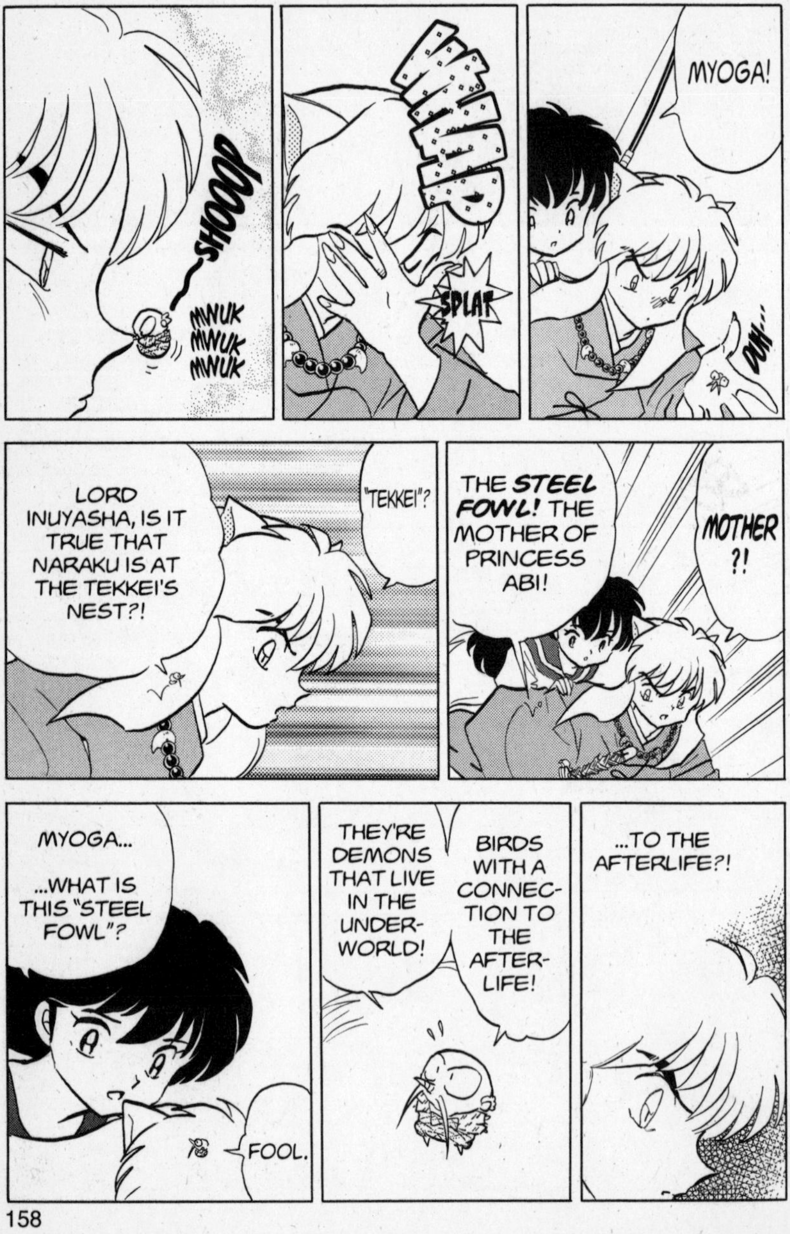
SHOOOP
MWUK MWUK MWUK
WHAP
SPLAT
MYOGA!
DUH...
LORD INUYASHA, IS IT TRUE THAT NARAKU IS AT THE TEKKEI'S NEST?!
"TEKKEI"?
THE STEEL FOWL! THE MOTHER OF PRINCESS ABI!
MOTHER ?!
MYOGA...
...WHAT IS THIS "STEEL FOWL"?
FOOL.
THEY'RE DEMONS THAT LIVE IN THE UNDER-WORLD!
BIRDS WITH A CONNEC-TION TO THE AFTER-LIFE!
...TO THE AFTERLIFE?!

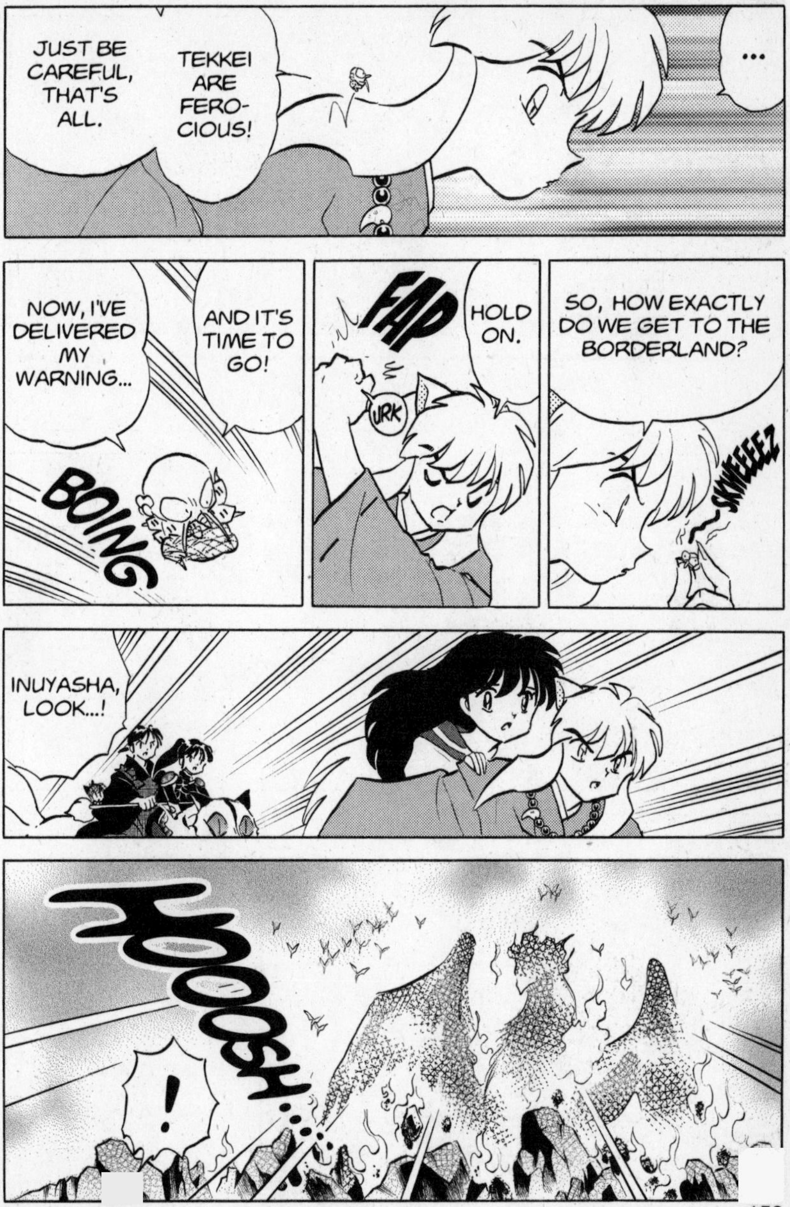
JUST BE CAREFUL, THAT'S ALL.
TEKKEI ARE FERO-CIOUS!
...
NOW, I'VE DELIVERED MY WARNING...
AND IT'S TIME TO GO!
BOING
FAP
URK
HOLD ON.
SO, HOW EXACTLY DO WE GET TO THE BORDERLAND?
SKWEEEEZ
INUYASHA, LOOK...!
WHOOOSH...
!

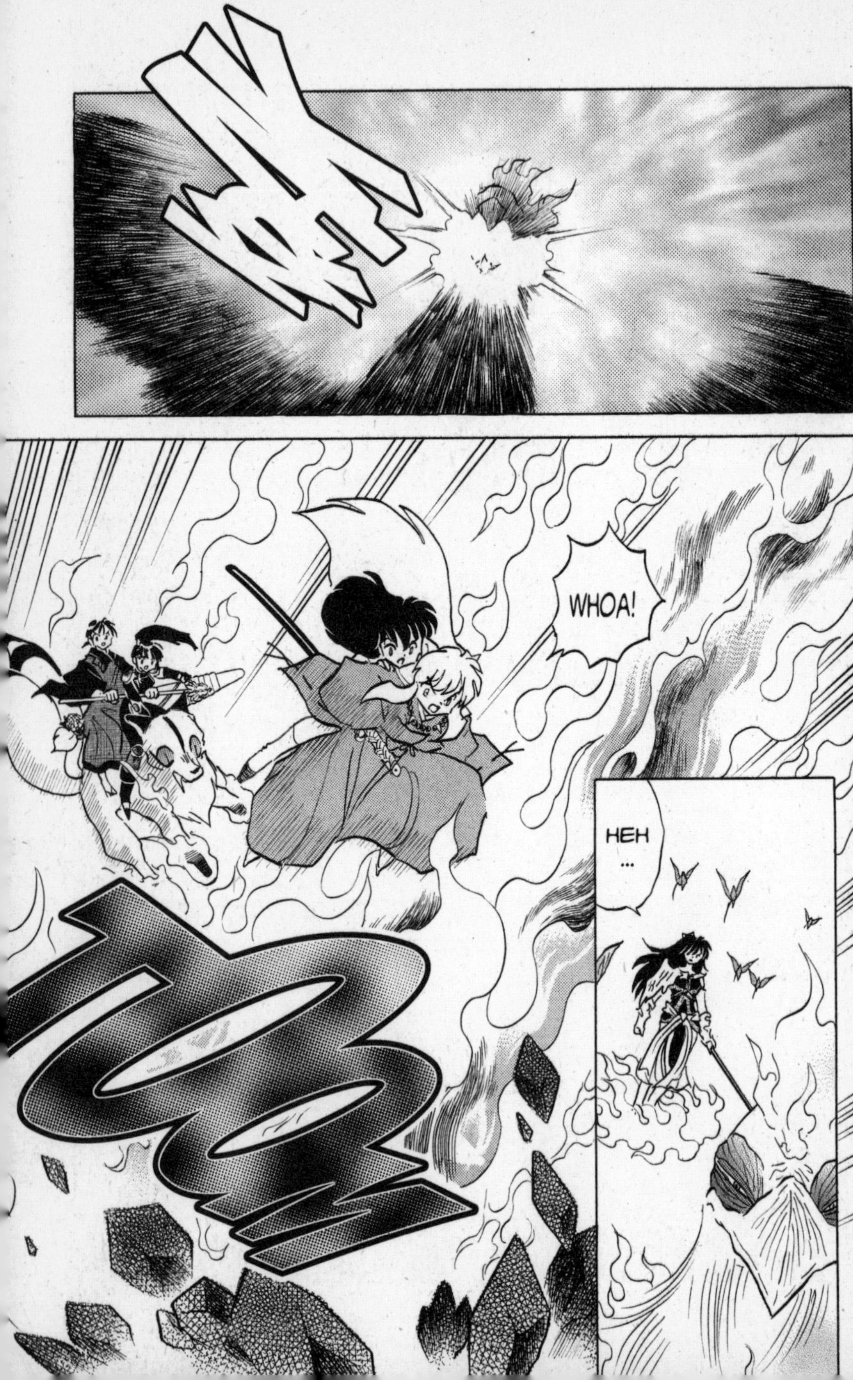
WHOA!
HEH ...

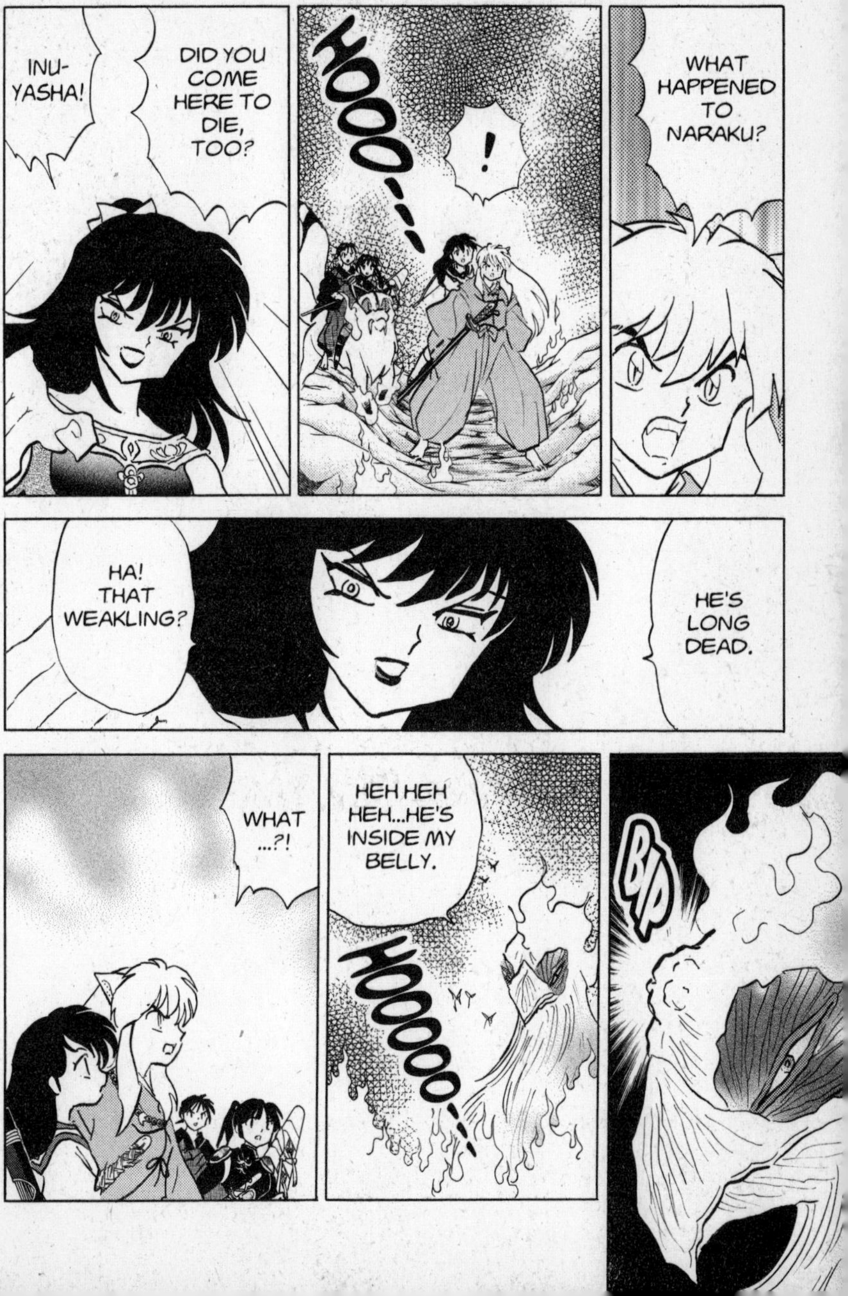
INU-
YASHA!
DID YOU
COME
HERE TO
DIE,
TOO?
HOOO...
!
WHAT
HAPPENED
TO
NARAKU?
HA!
THAT
WEAKLING?
HE'S
LONG
DEAD.
WHAT
...?!
HEH HEH
HEH...HE'S
INSIDE MY
BELLY.
HOOOOO...
BIP

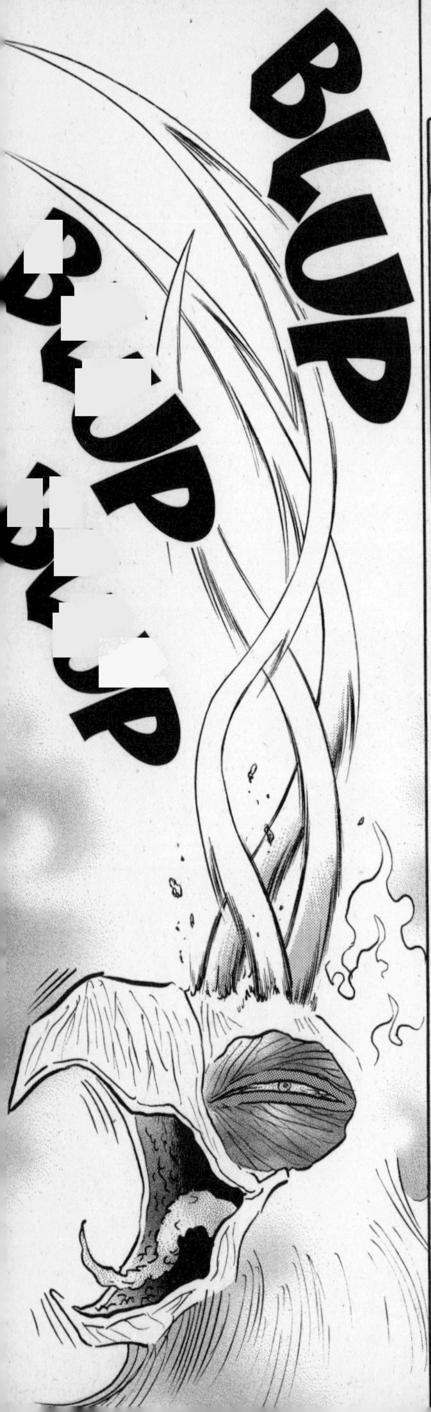
BLUP
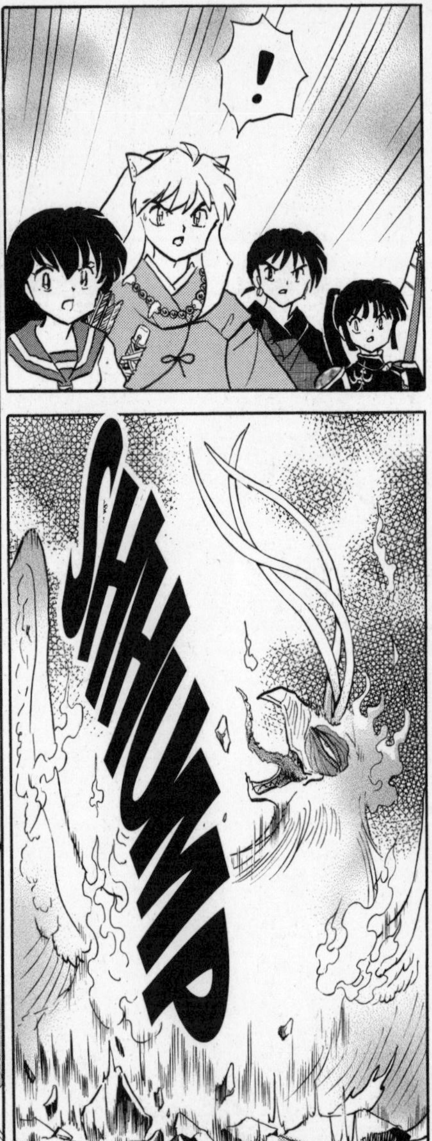
!
SHHUMP

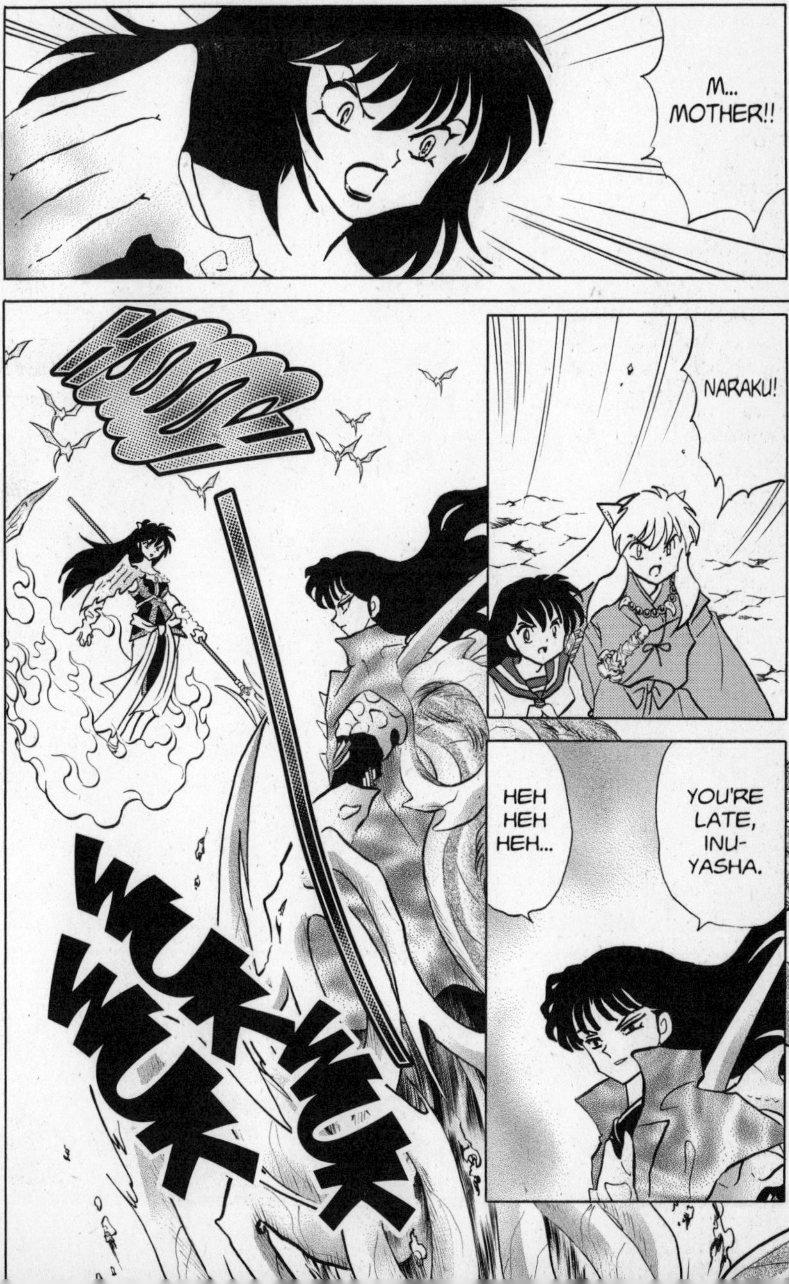
M... MOTHER!!
WUK WUK WUK
NARAKU!
HEH HEH HEH...
YOU'RE LATE, INU-YASHA.

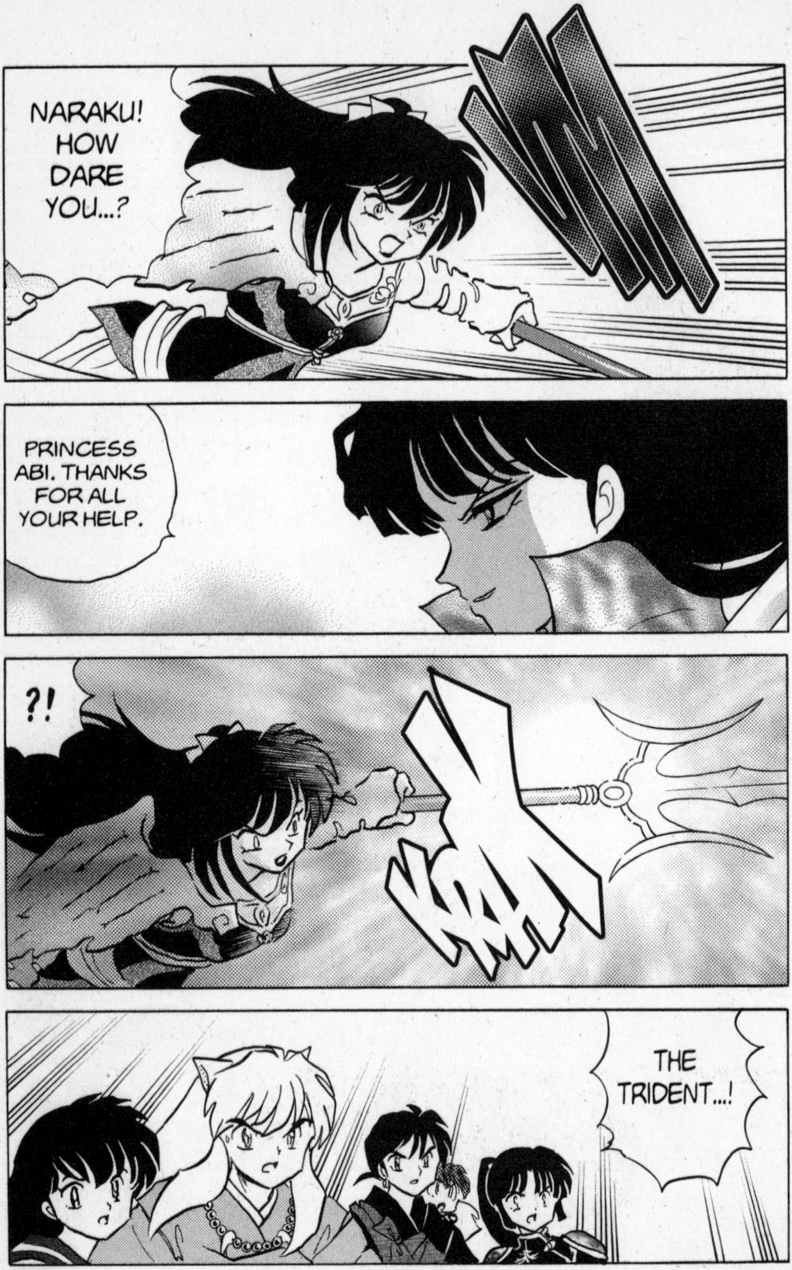
NARAKU! HOW DARE YOU...?
PRINCESS ABI. THANKS FOR ALL YOUR HELP.
?!
THE TRIDENT...!

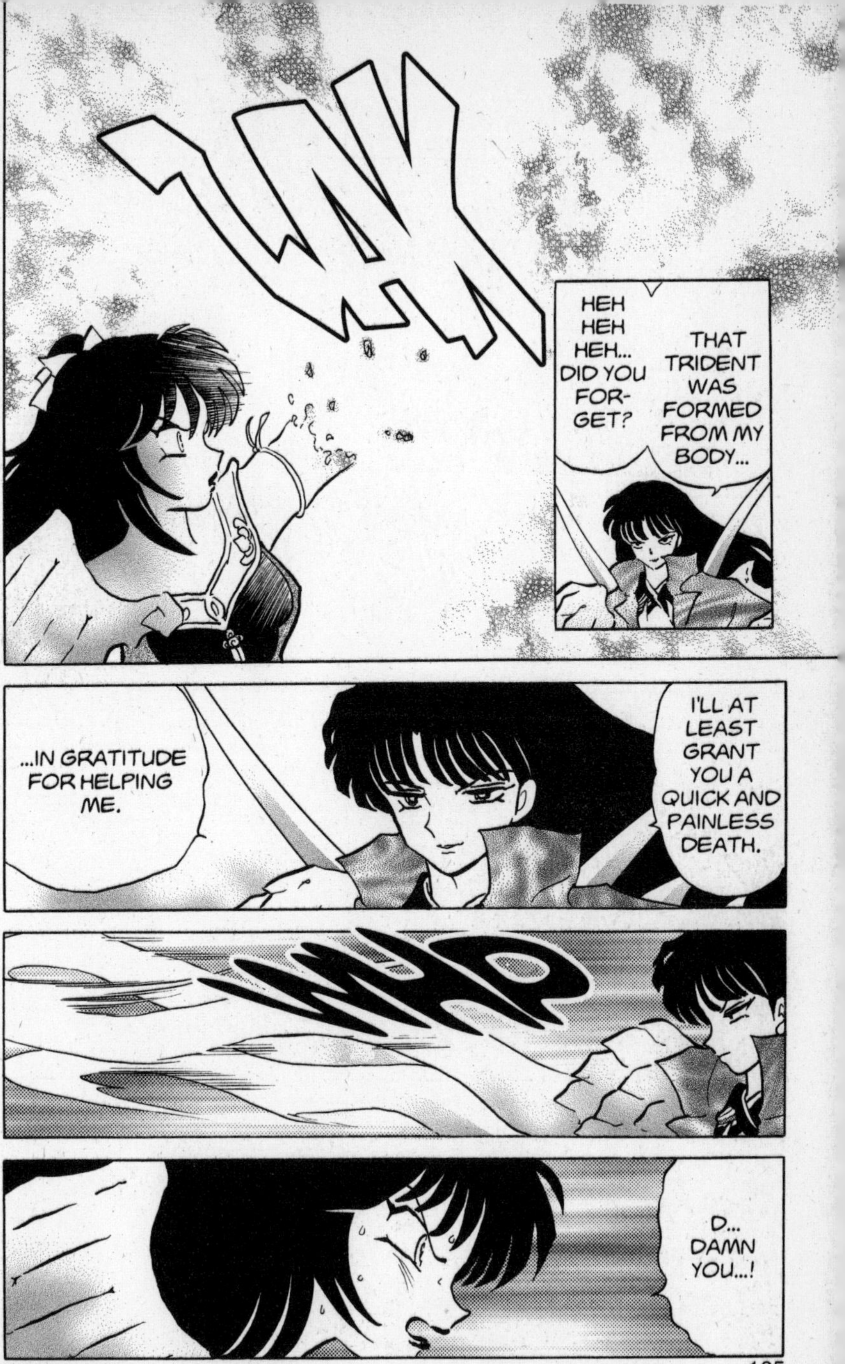
HEH HEH HEH... DID YOU FORGET? THAT TRIDENT WAS FORMED FROM MY BODY...
I'LL AT LEAST GRANT YOU A QUICK AND PAINLESS DEATH.
...IN GRATITUDE FOR HELPING ME.
WHIP
D... DAMN YOU...!

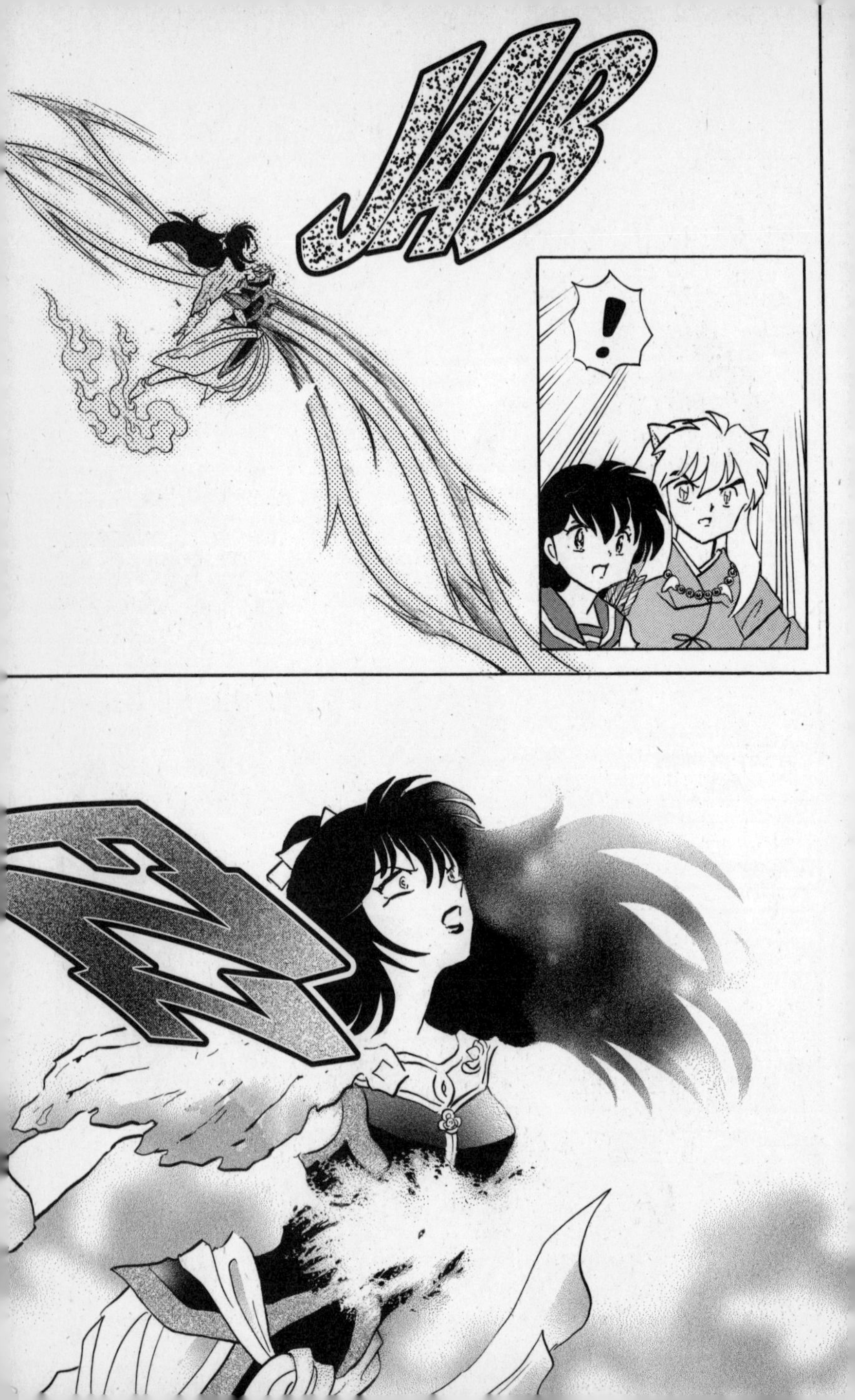
JAB
!

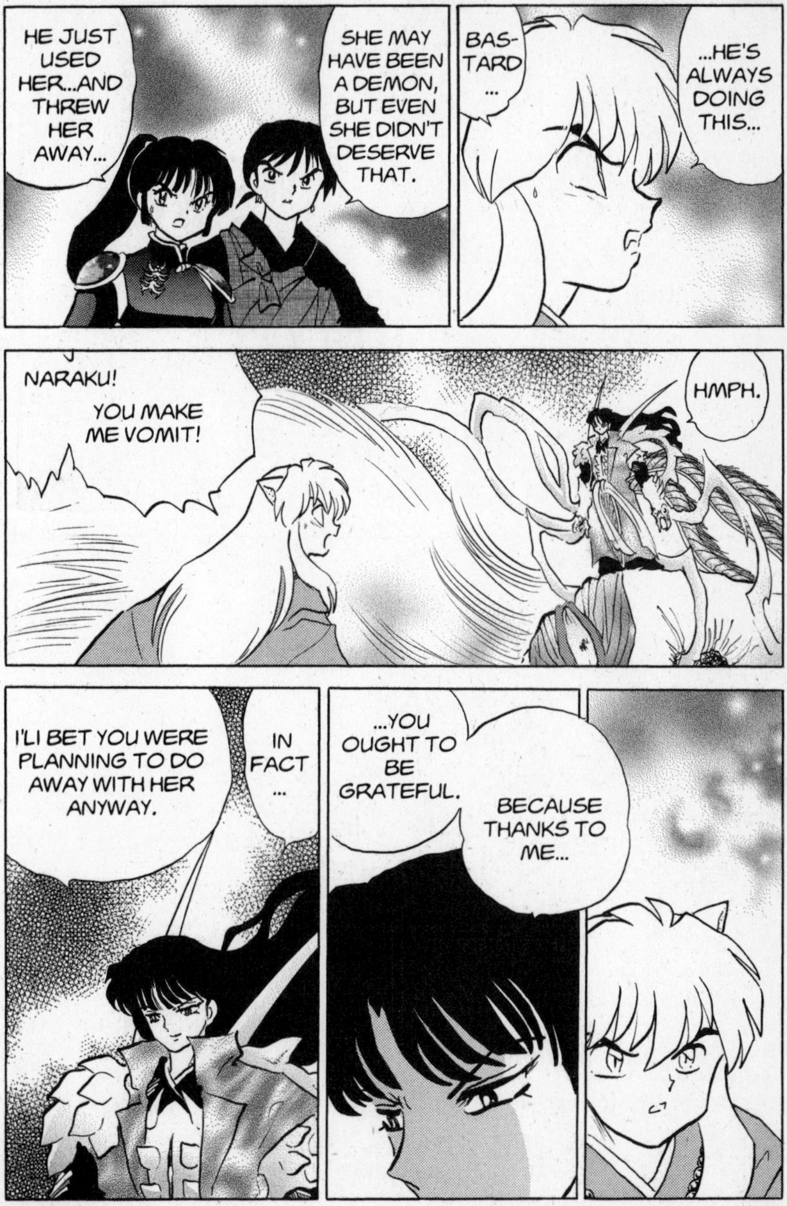
HE JUST USED HER...AND THREW HER AWAY...
SHE MAY HAVE BEEN A DEMON, BUT EVEN SHE DIDN'T DESERVE THAT.
BAS-TARD...
...HE'S ALWAYS DOING THIS...
NARAKU!
YOU MAKE ME VOMIT!
HMPH.
I'LI BET YOU WERE PLANNING TO DO AWAY WITH HER ANYWAY.
IN FACT...
...YOU OUGHT TO BE GRATEFUL.
BECAUSE THANKS TO ME...

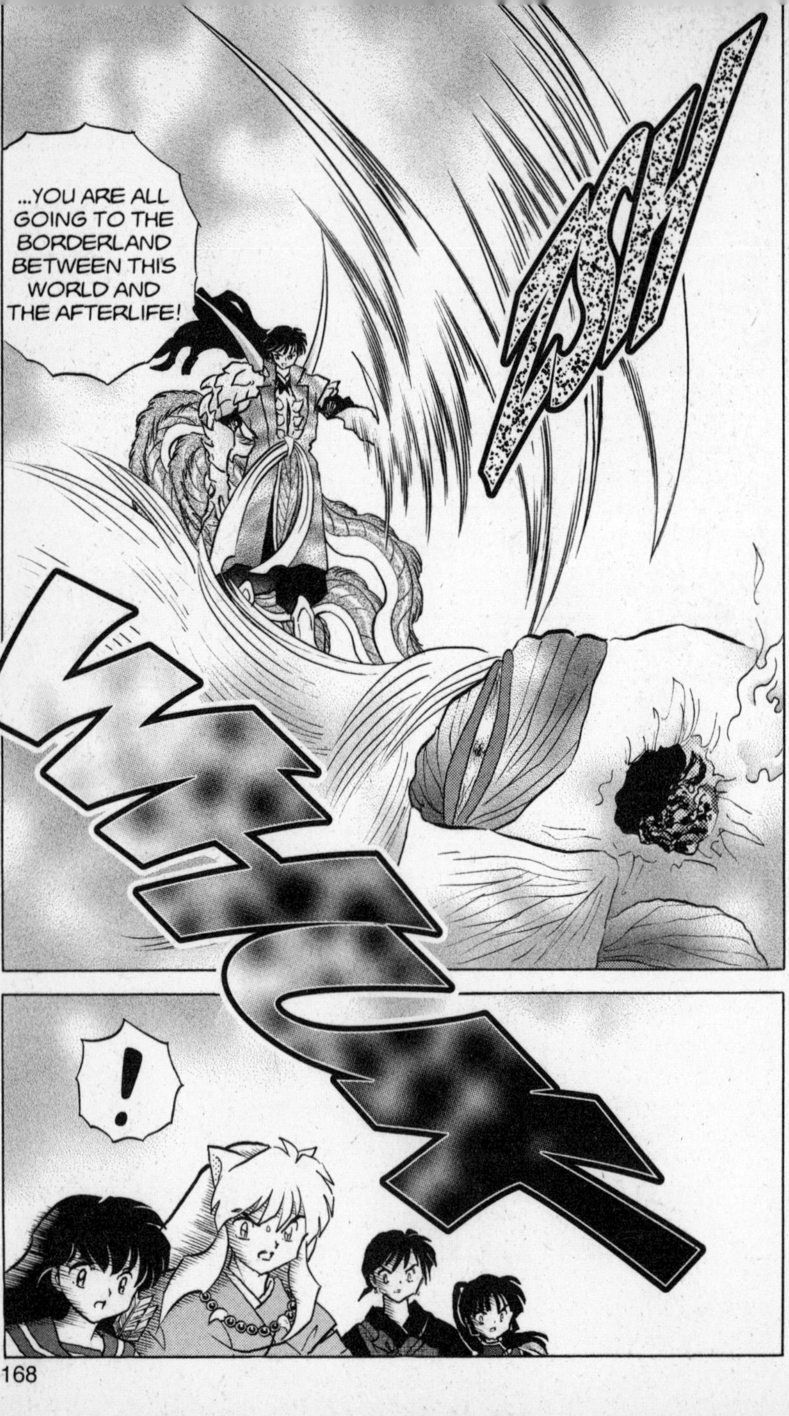
...YOU ARE ALL GOING TO THE BORDERLAND BETWEEN THIS WORLD AND THE AFTERLIFE!
!

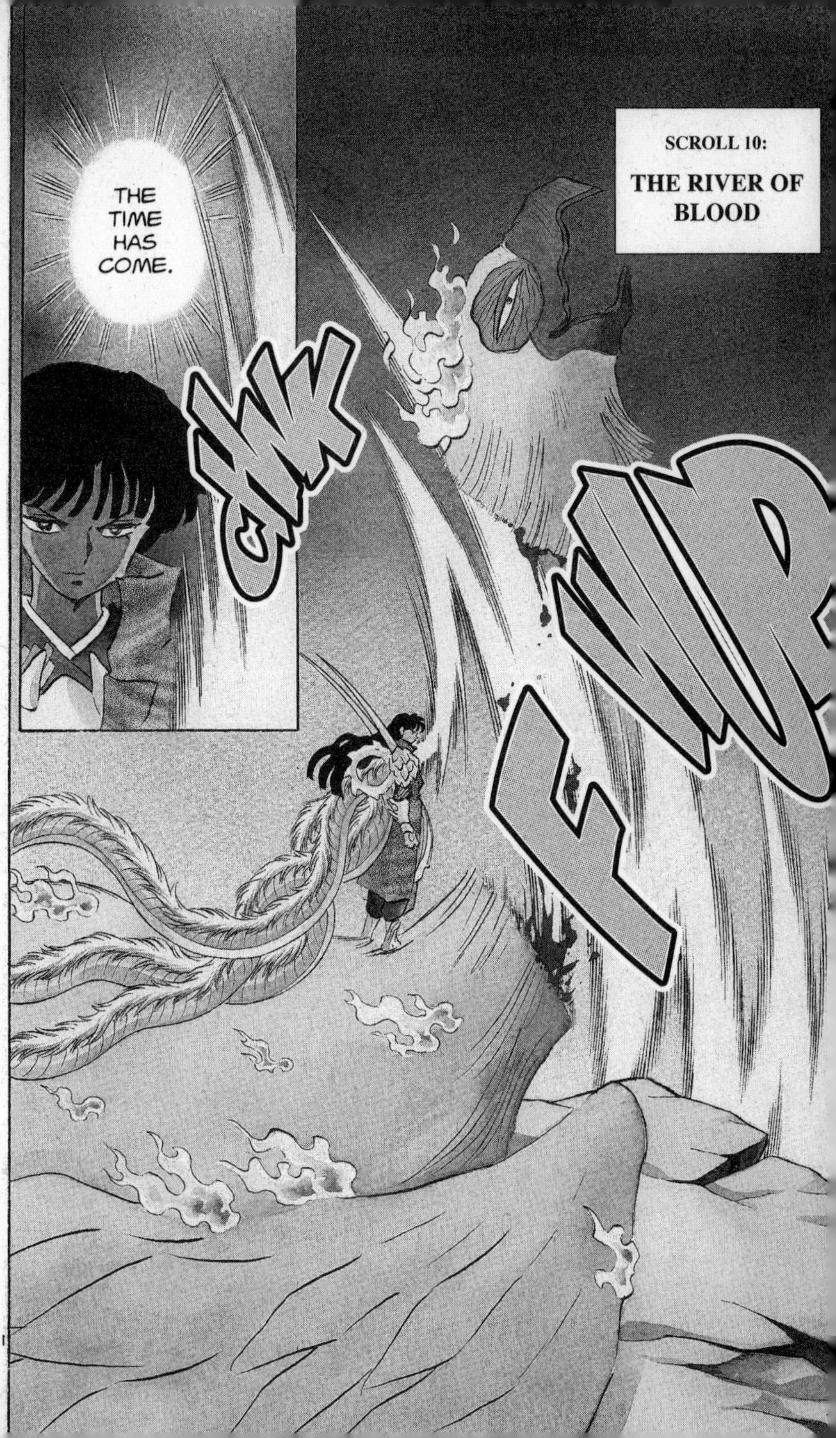
THE TIME HAS COME.
CHNK
SCROLL 10:
THE RIVER OF BLOOD
FWIP

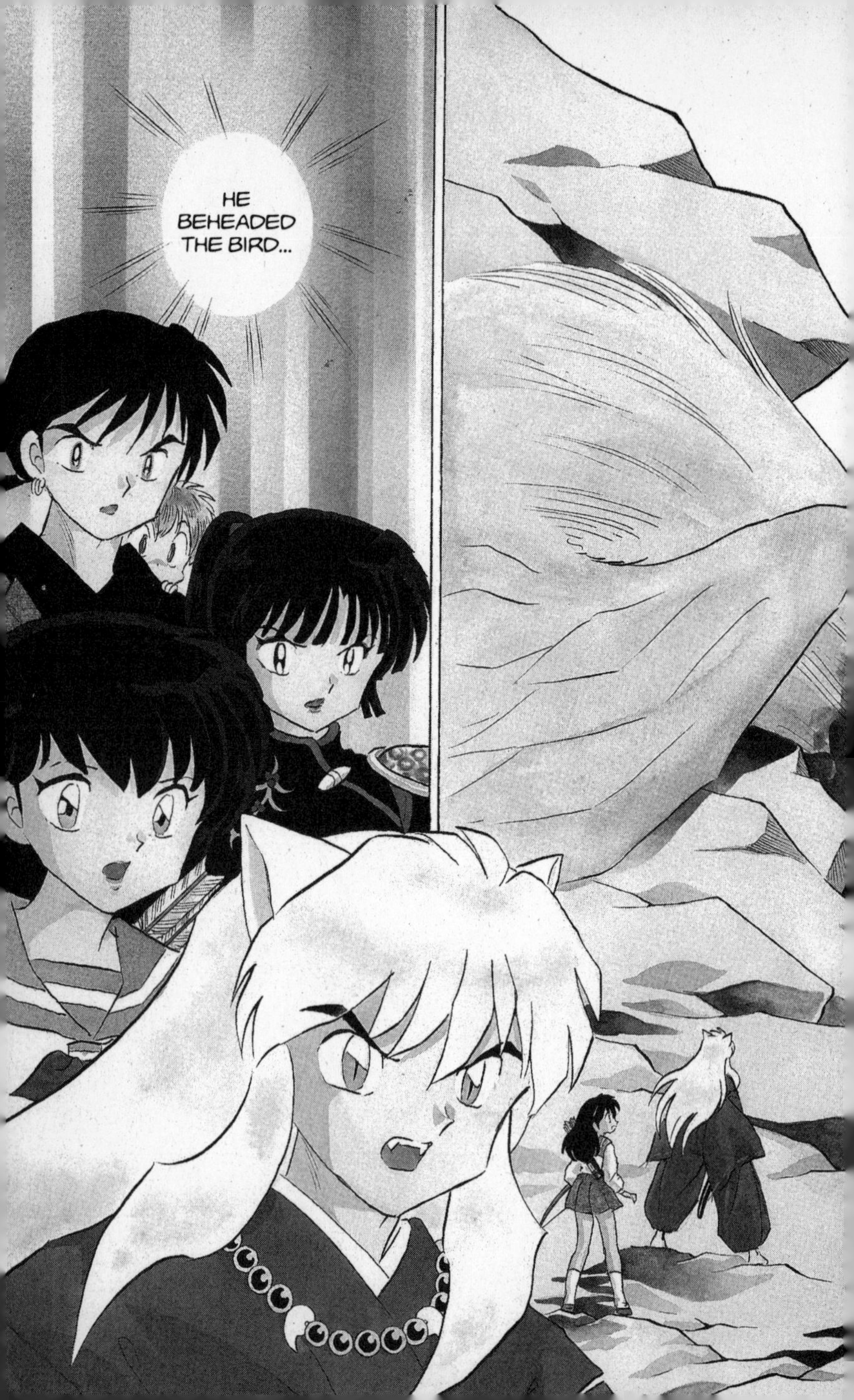
HE BEHEADED THE BIRD...

SCROLL 10:
THE RIVER OF BLOOD

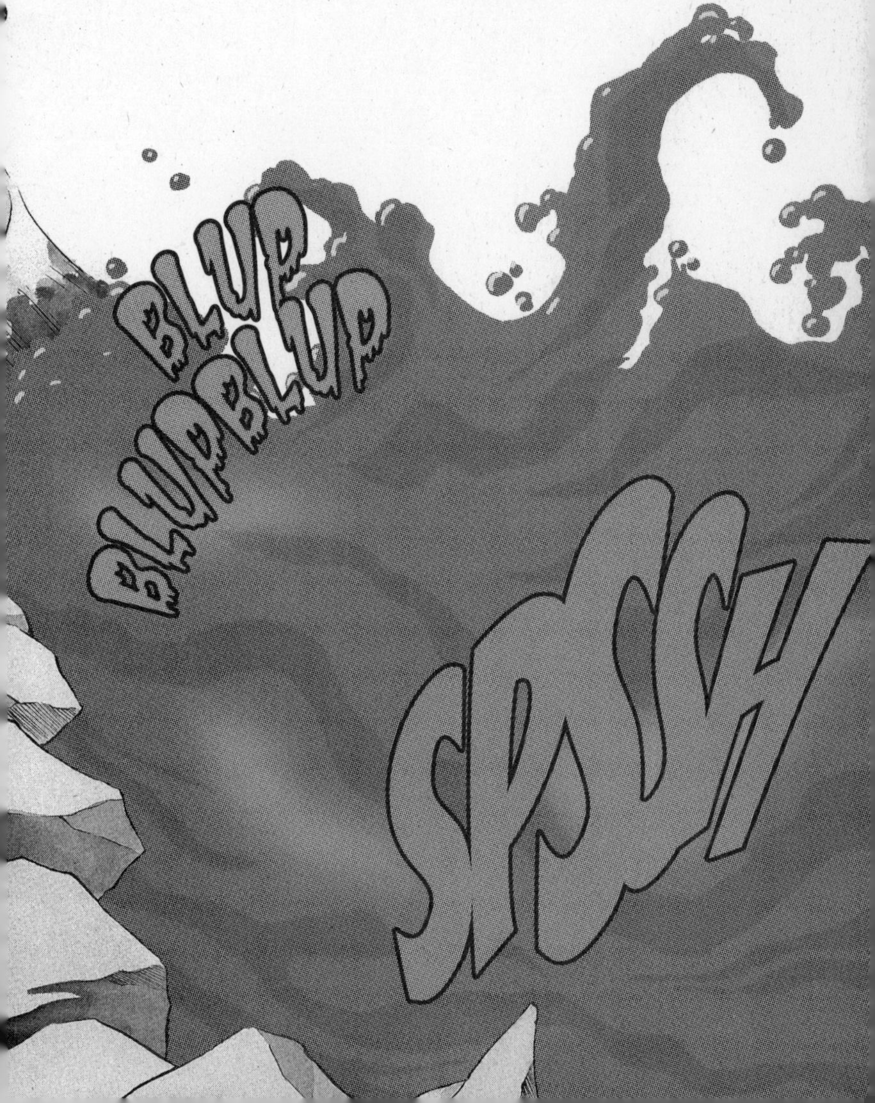

BLUP
BLUPBLUP

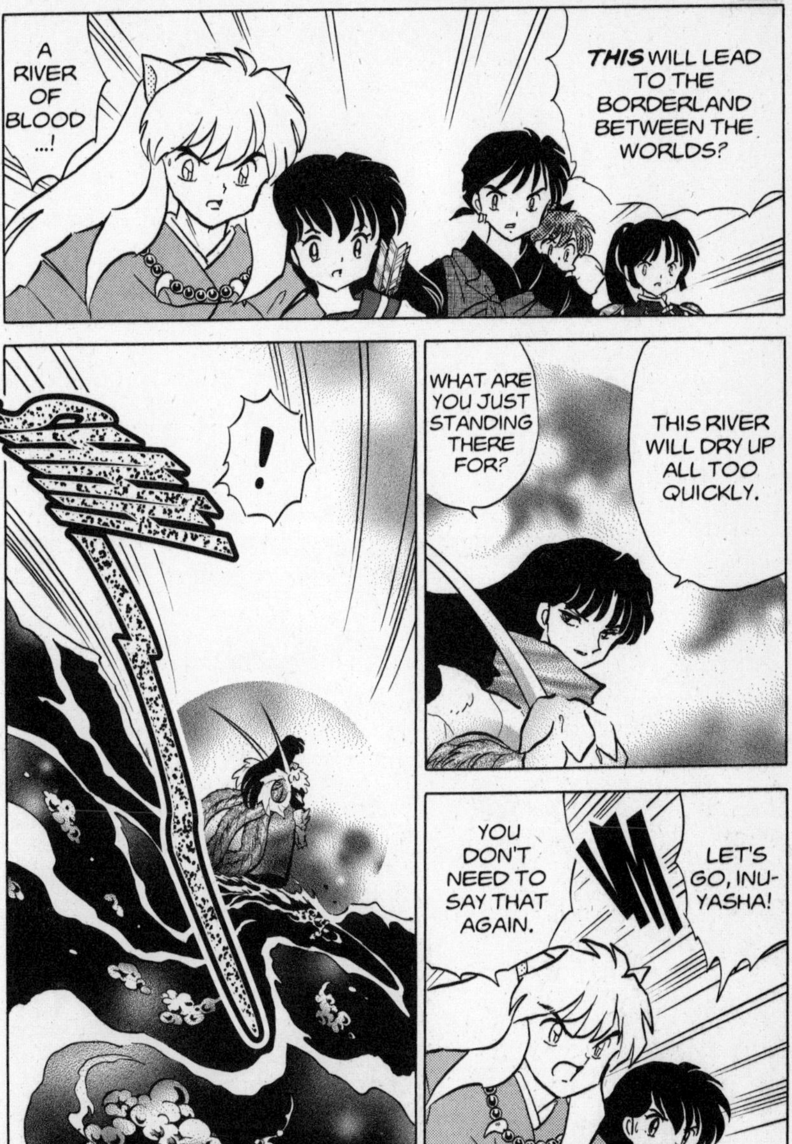
A RIVER OF BLOOD ...!
THIS WILL LEAD TO THE BORDERLAND BETWEEN THE WORLDS?
!
WHAT ARE YOU JUST STANDING THERE FOR?
THIS RIVER WILL DRY UP ALL TOO QUICKLY.
YOU DON'T NEED TO SAY THAT AGAIN.
LET'S GO, INU-YASHA!

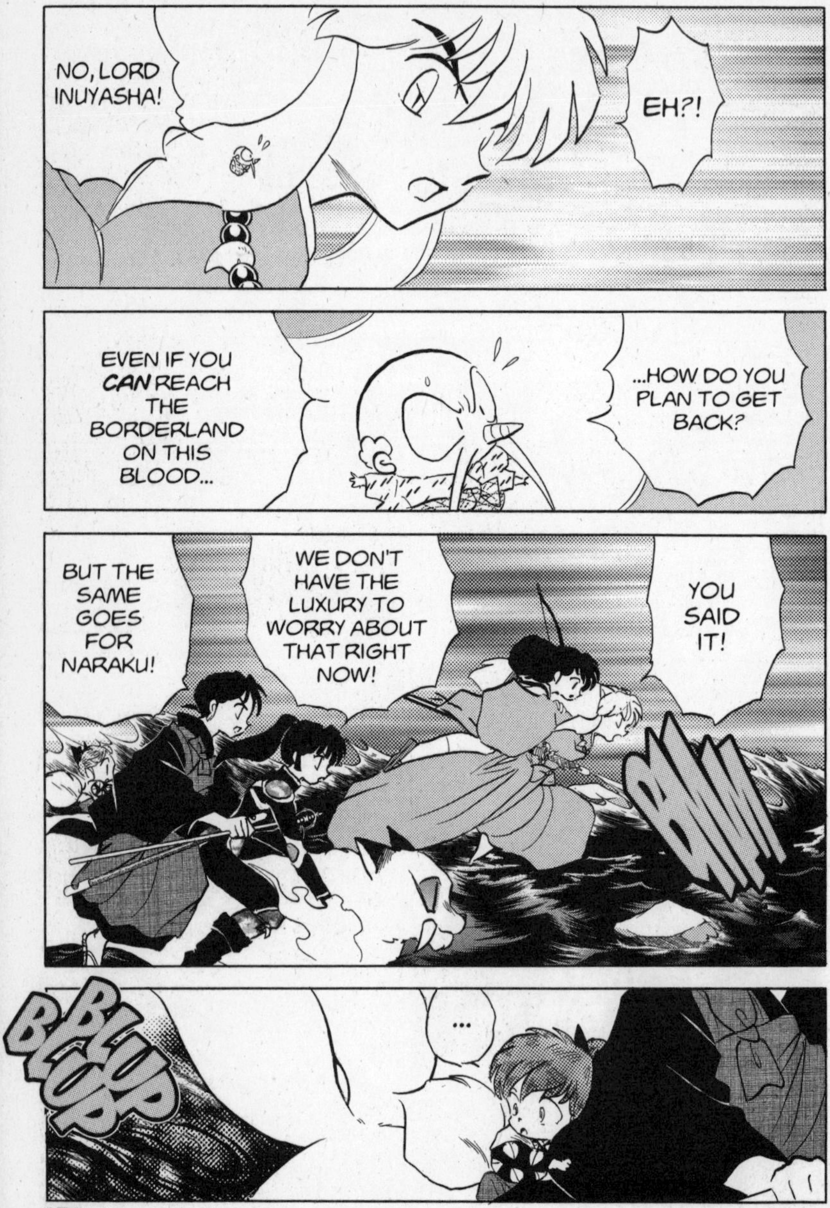
NO, LORD INUYASHA!
EH?!
EVEN IF YOU CAN REACH THE BORDERLAND ON THIS BLOOD...
...HOW DO YOU PLAN TO GET BACK?
BUT THE SAME GOES FOR NARAKU!
WE DON'T HAVE THE LUXURY TO WORRY ABOUT THAT RIGHT NOW!
YOU SAID IT!
BLUP BLUP
...

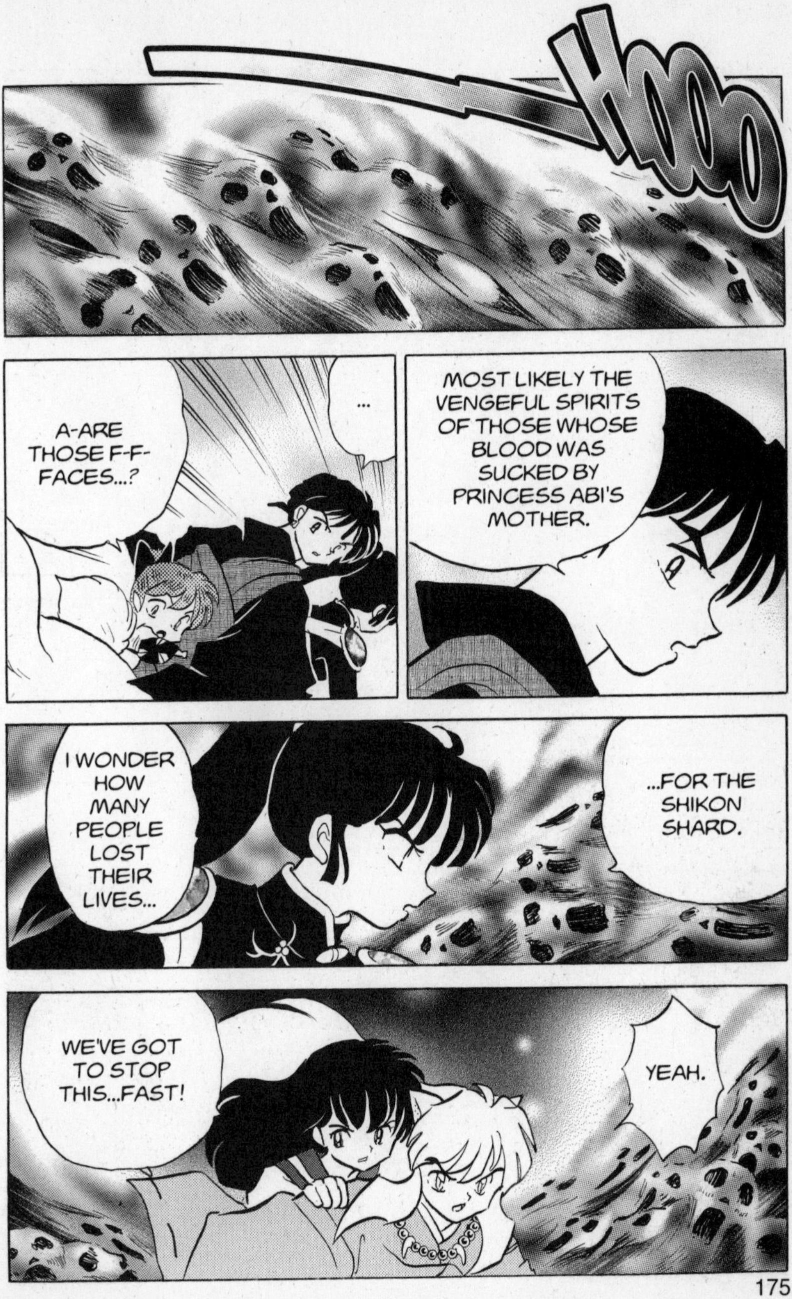
HOOO
A-ARE THOSE F-F-FACES...?
...
MOST LIKELY THE VENGEFUL SPIRITS OF THOSE WHOSE BLOOD WAS SUCKED BY PRINCESS ABI'S MOTHER.
I WONDER HOW MANY PEOPLE LOST THEIR LIVES...
...FOR THE SHIKON SHARD.
WE'VE GOT TO STOP THIS...FAST!
YEAH.

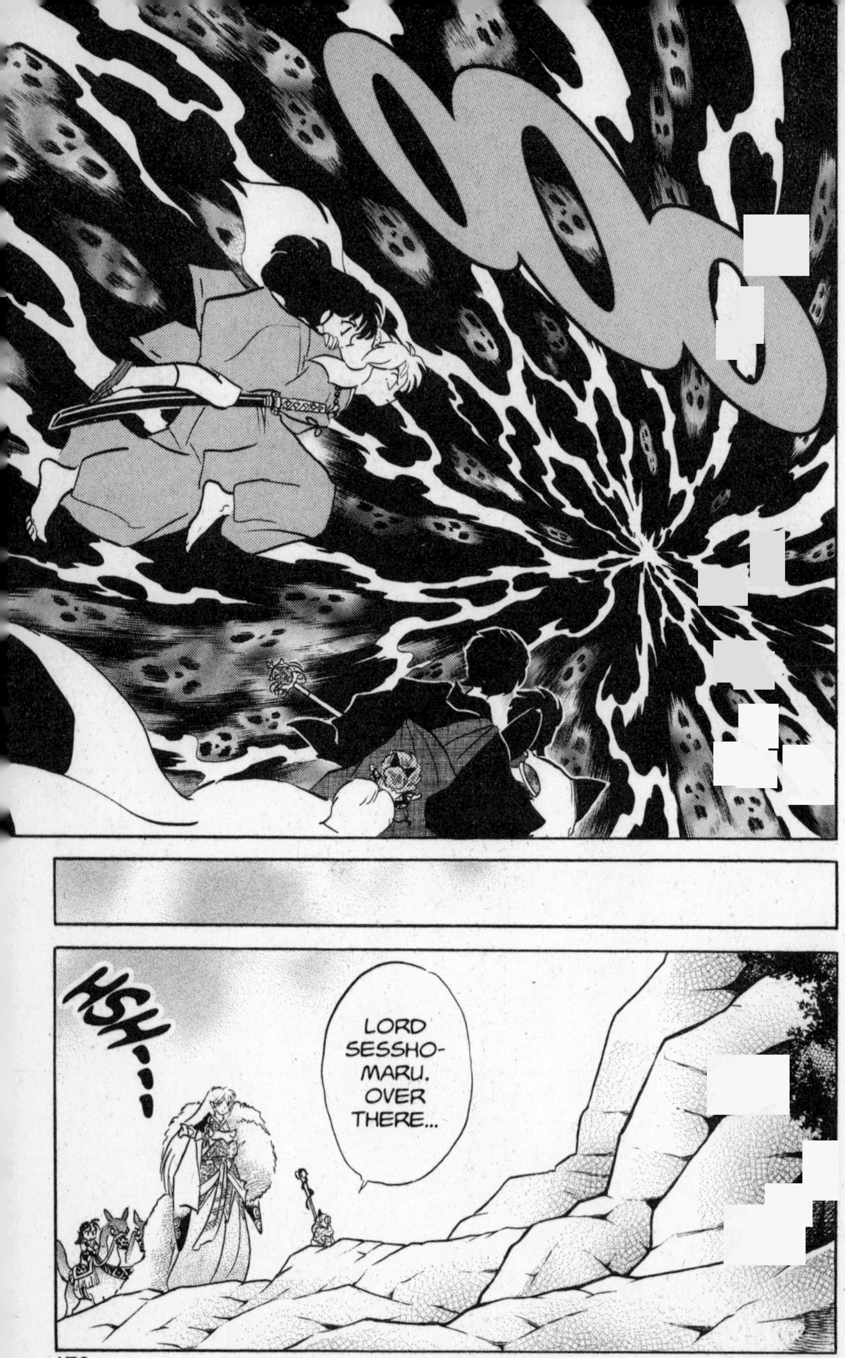
HSH...
LORD SESSHOMARU. OVER THERE...

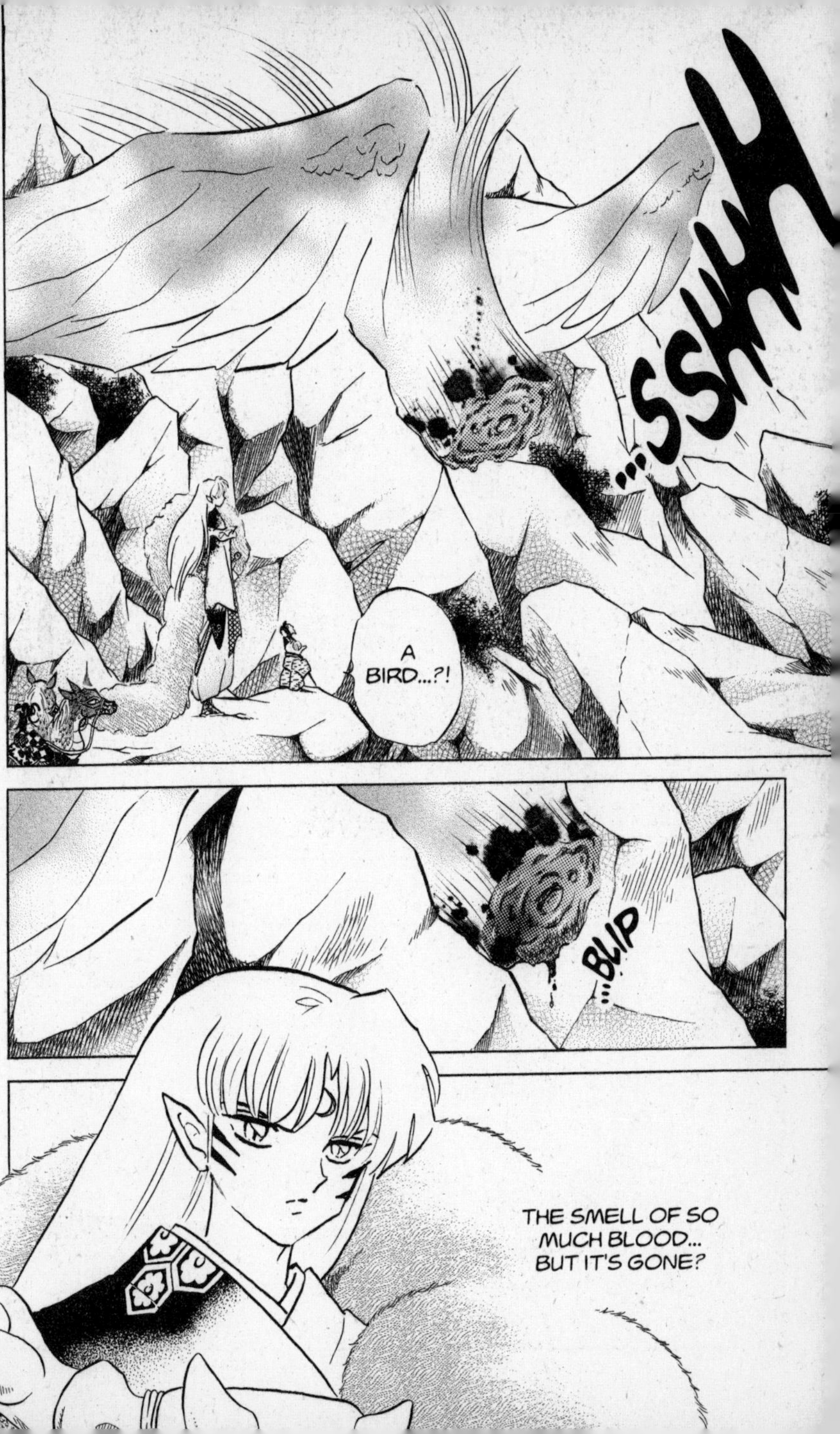
...SSHH
A BIRD...?!
...BLIP
THE SMELL OF SO MUCH BLOOD... BUT IT'S GONE?

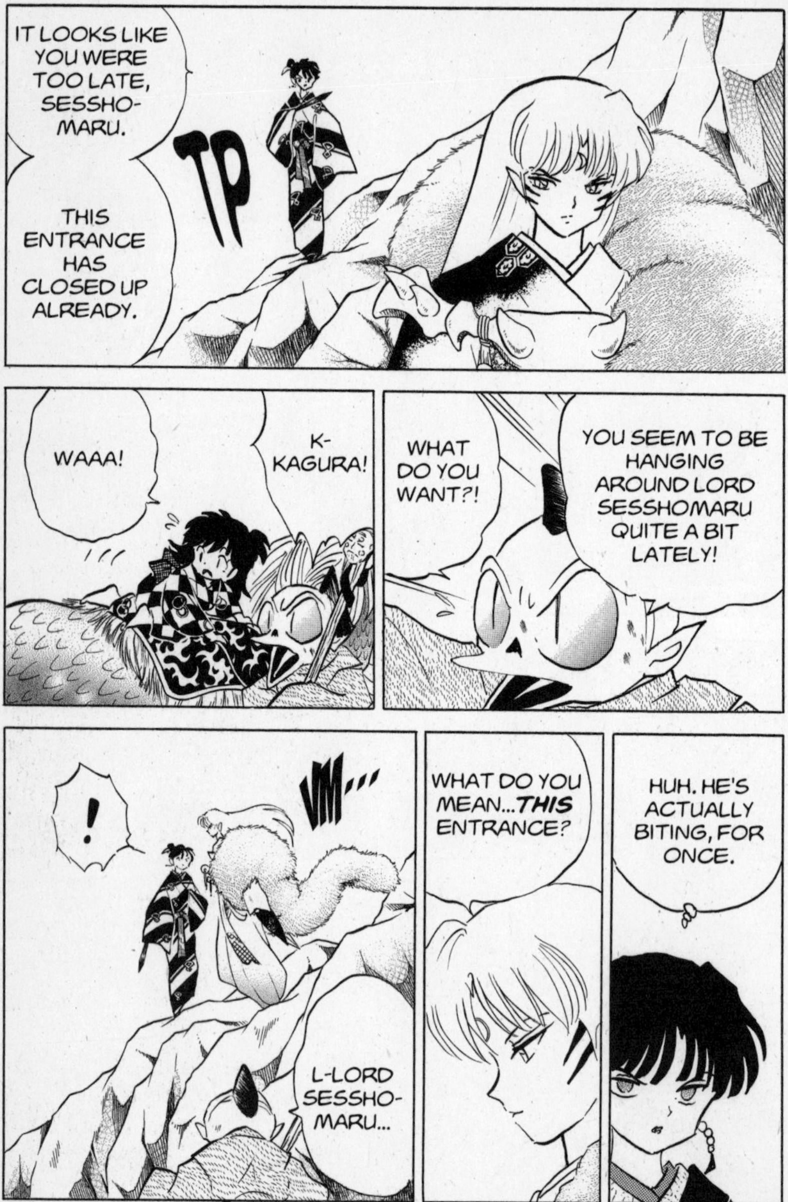

IT LOOKS LIKE YOU WERE TOO LATE, SESSHOMARU.
THIS ENTRANCE HAS CLOSED UP ALREADY.
TP
WAAA!
K-KAGURA!
WHAT DO YOU WANT?!
YOU SEEM TO BE HANGING AROUND LORD SESSHOMARU QUITE A BIT LATELY!
!
VM...
L-LORD SESSHOMARU...
WHAT DO YOU MEAN...*THIS* ENTRANCE?
HUH. HE'S ACTUALLY BITING, FOR ONCE.

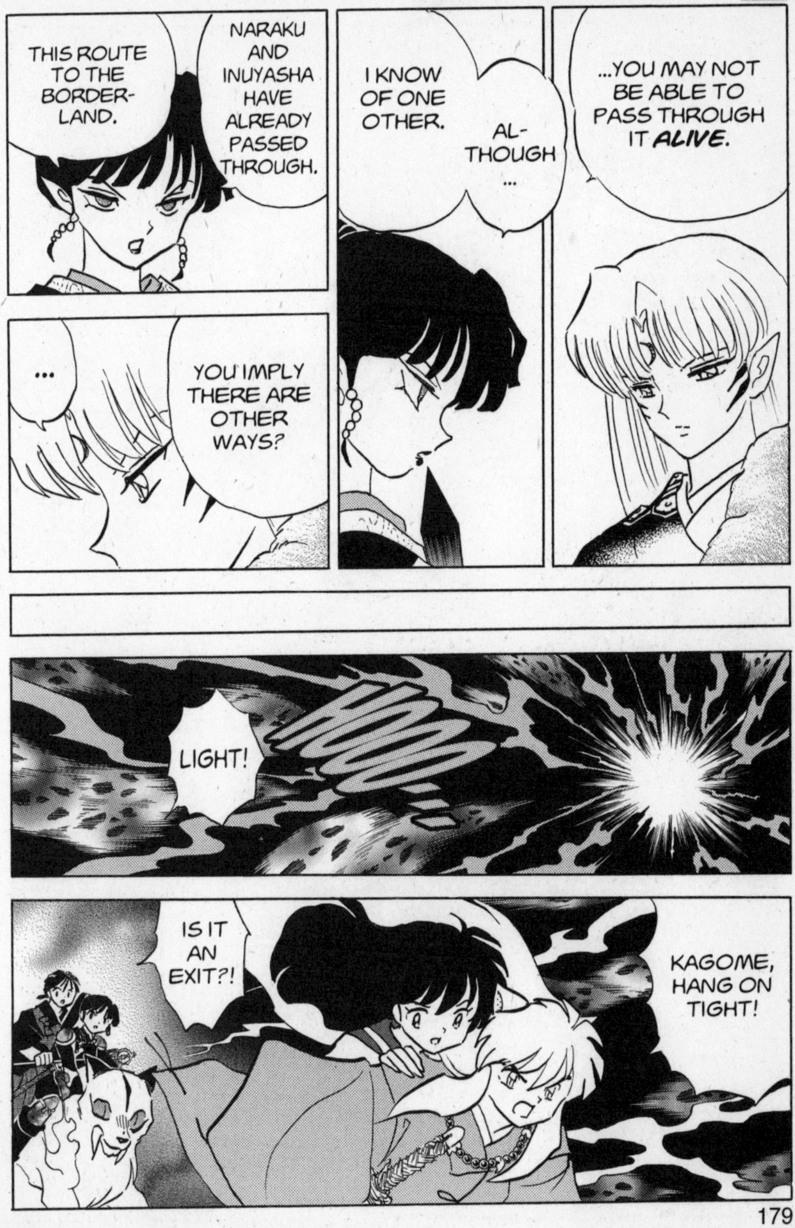
THIS ROUTE TO THE BORDER-LAND.
NARAKU AND INUYASHA HAVE ALREADY PASSED THROUGH.
...
YOU IMPLY THERE ARE OTHER WAYS?
I KNOW OF ONE OTHER.
AL-THOUGH ...
...YOU MAY NOT BE ABLE TO PASS THROUGH IT ***ALIVE.***
LIGHT!
IS IT AN EXIT?!
KAGOME, HANG ON TIGHT!

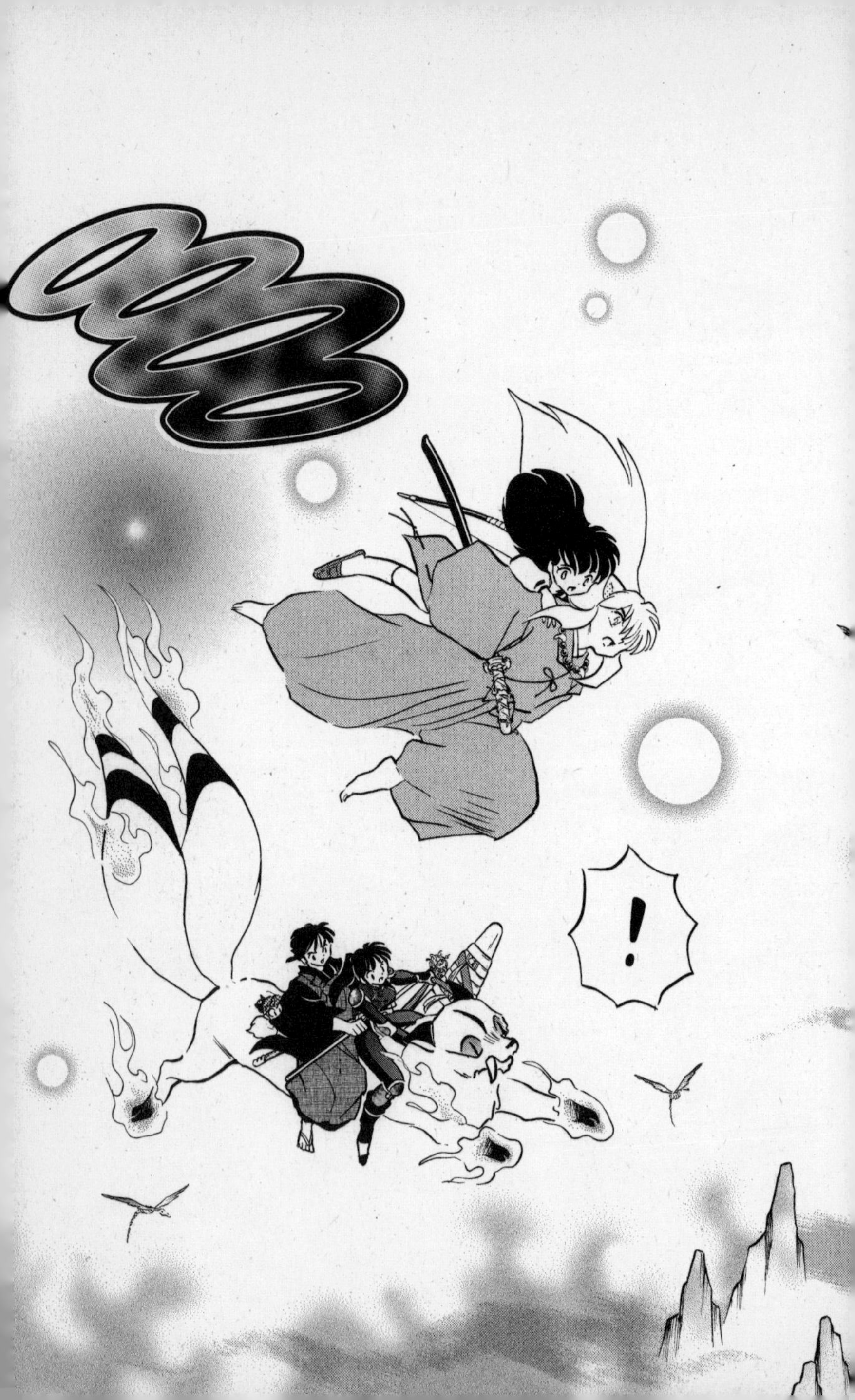
!

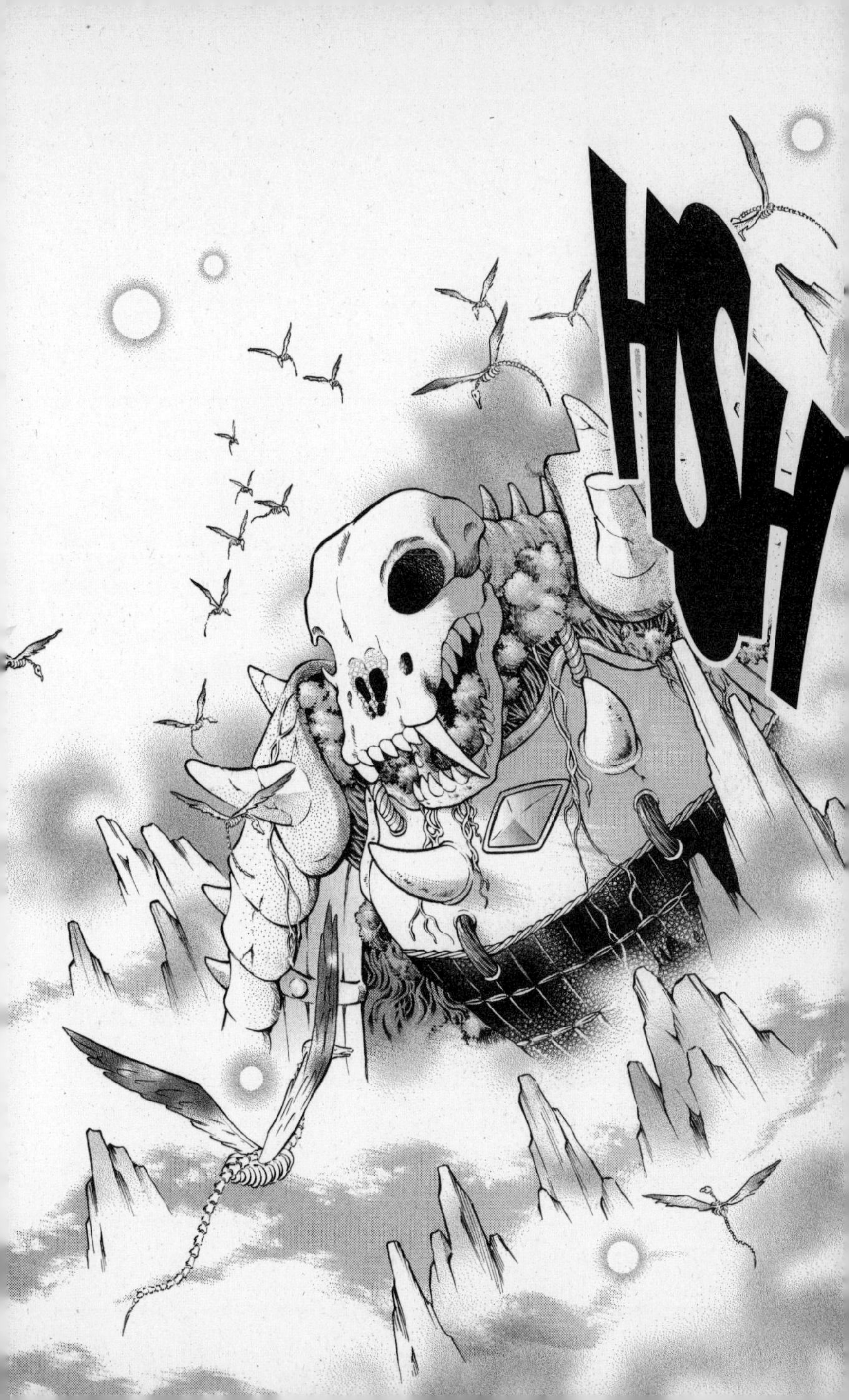
HOSH

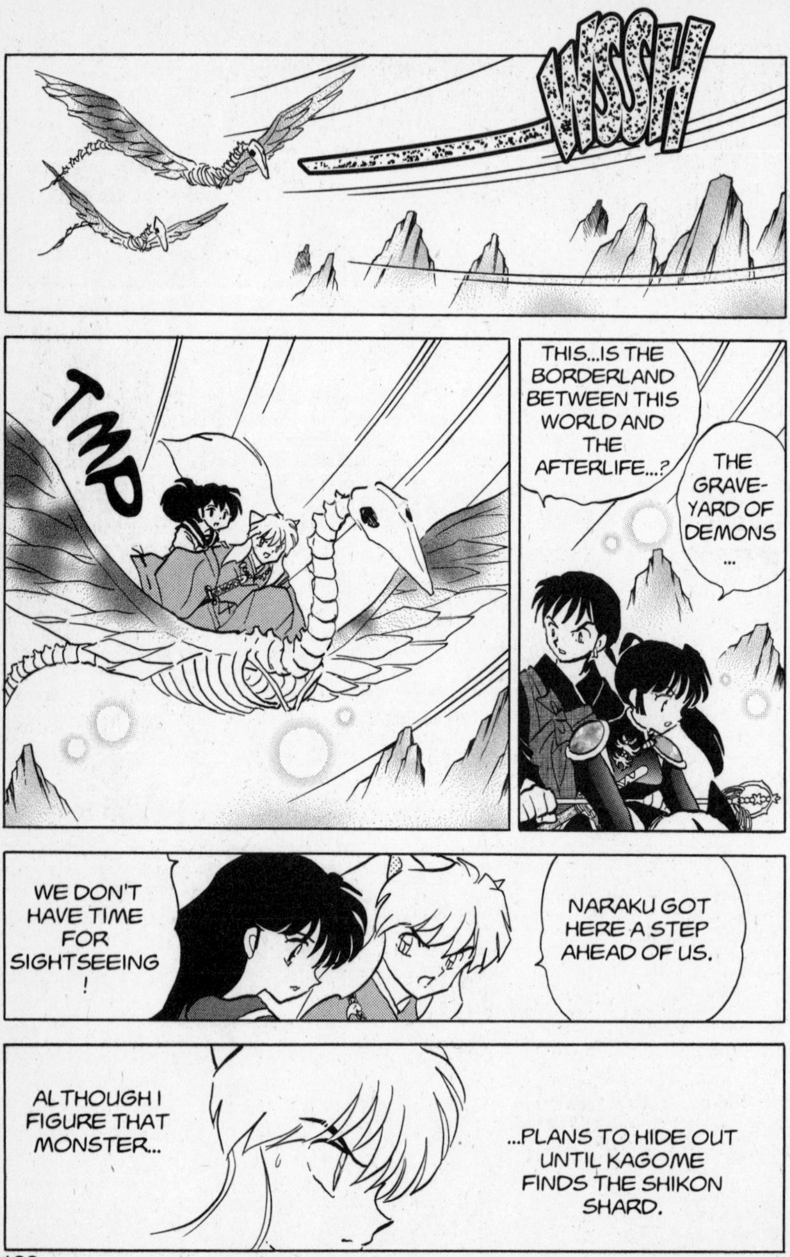
WSSH
TMP
THIS...IS THE BORDERLAND BETWEEN THIS WORLD AND THE AFTERLIFE...?
THE GRAVE-YARD OF DEMONS ...
WE DON'T HAVE TIME FOR SIGHTSEEING !
NARAKU GOT HERE A STEP AHEAD OF US.
ALTHOUGH I FIGURE THAT MONSTER...
...PLANS TO HIDE OUT UNTIL KAGOME FINDS THE SHIKON SHARD.

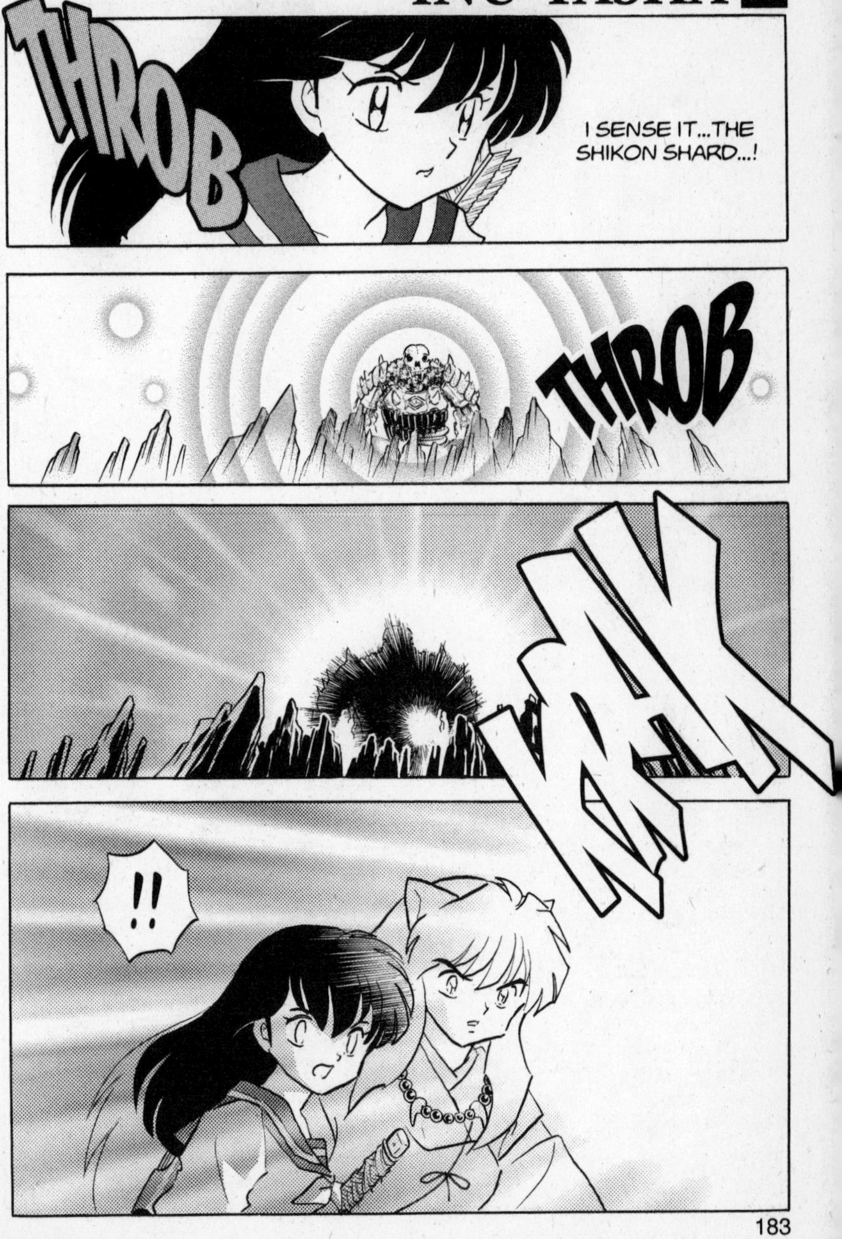
THROB
I SENSE IT...THE SHIKON SHARD...!
THROB
!!

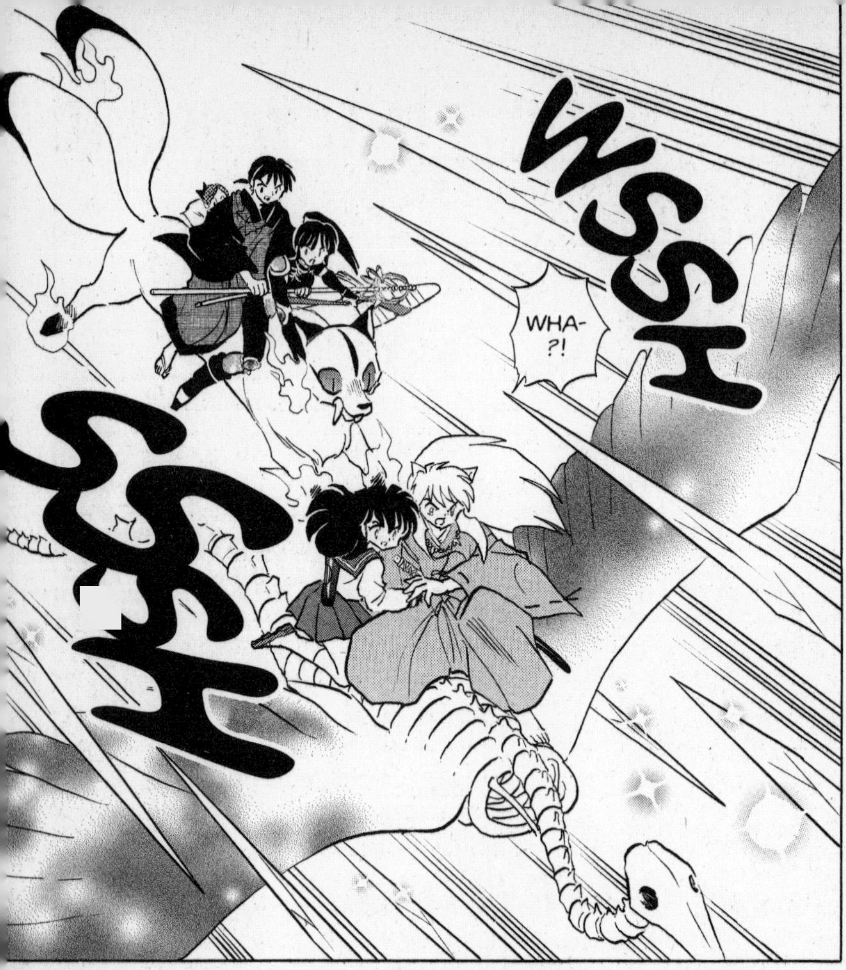
WSSH
WHA-?!
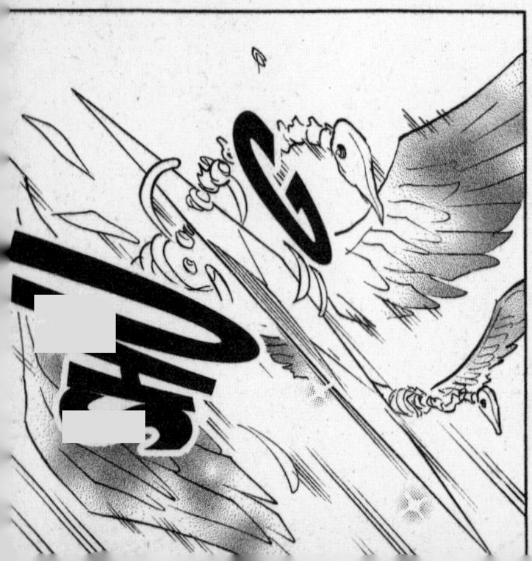
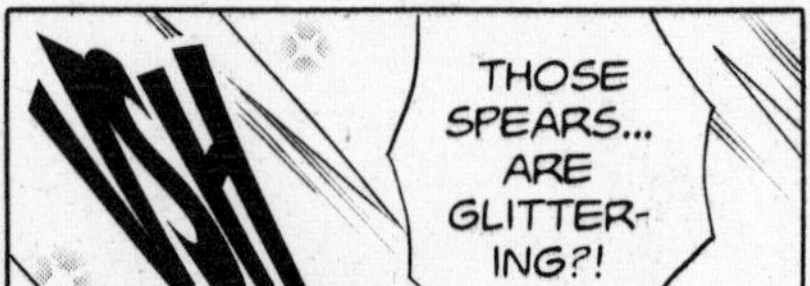
THOSE SPEARS... ARE GLITTERING?!

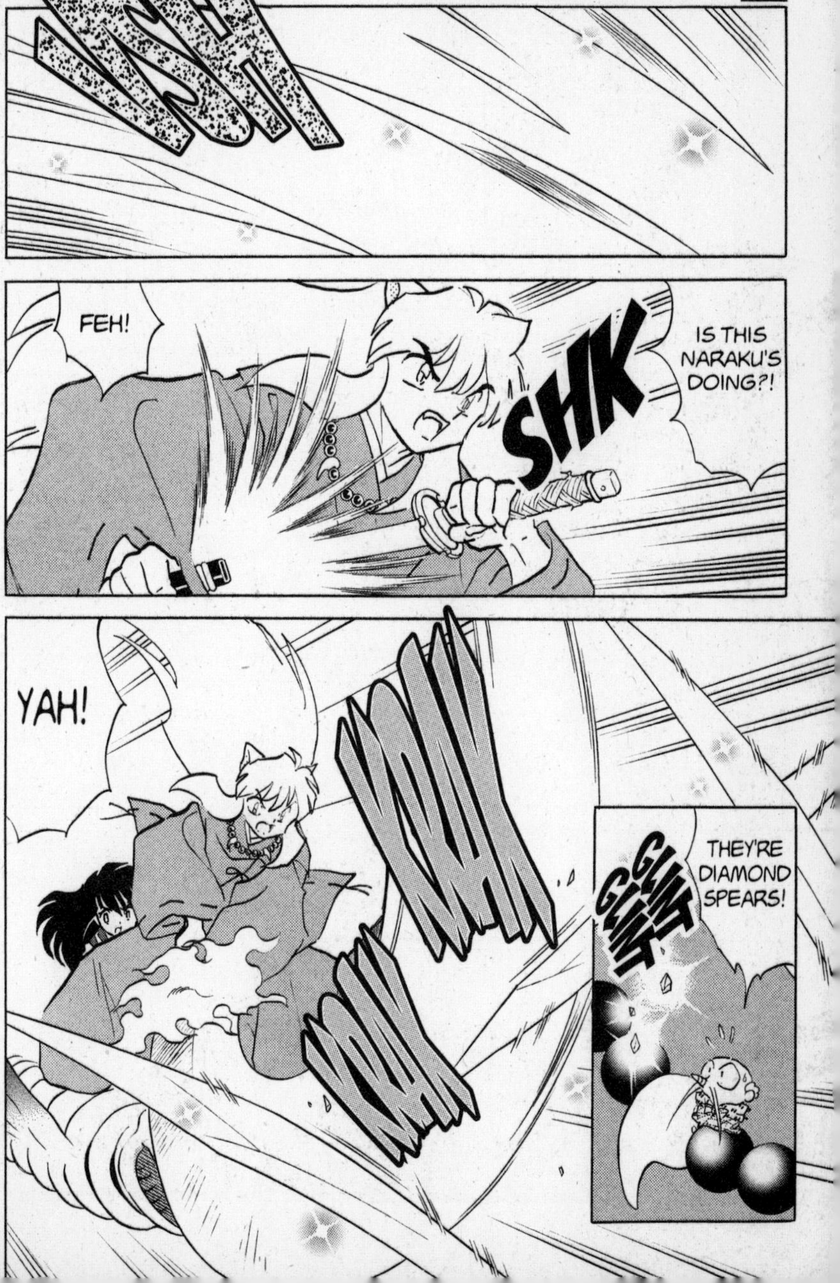
FEH!
SHK
IS THIS NARAKU'S DOING?!
YAH!
GLINT GLINT
THEY'RE DIAMOND SPEARS!

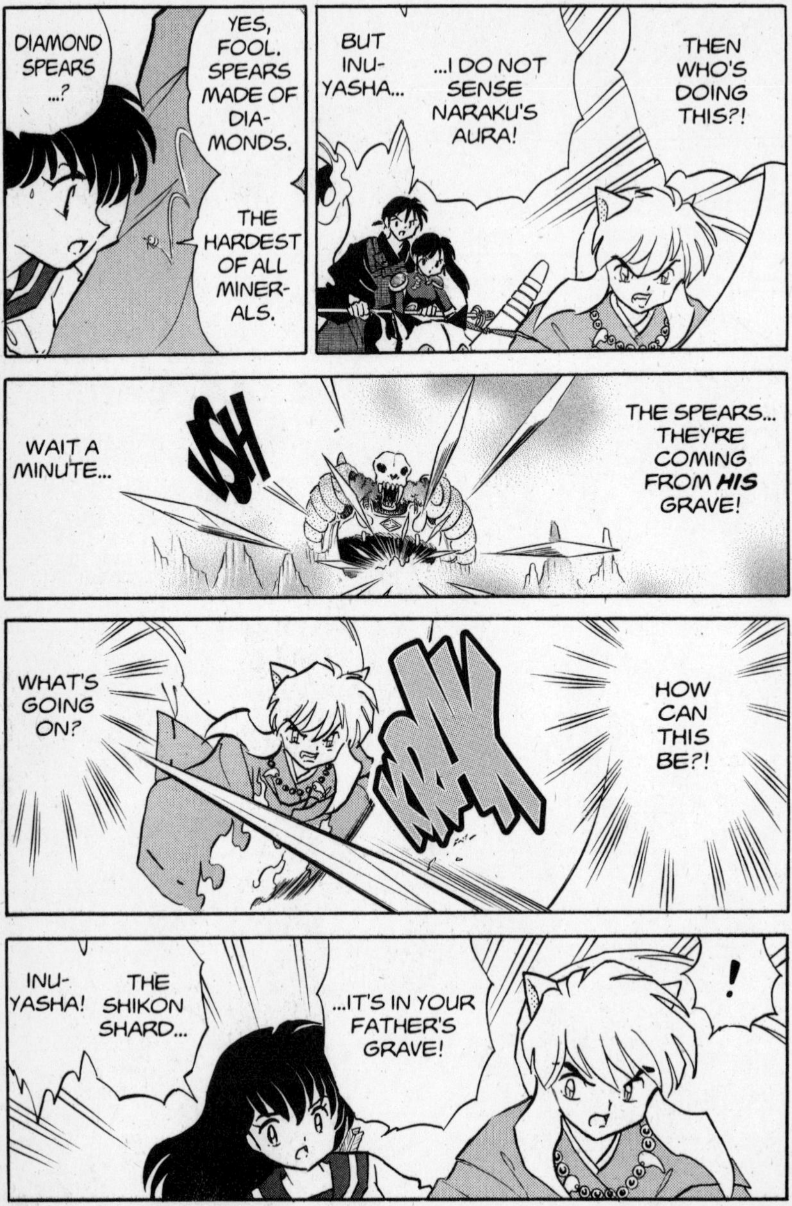
DIAMOND SPEARS ...?
YES, FOOL. SPEARS MADE OF DIAMONDS.
THE HARDEST OF ALL MINERALS.
BUT INU-YASHA...
...I DO NOT SENSE NARAKU'S AURA!
THEN WHO'S DOING THIS?!
WAIT A MINUTE...
VSH
THE SPEARS... THEY'RE COMING FROM *HIS* GRAVE!
WHAT'S GOING ON?
HOW CAN THIS BE?!
INU-YASHA!
THE SHIKON SHARD...
...IT'S IN YOUR FATHER'S GRAVE!
!

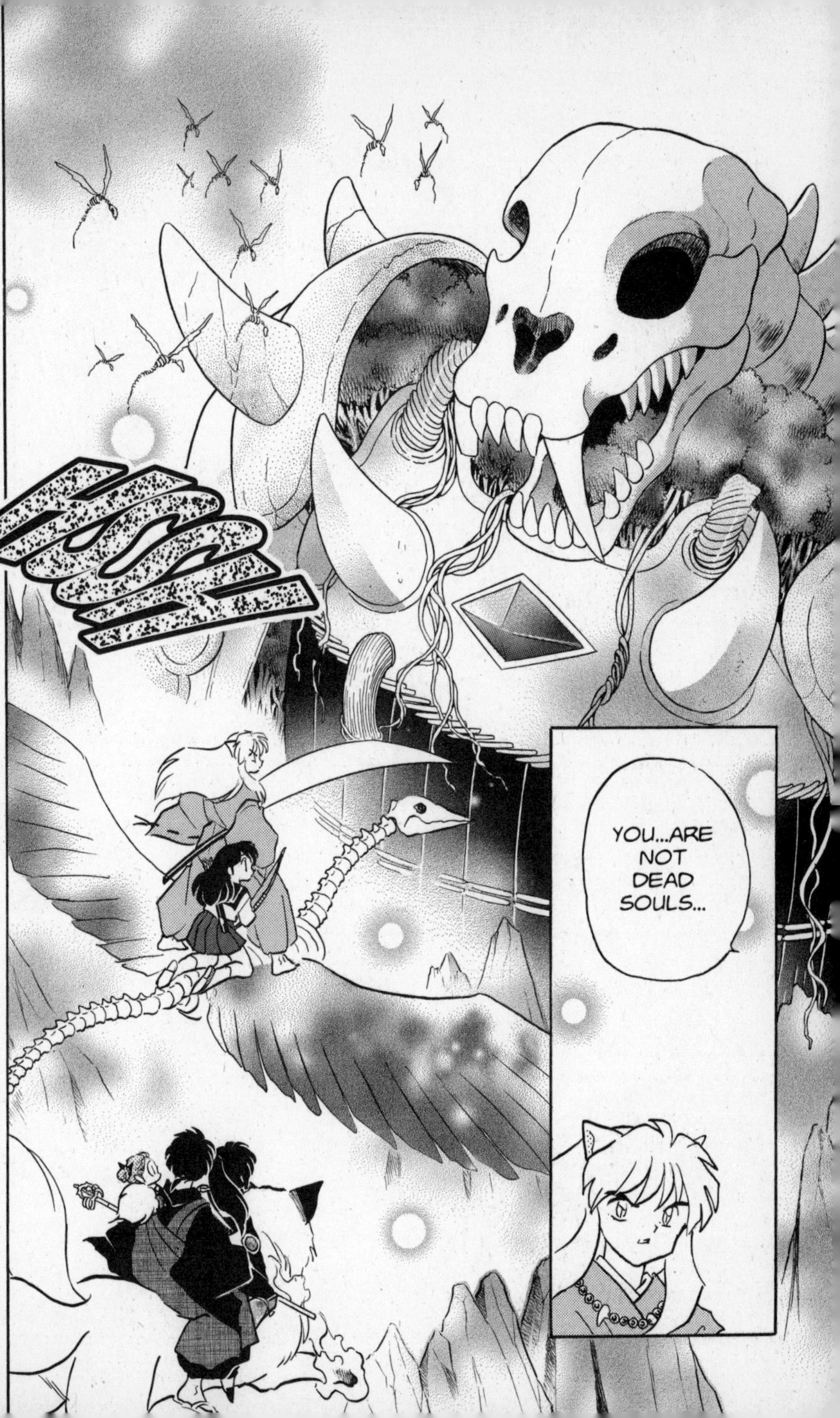
HSSH
YOU...ARE NOT DEAD SOULS...

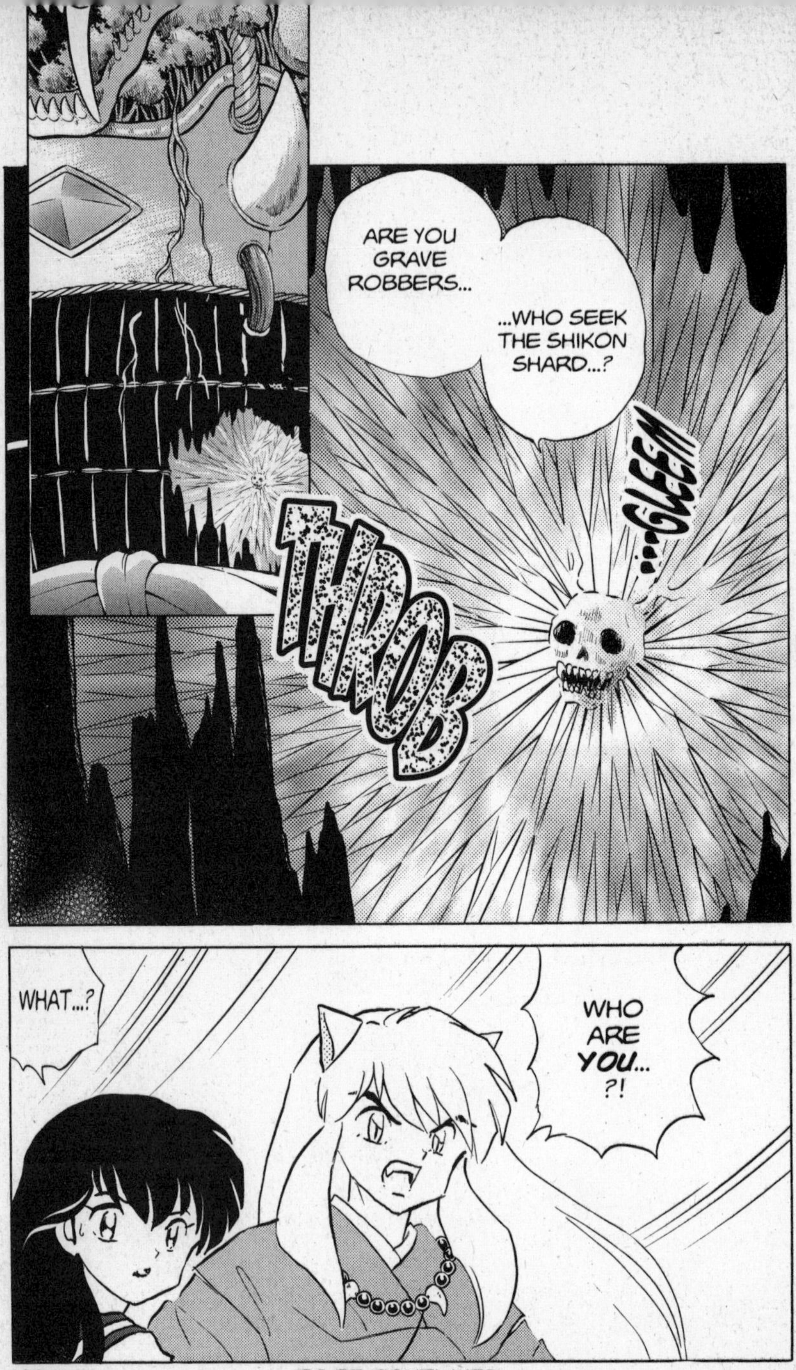
ARE YOU GRAVE ROBBERS...
...WHO SEEK THE SHIKON SHARD...?
THROB
GLEEM...
WHAT...?
WHO ARE YOU...?!

TO BE CONTINUED...

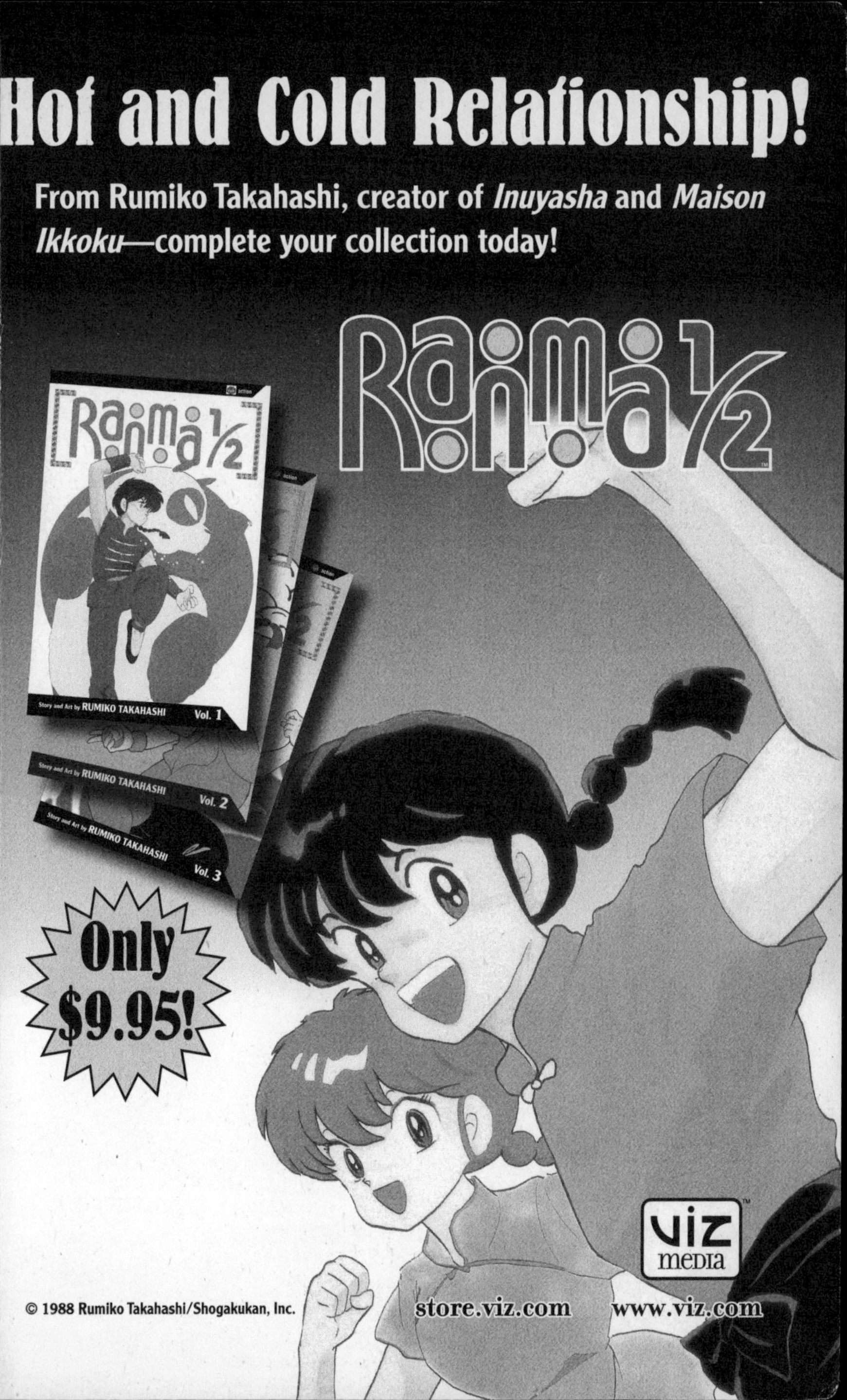
Hot and Cold Relationship!
From Rumiko Takahashi, creator of *Inuyasha* and *Maison Ikkoku*—complete your collection today!
Ranma 1/2
Ranma 1/2
Story and Art by RUMIKO TAKAHASHI Vol. 1
Story and Art by RUMIKO TAKAHASHI Vol. 2
Story and Art by RUMIKO TAKAHASHI Vol. 3
Only $9.95!
viz media
© 1988 Rumiko Takahashi/Shogakukan, Inc.
store.viz.com
www.viz.com

LOVE MANGA?

LET US KNOW WHAT YOU THINK!

OUR MANGA SURVEY IS NOW AVAILABLE ONLINE. PLEASE VISIT: VIZ.COM/MANGASURVEY

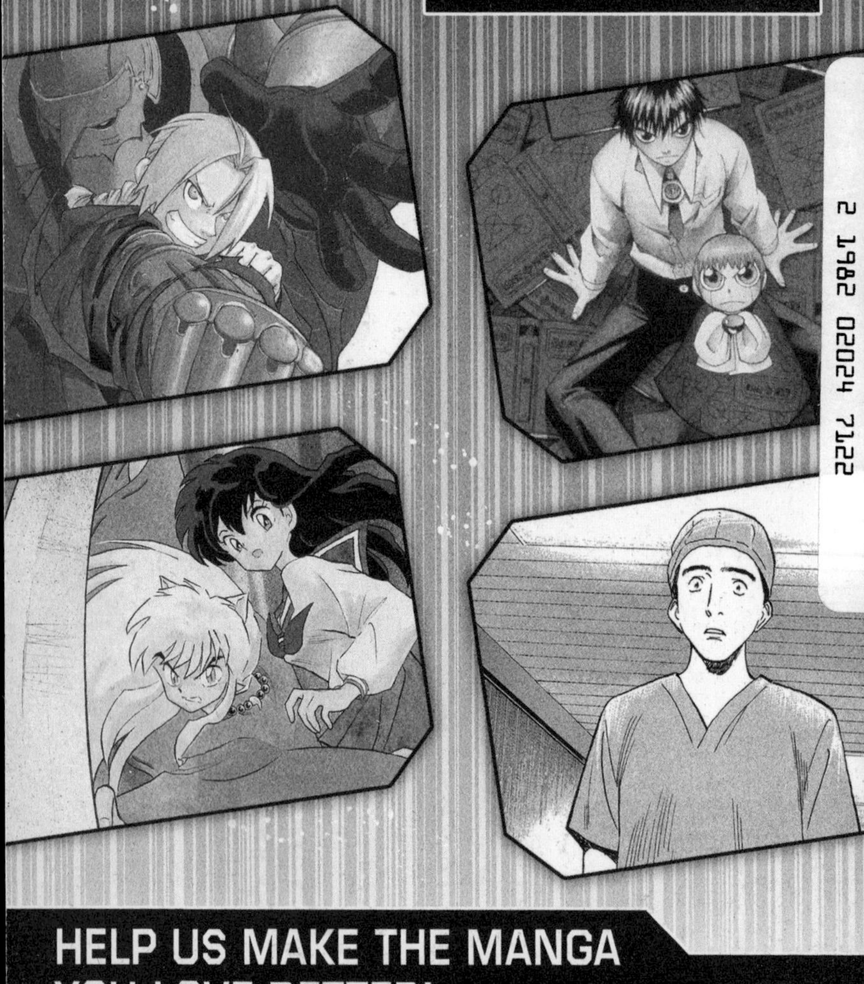

HELP US MAKE THE MANGA YOU LOVE BETTER!

viz media

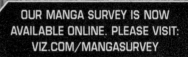